CATHOLICS
ON THE
INTERNET

BROTHER JOHN RAYMOND

PRIMA PUBLISHING

To Saint Albert the Great

Bishop, Doctor of the Church, Scientist

Library of Congress Cataloging-in-Publication Data

Ramond, John, Brother.
   Catholics on the Internet / John Raymond.
     p.   cm.
   Includes index.
   ISBN 0-7615-1168-7
   1. Catholic Church—Computer network   resources. 2. Web sites. I. Title.
BX842.5.R38 1997
025.06'282—dc21   97-27233
                                                            CIP

97 98 99 00 01 DD 10 9 8 7 6 5 4 3 2 1
Printed in the United States of America

HOW TO ORDER

Single copies may be ordered from Prima Publishing, P.O. Box 1260BK, Rocklin, CA 95677; telephone (916) 632-4400. Quantity discounts are also available. On your letterhead, include information concerning the intended use of the books and the number of books you wish to purchase.

Visit us online at www.primapublishing.com

CONTENTS

ACKNOWLEDGMENTS ▼▼▼

I would like to thank the following people for their permission to use the information compiled on their homepages: John Mark Ockerbloom (Catholic Resources on the Net); Father John Stryjewski (AlaPadre's Catholic Corner); Scott J. Fabian (Ecclesia); Danny Greene (Catholic and Christian Resources on the Internet); Peter J. Wagner (RCNet); Michael S. Rose (Catholic Kiosk); Tad Book (Catholic Resources on the Net); and J. Marcus Ziegler (The Search Page). As you can see, I had a lot of help!

Another important person to thank is Dr. Bob Rankin for the use of information from his wonderful article "Accessing the Internet by E-Mail." Without his pointers this book may never have gotten off the ground. Also, special thanks goes to Father Nicolò Suffi (Libreria Editrice Vaticana) for his permission to quote the statement made by Pope John Paul II in connection with the World Communications Day.

I am grateful to the following for their kind recommendations of this book: Michael Cox (reporter for the Catholic Free Press); Bud Macfarlane, Jr., M. I. (founder of CatholiCity); Owen Phelps, Jr. (director of Catholic Connect!); Father Peter Stravinskas, Ph.D., S.T.D. (editor of *The Catholic Answer*).

I would like to thank Peter Mirus of EWTN for providing me with information on their online services.

Others to whom I am grateful for their support include Michael Galloway (director of Catholic Online); Brother Craig Driscoll, my superior, for his help and encouragement; and the many who have prayed for this project.

Finally, thanks go to the two people who have made this book a reality in print: Paula Munier Lee (Associate Publisher, Lifestyles Division) and Karen C. Naungayan (Project Editor) from Prima Publishing.

INTRODUCTION

MY JOURNEY TO THE INTERNET

My journey really began with the *Catholic Twin Circle* newspaper. For the past few years I have been writing a bi-weekly column called "Prayer" for that publication. I began by mailing my articles, then the editor asked me to send them using a modem. Fortunately for me, I had worked on computers before becoming a monk.

Some Computer Background

I was exposed to computers during my electrical engineering studies at the University of Michigan. During a summer engineering co-op job at the Environmental Research Institute of Michigan, I worked under a man who had a doctorate in computer science—quite challenging with my introductory-level computer-programming background. When he talked to me using words such as *ASCII* and *bits,* I thought he was talking in a foreign language; he was—computer language. Some time later I worked for the Educational Computer Corporation in Orlando, Florida, where I really got to know the "guts" of a computer. They designed computer-simulated electrical power plant control panels, airplane cockpits, and such. The purpose of the simulators was to teach people what to do when a malfunction occurred. We programmed the computers in what is called "machine language," the basic language a computer understands. One engineer encouraged me to build a personal computer from scratch. So I ordered the parts and, following a blueprint, put one together. Unfortunately, it didn't work when I was done. But I did learn something from this experience—never to do it again!

This background in computers enabled me to install the modem in the computer at the monastery. I sent my first article by *e-mail* (electronic mail) back in 1991. E-mail is like having a post office box where people can send you letters except, instead of having a box at the Post Office, your space is in the memory of a large local network computer, where your letters are stored until you retrieve them with your home computer.

CompuServe

In 1995 the *Catholic Twin Circle* had an article about Catholic groups on the Internet. I learned that, among the access providers (the local networks), CompuServe had the biggest Catholic representation with its Catholic Online forum. Since my community does much writing for Catholic publications and publishes its own magazine, *The Tabernacle*, CompuServe seemed a good opportunity to reach more people. When I read that CompuServe had an audience of 10 million members, I was sure we would reach more people.

Outreach

After seeing an ad in which CompuServe offered a month's free trial, I decided to give it a try. I got the WinCim program (which CompuServe provides) up and running on my computer. Then I started looking around at the different forums—that is, places that provide information libraries and chat areas. I became good friends with some *sysops*, those in charge of forums. I started contributing articles, especially one I had written about Divine Mercy, to various forum libraries. One teacher of European religions liked it so much that he asked permission to distribute it to all his students. The forum dedicated to Masonry, however, was not interested in it. I was not surprised!

The Internet

CompuServe is a local network. But it offers members access to the Internet. Through this access I began contributing the Divine Mercy article to Usenet—that is, discussion groups on the Internet. There are many such groups, each formed around a particular topic of interest. For example, people all over the world can view or contribute articles to a group focused on Catholic news or information. The *address* for one that I'm most familiar with is: tnn.religion.Catholic.

A FREE HOMEPAGE

For some years my community had been mailing out our magazine, *The Tabernacle*. Having quite a few back issues saved on computer disk, I contributed them to the Catholic Online forum library on CompuServe. One of the sysops, Ray Reilly, liked them. He asked me if he could put the latest one, along with information about our community (for those who might be interested in joining) on an Internet homepage for us. And it would be free! Of course, I was elated and gave him permission. That began the process of our having a homepage on the Internet. "What's a homepage?" you may be asking. It looks just like a page in a book and may include pictures. Usually the opening page is like the book's table of contents. With your *mouse* you select the topic you want to view and the homepage will take you to another page with that information.

Mailing Lists

Next, I learned about mailing lists, that is, e-mail conversation lists on a particular subject on the Internet. I signed up for a few and contributed to them as well. But the e-mail from these lists became overwhelming. I fell behind in keeping up with the conversations. Months later I came across a conversation concerning me. "What happened to that monk?" someone was wondering, "Is he still on the mailing list?" Another person jokingly answered, "Maybe he has taken a vow of silence." I will discuss mailing lists in Chapter 2.

My Own Homepage

CompuServe, like many of the big access providers, offered its members a free site to set up a homepage and the computer program to create it. This allowed me to make my own homepage, which was not difficult to learn. I designed my homepage with a main menu (table of contents) for selecting over 150 articles that I had written on topics ranging from prayer to items for sale from our monastery gift shop. I also invited people to e-mail the monastery with their prayer requests.

Multiple Homepage Sites

RCNet, like some other Catholic groups on the Internet, offered to put our homepage on their site for free. So I moved the homepage I created on CompuServe to RCNet (http://www.rc.net/org/monks). I added a *hyperlink* (a button on the screen

you can click to transfer from one homepage to another) to our page on Catholic Online's Web site. I used my free homepage spot on CompuServe to post our magazine
and hyperlink to our other two homepages.

Catholic Resources—Where Are They?

As I learned various things about the Internet, I still was ignorant of many of its
Catholic resources. At one point I asked Ray Reilly, the sysop of Catholic Online, if
he had e-mail addresses for other Catholic groups on the Internet. He had very few.
Tracking down Catholics would take someone with detective qualities; I had just
the man—a friend, Mike Farrell, who is a policeman. In a short time Mike e-mailed
me a vast directory of Catholic groups put together by Timothy DeRyan. The list left
me amazed. Since then I have done my own detective work and compiled some good
resources.

I began on the Internet without the slightest idea what I was doing. Throughout
this book I will keep in mind people who are new to the Internet, as I once was. I will
also provide some information that hopefully will satisfy the Bill Gates types who are
interested in Catholic sites! I once sent a list of Catholic sites to a friend of the
monastery. She told me that the revelation of what was available left her mouth
hanging in amazement. She had previously known of very few resources for Catholics on the Internet. I then realized then the need for a book like this.

About Part I

The chapters in Part I of this book should be read in order by those unfamiliar with
the Internet and its terminology. Each chapter assumes you are familiar with the vo-
cabulary introduced in the preceding chapters. Even if you are already familiar with
the Internet, you may find helpful information in these chapters.

About Part II

Part II is primarily a reference to Catholic sites on the Internet. These chapters give
a detailed sampling of what's out there, but only a sampling. With such a vast amount
of information for Catholics on the Internet, I felt somewhat overwhelmed. Like the
Evangelist St. John, who wrote in his Gospel that if everything Jesus did were written
down, he didn't think the world itself could contain the books that should be written
(cf. Jn. 21, 25); so it seems to me with the ever-expanding information for Catholics
on the Internet.

Questionable Catholic Sites

Keep in mind that information on the Internet that claims to be for Catholics may in whole or in part deviate from authentic Church teaching. Cardinal Roger Mahony of Los Angeles wrote in a statement he presented to the Pontifical Council of Social Communications during a meeting at the Vatican, "There are too many Catholic Web sites and services that are questionable." The Cardinal, concerned about Catholic sites on the Internet that include material contrary to official Church teaching, recommended to the Council, "The Church needs to take immediate steps to authorize and authenticate electronic services that utilize the name 'Catholic,' while disallowing those that are illegitimate and so informing unsuspecting users." The Cardinal also expressed concern over individuals on the Internet who use the title "Father" or "Reverend" to give credence and strength to their viewpoints. The Cardinal urged a greater official Church presence on the Internet. I hope this book will help further this goal.

Readers' Discernment

I do not claim to endorse any groups or locations on the Internet for Catholics mentioned in this book. I tried to delete questionable sites and information or, at least, point out that the site has questionable material. But, with all the sites mentioned in this book along with their many links to other information, I could not pull all the weeds from the wheat field. So I advise the reader to discern what is in keeping with the Faith, with, I hope, the help of the Catechism of the Catholic Church. The Catechism is widely available and can be purchased at your local Catholic bookstore. The Catechism of the Catholic Church for personal computers (Sheridan Electronics) can be ordered on disk from the United States Catholic Conference Publishing Services, 3211 Fourth Street NE, Washington DC 20017-1194 (Phone 800-235-8722 or FAX 301-209-0016). Further, the Catechism is available on the Internet (cf. Part II).

Another resource for the Faith is "Welcome to The Catholic Church on CD-ROM" (Harmony Media). It is a comprehensive, fully integrated reference to the Catholic Faith. Parents, priests, teachers, students, or those who simply want to know more about the Catholic Faith will find this program valuable. It includes an illustrated Catholic Bible (RSV edition), Catholic Encyclopedic Dictionary, all Vatican II documents, *The Way of the Lord Jesus* by Germain Grisez (a two-volume work on Church moral teachings), *The Sources of Catholic Dogma* by Denzinger, *Lives of the Saints* (three complete volumes), *The Sacraments and Their Celebration* by Nicholas Halligan, O.P., *Catholic Church History* by Msgr. Eberhardt (a two-volume set), *The*

Catholic Catechism by Fr. John Hardon, S.J., *My Daily Bread* by Fr. Anthony Paone, S.J., *Chart of Church Structure, Maps of Historic Periods and Places, Liturgical Music,* hundreds of color illustrations by turn-of-the-century painter J. Tissot, plus photographs and other works of art. It can be ordered from Frank Pollicino by mail at: The Catholic Shopper, 550 Smithtown Bypass #224, Smithtown, NY 11787; by phone: 516-366-4928; or by homepage: http://www.catholicshopper.com. Any items mentioned in this book can also be ordered from The Cloister Shop, The Monks of Adoration, P.O. Box 546, Petersham, MA 01366-0546.

A Sure Catholic Guide

The sure guide for authentic Catholic teaching is from the Magisterium of the Church—that is, the bishops in union with the Pope. "The faithful . . . are obliged to submit to their bishops' decision, made in the name of the Church, in matters of faith and morals, and to adhere to it with a ready and respectful allegiance of mind. This loyal submission of the will and intellect must be given, in a special way, to the authentic teaching authority of the Roman Pontiff." (Vatican II Documents, "Dogmatic Constitution on the Church," paragraph 25).

ICONS

Beside each Web site name and address, you will find an icon. These icons are provided so you can easily flip through this book and find information on specific subject matter. (Please note: Some Web sites fall under more than one category.)

Apostolates
(The heart is a symbol of charity.)

Books, publications, radio, and television

Catholic culture

Catholic information, references, and resources

Catholic organizations

Church teachings and Catechisms

Catholic writings

Dioceses and churches

Liturgy and prayer

Our Lady, saints, and holy people
(Saints receive a crown, as a reward, in Heaven.)

Sacred Scripture

Schools and campus ministries

The Vatican

Theology

Odds and ends

PART 1

▲▲▲

Internet Information You Need to Know

1

▼▼▼

The Internet

WHAT IS THE INTERNET?

Almost every book or article on the Internet begins by explaining what it is—so why should this book be different? What is it? Let's begin by considering something we are familiar with—our telephone system. We think nothing of using the phone all the time. We can even talk to people on the other side of the world. From our phone bill, we know there is a difference between a local call and a long-distance call. A local call involves a local network of phone lines that converge somewhere so that two people calling can be connected. Long-distance lines connect all these local phone networks. The long-distance lines enable two people on different local networks to talk to each other. Now let's replace the people by computers. Suppose your local network's telephone lines converged to a large computer instead of your telephone company. If you have a computer at home, it can call this local large computer and "talk" to it. Many home computers doing this form a local network of computers. If someone were to connect the local networks that exist all over the world, just like long-distance phone lines, then someone with a computer in a United States network could communicate with someone on a network in Japan. The Internet has done this—connected all these large computers that control local networks to form a network of networks.

QUESTIONS ABOUT THE INTERNET

You may have many questions about the Internet that this book does not address. A good place to look, whether you are an expert or novice, is the "World Wide Web Frequently Asked Questions" site on the Internet. The address of this homepage is http://www.boutell.com/faq/. If you use either the Internet Explorer or the Netscape Navigator browser, look under "Help" on the menu to learn more about the Internet. If you don't have the slightest idea of what a homepage is, don't panic—read Chapter 3!

SCREENING THE INTERNET

Some people are afraid of the Internet, mainly because of horror stories they hear on the news about bad things on it—such as pornography, bomb-making instructions, and suicide groups. Realize that a person has to go looking for bad things on the Internet; these topics do not just pop up on your computer screen. If you are worried about what you or your children may see on the Internet, several computer programs on the market can filter out immoral material. *Surfwatch* from Surfwatch Software keeps children out of certain Internet sites, newsgroups, chat areas, and FTP sites that contain sexually explicit material. You can download it at http://www.surfwatch. com/. Another program called *Cyber Patrol* from Microsystems Software (800-489-2001 or http://www.microsys.com) allows parents to block sites that contain any of the following: partial nudity, nudity, reference to sexual acts, gross depictions, racist/ethnic slurs, gambling, satanic/cult references, use of drugs, drug culture, militant/extremist rhetoric, violence, profanity, and questionable/illegal activities. Parents can also block sites where alcohol, beer, wine, and tobacco use are encouraged. Both *Surfwatch* and *Cyber Patrol* can be used with standard homepage browsers.

TECHNOLOGY AND CATHOLICISM

Technology can be used for God's glory. The Catechism of the Catholic Church tells us, "Science and technology are precious resources when placed at the service of man and promote his integral development for the benefit of all" (paragraph 2293). The Internet has many wonderful resources on it for the Catholic Faith. It can be a great tool for bringing Catholics together and for evangelizing the world. In this book I will show some of the resources that are available for Catholics who are on the Internet.

GETTING ACCESS

By now you are aware that you need a computer to get on the Internet. I began on the Internet with an IBM-compatible computer that had a 486SX-25 megahertz processor, 4 megabytes of RAM, a monochrome VGA display, a 40 megabyte hard drive, and Windows 3.1. It was sufficient for a time. But most new computer programs demand bigger hard drives, use more graphics, and need faster processors and more RAM. So if you are buying one, get the most you can afford. (If you want to hang on to a computer you already have, see Chapter 4.) I strongly recommend you get at least a 28.8-Kbps modem. Otherwise communication between computers can be very slow. There are now Internet connections offered by television cable and satellite companies, which can be very fast; however, at present they only allow fast communication one way, from the Internet to you. To send something, you have to use the regular phone line or a slower speed.

My little 486 computer died when I tried getting on America Online and Prodigy (I believe the graphics were just too much for the little guy) so I bought a new one. I now have a Pentium Pro 200 megahertz machine with a 1.6 gigabyte hard drive. With this machine I notice a drastic difference in downloading files from the Internet compared to downloading from my old 486. By the way, if you have to buy a computer, I recommend looking in some of the many good computer magazines that rate computers. I bought mine after studying computer charts that rate computers in *PC World* magazine and am very satisfied with the results. I have heard terrible stories of people having problems with new computers, warranties, and such. So many factors must be taken into account when buying a computer that I believe it's safer to let experts advise us. Now where was I . . . ?

Oh yes . . . getting access. If you don't own a computer and are new to this, you can probably go to your local library and play around on the Internet. Some libraries even offer Internet classes. Now, presuming you have a computer, you want to get "access" to the Internet. Where should you look? For those completely unfamiliar with the Internet, the big access providers are a great help. CompuServe and America Online provide free both the software to get started and one month's trial service. In many places they can provide local phone numbers for access. The cost is minimal. If you decide to join the service, you can either sign up for a limited amount of hours each month, or for slightly more money, some providers offer unlimited access for a flat monthly rate. Some also provide free programs to browse homepages on the Internet. In addition, you can even create your own homepage for free.

CompuServe

CompuServe, which has forums with extensive libraries on many subjects, is, I believe, one of the best sources for reference material. Note: if you want information in a hurry, turn off the graphics on the program CompuServe gives you to access its service. CompuServe has the Catholic Online Forum (GO CATHOLIC), where you can meet other Catholics and look at their libraries, which include many articles, computer programs, and recent news. Following is a specific listing of what you will find there.

Catholic Online Forum

The Library

The library portion of the Catholic Online Forum contains programs, text files, and graphic files. The library is the Forum's reference resource. It is a collection of files organized into sections for your convenience. These materials can be read *online* (while you're connected over the phone) or *downloaded* (put on your computer hard drive to look at later). You can also share with others by *uploading* or *contributing* files from your computer to their library. Catholic Online has stored, and provides access to, thousands of files not found in the library. If you do not see a file or file area you want, they will help you locate the file or files you need.

Here are the title headings of sections in the Catholic Online Forum library: General Area (contains files of a general nature and those relating to the forum), Church Documents (contains a collection of files related to the Catholic Church and the popes of the past), Bible, Pro-Life, Church History and Saints, John Paul II, Graphics/Discovery, Book Club/Religious Education, Spirituality/Prayer, Current Issues, Media/Entertainment, Vatican II, Church Fathers, Catholic Market Place (Catholic products), Catholic Discovery (reveals exciting historical and contemporary facets of our culturally rich Catholic heritage; includes hundreds of magnificent photos with text), CPI/Publications (Catholic Online news updates), Liturgy/Sacred Music, Apologetics (defense of the Catholic Faith), PC/Internet Utilities, Catholic Digest, Engaged Encounter, Biblioteca, and 1995 Papal Visit to the United States.

Conference Rooms

Catholic Online conference rooms are a great way to meet new people or talk to old friends. In the conference rooms, members gather for "live" conversation. Here you may find several members participating in a regularly scheduled meeting or in a special conference hosted by a guest speaker. The different rooms are General Chat Room (general chat, scheduled meetings, and guest lectures), Pro-Life Room, Rectory, Singles Space Youth Room (general chat, scheduled meetings, and guest lectures related to subjects involving the youth of our Church and the world of today), Spirituality Room, Scripture Room, and Family Conference Room.

Bulletin Board

Catholic Online's message section is similar to posting notes on a bulletin board. People respond to what others have posted, resulting in a "thread" of messages. Message sections are New Member/General, Pro-Life, Sacred Scripture, Saints and Calendar, Marriage and Family, Spirit & Prayer, Liturgy/Sacred Music, Doctrine/Canon Law, Blessed Virgin Mary, Apologetics, Books & Reviews, Youth/Vocation, Eastern/Orthodox (provides the Eastern and Western halves of our Catholic Church the opportunity to meet and share spiritual traditions), Español/Spanish, Catholic Singles, Catholic Ecumenism, Engaged Encounter, and Speculation.

WOW

If you are truly new to computers, you might consider buying *WOW*, an online access program designed for inexperienced users. *PC World* magazine says it's easier to use than America Online's program. Designed for the whole family, you register each user as an adult or child at sign-up. It gives parents control over Internet access and the option of screening their kids' e-mail. One account can have up to six users. You receive unlimited access time.

Catholic Online

Catholic Online is an international Catholic organization that currently provides services to 180 countries. They are working on becoming an Internet access provider for Catholics and are putting together what is called the "Catholic Communications Network." Catholic Online is certainly qualified to become an Internet provider as their core business and expertise is in electronic communications and networking, as well as Internet systems design and construction. This network, which will connect Catholic dioceses around the world, will be a specifically Catholic network that still will allow people to browse the Internet. Catholic Online will offer many of the services that big access providers now have. This network has already been established in 25 dioceses in the United States. Catholic Online already provides free Internet access, which they subsidize, and a homepage to any Catholic parish in the United States. For those interested in getting access, Catholic Online can be reached at 805-869-1000; or see their homepage at http://www.catholic.org. If you do not have access to the Internet, you may be able to go to your local library and get access to their homepage. Or, you can simply telephone them.

Netcom

Although this is not a stand-alone Catholic access service, Catholic Online, in association with Netcom access provider, has NETCOMplete Netscape (Windows and Mac versions)—Internet software that opens directly to Catholic Online's World Wide Web homepage (See Chapter 5 for details). Besides this, you will have direct access to the Web, FTP, e-mail, Listserv, Usenet, Gopher, Internet Relay Chat (IRC), and other services.

You will receive unlimited access to the Internet. NETCOM has over 300 local access numbers throughout the U.S. and Canada, 800 # Service, 28.8 Kbps modem access, domain name registration, customized Catholic Online Netscape software (Windows and Mac Versions), and sites on which you can develop your personal or organization's homepages.

Computer system requirements: 386 or greater IBM PC-compatible 4MB RAM, VGA recommended, mouse or other pointing device, modem with 9600 or greater baud rate, 4MB free hard disk space, DOS 5 or above, and Windows 3.1 or greater. Call 800-295-3004 to request your copy of Catholic Online/NETCOMplete Netscape Software or e-mail them at 76711.1715@compuserve.com. Include your name and postal address.

If you are part of a business operation, ask about their direct Internet connections—that is, their leased lines and dial-up connectivity: T-1 ULTRA high-speed dedicated lines at 1.544 Mbps direct Internet access, 56K-frame connect leased-line access, and LAN dial connections.

America Online

America Online is the biggest access provider. Again similar to CompuServe, you can turn off the graphics for better speed. To do this simply look for "Preferences" under "Members" on the title bar of the program you receive. Select "Graphics" and turn off pictures and sound. Also under "Members," you will find "Parental Control." America Online allows up to five different names on the same account and lets you control the access of each user. Say, for example, you have a son named Peter. You can lock Peter out from accessing things you don't want him to see. As on CompuServe, you will find a Catholic presence on America Online with a library, bulletin boards, and chat rooms.

The Catholic Community

The "Catholic Community," as it is called (KEYWORD CATHOLIC), has a variety of Catholic resources. Catholic Community is composed of a group of priests, religious and laity, who come together with the common belief in this new kind of online ministry. The main screen you will see when you access Catholic Community will give you

▼▼▼

CATHOLIC NEWS SERVICE

In case you've never heard of CNS, here is a little background. Catholic News Service is the primary source of national and world news that appears in the U.S. Catholic press. It is also a leading source of news for Catholic print and broadcast media throughout the world. Almost every English Catholic newspaper in the world uses CNS. Approximately 170 U.S. Catholic newspapers and broadcasters and the more than 70 other news organizations in more than 35 countries rely on CNS. Even the Vatican Radio uses their daily news report.

CNS, created in 1920 by the bishops of the United States, is editorially independent and a financially self-sustaining division of the U.S. Catholic Conference. The CNS Rome bureau, which provides Vatican coverage, gives CNS an international appeal. They have contacts with correspondents and smaller Catholic news agencies in Europe, Asia, Africa, Australia, and Latin America.

The CNS Photo/Graphics Service provides images from wherever news is happening. Photos are available in digital form via a bulletin board and in print form by mail.

CNS also produces a service called *Origins,* which provides complete texts of news-making documents, and it offers movie and TV reviews from a Catholic perspective through the *TV & Movie Guide* and *Movie Guide Monthly.* Its biweekly publication, *Catholic Trends,* provides an overview of church news affecting decision makers. CNS can also be reached at its homepage: http://www.catholicnews.com.

the following selections: Catholic News, Catholic Chat, Message Boards, Web Resources, and the Catholic Community Software Library (software and applications).

Catholic News

Under Catholic News, you will find the Catholic News Service (CNS); *National Catholic Reporter* (NCR), which is known as a liberal newspaper with nonacceptance of some Church teachings; and Papal News Update.

Bulletin Board

Under Message Boards, you will find the Catholic Community Message Board, Catholic Community Prayer and Spirituality Message Board, Catholic Issues and Doctrine, Catholic Life and Worship, and Vatican Resources.

Listed under Web Resources are certain Catholic homepages, including Alapadre's Catholic Corner (described in Chapter 7 of this book) and Web Talk message board.

Chat Areas

At Catholic Chat you will find Apologetics, Book Kritik Korner, Catholic Daughters, Catholic Exploration Center, Catholic Priest Online (not limited to just priests), Catholic Youth Online, DRE Chat, Eastern Rite, Free Zone (free discussion times), Knights of Columbus, Legion of Mary, Living Rosary, Teen Chat (ages 10–19 are welcome), Young Adults, Youth Ministry, Church Law and Liturgy, Lunch Bunch Chat, Praise and Prayer, Rite of Christian Initiation for Adults (for those interested in becoming Catholic), RCIA Team Chat (for team members and RCIA instructors), Secular Orders, Sunday Evening Chat, and Vocation Chat.

The most recent chat schedule can be obtained from the Catholic Community homepage at: http://members.aol.com.

The Eternal Word Television Network

The Eternal Word Television Network (EWTN) online service is an all-Catholic local network. You can telephone 703-791-2576 for help to set up an account. Although no one is required to pay for the service, there are recommended donation levels based on the time a person spends on the network. Suggested donations range from a "Light User" level to a "Sustaining User." The online services are divided into subject areas called Information Centers, each hosted by an organization (or priest) with expertise in a given subject. Each center has its own libraries containing large numbers of text files that you can either read online or download to your computer. Catholic books, articles, position papers, lists, and Church documents are all available in the file libraries. Each center has a public message area or forum, like CompuServe, where you can ask questions or discuss Catholic issues. Of course, you can send e-mail to anybody. Special features on EWTN include catalogs of major Catholic publishers from which you can place orders, daily dispatches of the Vatican Information Service, and EWTN's own daily Catholic news wire. You can get canonical advice or spiritual counseling online. You can also ask questions of the Christendom College faculty.

Other Ways to Access EWTN

Should those of you who already have Internet access regret not having EWTN on-line, don't despair. Most of their material is available through Telnet, which is most likely available through your access provider. With Telnet you can connect to EWTN at: ewtn.com. If you are looking for software, use FTP (your access provider will probably have this as well). You can download software from EWTN at the FTP address: ftp.ewtn.com. EWTN resources are also available through their homepage on the Internet. You can look at this site at http://www.ewtn.com (see Chapter 5 for more details). For those who have questions about all this you can even e-mail them at: sysop@ewtn.com.

Catholic Connect!

Catholic Connect! is another all-Catholic service provider. It has been set up by the Office of Communications and Publications of the Diocese of Rockford, Illinois, which focuses on serving the Church and its members. This service provider has weekly TV previews from a Catholic perspective, along with movie, video, and book reviews from the Catholic News Service. It has games for children that you can download and hundreds of handy, powerful utilities for your computer. You'll find a full-feature electronic daily newspaper. You can select only the sections that interest you and download them if you wish. The service allows members to interact with one another, live or in forums, and provides Internet e-mail. You can download any files from Catholic Connect's file areas, many of which are of special interest to Catholic parents, couples, and ministers working in the Church. For more details on their forums and library, see Chapter 5.

How to Access Catholic Connect!

You can access this service in three ways:

1. Directly by modem: Telephone 708-993-1297
2. By Internet (if you have access): Telnet to them at 205.243.101.43
3. Via their homepage: Reach them at http://www.cathconnect.org

No special software is required to access this service. But, if your computer runs Windows 3.1 or higher versions and you have a 14.4 Kbps or faster modem, Catholic Connect! provides special free software that you can get by accessing them in any of the three ways mentioned above—or they can mail it to you.

Cost

Catholic Connect! is the online service designed to serve Catholic families and professional ministers at very low cost!

The service is not yet large enough to provide you with free local access phone numbers. But they are devoted to keeping costs low by offering fast 28.8-modem access, off-line read-and-write e-mail, and auto high-speed download from your favorite forums and file areas.

If they grow just a little more, Catholic Connect! will offer subscribers toll-free connectivity via the user's Internet access number (be it AOL, CompuServe, Prodigy, NETCOM, or other access service).

To subscribe, call 800-817-4455 or write to: Catholic Connect!, 921 W. State St., Rockford, IL 61102.

Like the big commercial services, they offer point-'n-click access for Windows and for Macs; but unlike the big commercial services, they also offer a basic, menu-driven interface for those (such as missionaries) who can't afford new computers but "who need and deserve to be in touch with their Church." They did this in consultation with missionaries who begged them to keep their needs and difficulties in mind.

Free Catholic Organization Services

Catholic Connect! allows organizations to maintain forums and file libraries. Dioceses and Catholic professional organizations are provided a file and forum area at no cost, but they must agree to update it on a regular basis and advertise it in their diocese. In fact, they offered our contemplative community a free forum while I was gathering this information from them! Catholic Connect! can set up and maintain a homepage for you, too, but there is a cost for this service. If the national professional ministry organization(s) to which you belong, your state Catholic conference, or your diocese decides to take advantage of their offer of free space on Catholic Connect!, you will help them to grow more quickly. For details, call 815-963-3471.

The Peace Communication Network

Another access provider is The Peace Communication Network—a consortium of institutions established formally under Italian law. It was founded in 1995 by men and women who are members of Roman Catholic religious groups. The goal of the PCN consortium is to provide the member institutions with modern means of communication so that the Gospel of Jesus Christ can be spread throughout the world. In addition, they offer, to all members, a global networking connectivity that respects the needs of each group at a very reasonable cost. This is done by offering various levels of service tailored to the requirements of each institution.

In its short lifetime, the PCN consortium has grown at an extremely rapid rate. Already up to about seventy member institutions worldwide, the consortium has potential to provide services for over 500 member institutions.

Who Can Join

According to their Articles of Incorporation, any group listed in the Vatican's official directory, The *Annuario Pontificio,* or any organization connected with a listed group is eligible to be a part of PCN. Not only are Roman Catholic religious orders of both men and women eligible to join PCN, but congregations, institutes, sodalities, dioceses, parishes, schools, novitiates, provinces and houses of religious orders, research centers, and museums are eligible to join. If desired, the member institution can have its own World Wide Web homepage on the PCN server with 3MB of disk space available at no charge to the organization.

System Requirements

Your equipment does not have to be sophisticated. For the simplest access, your computer should be at least a 386-DX. Shareware software and instructions are available to get you started. If you want to get more sophisticated and use PCN on your local area network (LAN), you will need an analog modem connection from your local area network to the telephone line. Or use the special digital card for the LAN to ISDN line connection. You can set up your local area network so that your server communicates with the server at the PCN node site via a dedicated Telecom Italia digital line. You can apply to InterNIC for your own domain name, then use your own server to provide everything the people in your institution need for Internet communication.

Dial-up Numbers

PCN has local telephone dial-up from almost 600 major cities around the world, as well as 80 local telephone dial-up access points in Italy. Possible accesses include local Roman dial-up at analog modem speeds, local and distance ISDN dial-up at digital speeds, international local dial-up at analog modem speeds, and 24-hour dedicated line connection at digital speeds. See their homepage for more details.

Cost

The basic costs to get PCN services are as follows: 1. Membership fee (a one-time expense that does not vary from year to year). This membership fee opens the door to available services and privileges for your institution. It also gives the official representative of your institution full voting rights at the annual General Assembly meeting where budgets, goals, and directions for the PCN are set for the following year. 2. Annual service fee (can vary from year to year). This income is used by PCN to pay for its internal expenses. Operating costs (those incurred by the user institution during the course of using the PCN services). Exactly how much these costs are will depend on the kind of telephone service you are using to connect to the PCN server computer in Rome.

For More Information

To find out how your organization can be a part of PCN, take one of the following no-obligation routes for more information: Send an e-mail inquiry to info@pcn.net or see their homepage at http://www.pcn.net; or personally contact one of the following members of the board of directors: Fr. Angus Cooper, OFM, at a.cooper@ofm.org; Sr. Marie Gannon, FMA, at m.gannon@cgfma.org; Sr. Marialuisa Leggeri, FdCC, at m.leggeri@pcn.net; Fr. Paul Leung Kai Kwong, SDB, at p.leung@sdb.org; Fr. Raffaello Lombardo, IMC, at r.lombardo@pcn.net; Fr. Bernard Rosinski, SCJ, at bernie@scj.org; or Fr. Richard Todd, CMF, at r.todd@pcn.net.

2

▼▼▼

Mailing Lists

Mailing lists exist on the Internet. What are they? First, someone initiates an e-mail address concerning a particular topic of interest, then others sign up to be on the mailing list. Anything sent to this address is sent to all those who signed up to be on the list; they in turn usually respond to messages they receive. What results is a running e-mail *conversation.* To clarify what occurs, let me give an example from an actual mailing list.

First, though, I should explain that when using e-mail, it is customary to repeat some of the original message so the original sender can make sense of your response. The symbol ">" is used to distinguish your response from what you are responding to. In the example following, because Terrye is responding to what Ken previously said, she precedes his words by ">" and omits the symbol when she is talking. These conversations can go back and forth for days and many different people can put in their two-cents' worth.

E-Mail Example 1

From: Terrye
Subject: Real Presence

Dear Ken,
Your post brought back so many memories!
>But I have *never* felt anything so powerful as
>receiving the Holy Eucharist in the chapel at Seton Hall
>university. A small chapel, but the power is there! I

>don't know what it is, there's got to be a name for it, or
>perhaps you've all been saying it all along . . . but during
>the Eucharist, and the kneeling afterwards, I find I leave
>the chapel with an amazing peace, a happiness, a sense of
>being part of something vastly greater than myself and my
>immediate surroundings.

After my conversion experience (which happened
during the first Mass I attended), I visited many churches
in an effort to bargain with God ("OK, I'll be a *Christian*,
but do I have to be a *Catholic*?") Like you, I received
Communion at that first Mass, and was flooded with joy,
peace, and, most of all, a Real Presence I knew could only
be Christ. I knew *nothing* at all of Catholic theology at
that point; it wasn't that I "believed" in the Real Presence—
I *felt* it . . .

I know a couple of people have reminded you that it
is not licit for non-Catholics to receive Communion. That's
true. I also know what it felt like for you when you did. Ken,
with faith like yours in the Blessed Sacrament, you will never
feel satisfied in any other church. Ask to be received, and
soon! You'll be in my prayers.

       Terrye

Here is another example that I would like to share. It is just from ordinary
e-mail rather than a mailing list. The names have been changed for privacy. What
comes first is the message sent to me from "Jane." This is followed by the message I
had previously sent her. Notice all lines are preceded by ">" in the message I sent
her. Because my message to her included her previous message to me, you will see
">>" in front of those lines to show that it is two messages back. It's much like quoting a quotation. I also wanted to include this particular e-mail message to show you
the Internet's great potential for bringing people together to help other people.

E-Mail Example 2

Dear Brother John,
Thank you very much for including Helen in your prayers. I have
forwarded your message to her family and I have been informed that a priest

is going to anoint her today. Your prayers and thoughts are appreciated.
Sincerely,
Jane

At 08:14 PM 3/6/97 -0500, you wrote:
>>Message text written by Jane Doe
>>Would you please include Helen in your daily prayers. She was
>>diagnosed with lung cancer last week and is weakening fast. She is 76
>>and is my best friend's mother. Thank you very much.
>>
>>jtm<
>
>Dear Jane,
>
> We will be praying for Helen and have placed your intention in the
>prayer basket behind the tabernacle in our chapel. Please join us in praying
>for Helen by praying the Chaplet of Divine Mercy with her if possible or
>at least for her.
>   Also, if she is Catholic, consider finding out if she has received
>the sacrament of the Anointing of the Sick. If she desires this healing
>sacrament that has been known to bring physical healing but always gives
>spiritual strength during these difficult times, then contact the priest at
>the nearest parish or ask the hospital nurses if a priest is assigned there.
>
>   God bless,
>Brother John

E-MAIL EMOTIONS

With regard to mailing lists, e-mail, and chat rooms, it is important to remember that people can misinterpret what you say. A joke may be taken seriously. That is why emotion symbols and abbreviations such as the following have been developed:

<g>	=	Grin
<vlg>	=	(Can you guess this one?) Very Large Grin
:-)	=	(Look sideways!) Smile face
:-(	=	Sad face

There are many more and they are usually easy to figure out. Here are the common ones:

:)	=	Smile
:D	=	Smile/Laughing/Big Grin
:*	=	Kiss
;)	=	Wink
:X	=	My Lips Are Sealed
:P	=	Sticking Out Tongue
{}	=	A Hug
:(	=	Frown
:'(	=	Crying
O:)	=	Angel

E-MAIL SHORTHANDS

Here is a list of common shorthands to use in e-mail, mailing lists, and chat rooms:

LOL	=	Laughing Out Loud
ROTF	=	Rolling On The Floor (Laughing)
AFK	=	Away From Keyboard
BAK	=	Back At Keyboard
BRB	=	Be Right Back
TTFN	=	Ta-Ta For Now!
WB	=	Welcome Back
GMTA	=	Great Minds Think Alike
BTW	=	By The Way
IMHO	=	In My Humble Opinion
WTG	=	Way To Go!

VOICE E-MAIL?

With voice e-mail (you send a voice message into the microphone on your computer and the other person listens to it) and video conferencing (you both see and hear the person you are talking to live), there is no need for emotion indicators; the person's voice or facial expression expresses emotions.

TYPES OF LISTS

A Manual List

There are two types of mailing lists—manual and automatic. With a manual list, you send your request to be on the list to a human being who manually updates the files that put people on (or take people off of) a list. For instance, if I had a list, the address might look like John-monks@compuserve.com. To be added to the list, you would add "-request" to the address. So you would send a note saying you would like to be on the list to John-monks-request@compuserve.com.

An Automatic List

An automatic list is run by a computer software program—so don't expect to have much of a conversation. If you see "Listserv" in the address, you are dealing with such a list. For example, the Catholic Spirituality List, abbreviated Spirit-L, is located at Listserv@american.edu. To subscribe, I would send an e-mail to this address. In the body of the message, I would put only: SUB Spirit-L Brother John.

Digest Mode

With either manual or automatic lists, your mailbox can get very full. I subscribed to four mailing lists and sometimes got 100 messages in a day. So I got smart and started receiving them in digest form. What's that? Instead of receiving each response to a mailing list separately, digest form collects them into one big file for you. You can still respond to individual messages in the file. So, if you are on a manual list, use the address you subscribed to and send an e-mail saying you would like to receive the list in digest form. For an automatic mailing list, you have to send a specific command to the software program. In the previous automatic list example, I would send an e-mail to Listserv@american.edu. In the body of the message, I would type only: SET Spirit-L DIGEST.

Getting Off a List

How do you get off a list? For manual lists, just send an e-mail to the address under which you subscribed and say you want to be removed. For me to get off an automatic list like Spirit-L, I would send an e-mail to Listserv@american.edu and in the body type only: SIGNOFF Spirit-L. Now wasn't that easy?

Majordomo Lists

There is another automatic mailing system out there called *Majordomo*. Although I have not seen many lists that use this system, you will easily recognize this type of mailing list because the word "majordomo" appears in the e-mail address. For example, the address for the College Theology list looks like this: majordomo@sbu.edu. To simplify things, if you want to join such a list, just send the command HELP in your e-mail to the address of the list you are interested in. You will receive instructions on the commands for Majordomo.

Monitored Lists

Some lists can be monitored. What does that mean? Two things can happen with these type of lists. The list owner may read or screen all messages posted to the list. If the list owner reads all the messages and finds something posted that he or she does not like, the sender of that message may hear about it. If the list owner screens the messages, then he or she actually controls what is posted. For example, you may send an e-mail to the list saying "Today is Tuesday." The list owner may read that and say, "Nice to know, but useless information." So your e-mail may be thrown away and never seen on the mailing list.

Lists of Lists

Here are three of the many homepage addresses that maintain lists of mailing lists and instructions on how to use them:

> http://www.nova.edu/Inter-Links/listserv.html
> http://tile.net/lists/
> http://www.ucssc.indiana.edu/mlarchive/

Some Catholic Mailing Lists

Here is a sampling of what's out there:

Apparitions List
apar-l@ubvm.cc.buffalo.edu

To subscribe, write to: listserv@ubvm.cc.buffalo.edu
Concerns apparitions and messages of Jesus and Mary.

Catholic Campus Ministry List
Newman-L@Listserv.american.edu

To subscribe, write to: listserv@listserv.american.edu
A list for those involved in Catholic Campus Ministries around the world.

Catholic List

To subscribe, write to: Catholic-request@sarto.gaithersburg.md.
For discussions of orthodox Catholic theology by anyone, under the jurisdiction of the Holy Father, John Paul II.

Catholic-Action

To subscribe, write to: rfreeman@vpnet.chi.il.us
A moderated list concerned with Catholic evangelism, Church revitalization, and preservation of Catholic teachings, traditions, and values.

Catholic Spirituality List
spirit-l@listserv.american.edu

To subscribe, write to: listserv@listserv.american.edu
A forum on spirituality in secular life in the context of the Roman Catholic Faith.

Catholic Web Announcement List
catholic-web@press.smp.org

To subscribe, write to: catholic-web@press.smp.org
Announces new Catholic Web sites to all members of the list.

Christianity in Late Antiquity List
enchlus@acadvm1.uottawa.ca

To subscribe, write to: listserv@acadvm1.uottawa.ca

CIN Ask Father

cinaskf@catinfo.cts.com

To subscribe, write to: listserv@catinfo.cts.com
Questions and answers on the Catholic Faith.

CIN Bible

cinbible@catinfo.cts.com

To subscribe, write to: listserv@catinfo.cts.com
Discussion of Bible topics and scholarship.

CIN Carmelite Spirituality

cincarm@catinfo.cts.com

To subscribe, write to: listserv@catinfo.cts.com
Discussion of Carmelite topics.

CIN Catholic News

cinnews@catinfo.cts.com

To subscribe, write to: listserv@catinfo.cts.com
Read-only message area.

CIN Charismatic

cinchar@catinfo.cts.com

To subscribe, write to: listserv@catinfo.cts.com
Addresses topics of interest for Charismatic Catholics and Christians.

CIN Eastern Rite Conference

cineast@catinfo.cts.com

To subscribe, write to: listserv@catinfo.cts.com
Primarily an area of discussion about the various Eastern Catholic Churches. Also a discussion area relating to all Eastern Christian Churches.

CIN Education/Homeschool

cineduc@catinfo.cts.com

To subscribe, write to: listserv@catinfo.cts.com
Discusses educational and family support issues.

CIN Ethics

cinethc@catinfo.cts.com

To subscribe, write to: listserv@catinfo.cts.com
Discusses anything that fits in the broad area of human ethics.

CIN General Discussion

cinmain@catinfo.cts.com

To subscribe, write to: listserv@catinfo.cts.com
Discussion on Catholicism pertaining to faith, morals, and living the Christian life. Open to all.

CIN Prayer & Spirituality

cinpray@catinfo.cts.com

To subscribe, write to: listserv@catinfo.cts.com
One can submit prayer requests to this list.

CIN Pro-Life Information

cinlife@catinfo.cts.com

To subscribe, write to: listserv@catinfo.cts.com
Read-only conference.

CIN Technical

cinpray@catinfo.cts.com

To subscribe, write to: listserv@catinfo.cts.com
Discussion area for telecommunication and computer topics as they pertain to religious electronic communication.

CIN Totus Tuus

cintuus@catinfo.cts.com

To subscribe, write to: listserv@catinfo.cts.com
Papal addresses.

CIN Youth

cinyth@catinfo.cts.com

To subscribe, write to: listserv@catinfo.cts.com
Self-evident.

College Theology Society

cts@sbu.edu

To subscribe, write to: majordomo@sbu.edu
A mailing list sponsored by the College Theological Society.

Discern List

discern@pwa.acusd.edu

To subscribe write to: listproc@pwa.acusd.edu
For those who are discerning a vocation. Open to vocation directors also.

Dominican Family Mail List

dom-fam@catinfo.cts.com

To subscribe, write to: listserv@catinfo.cts.com
Open discussion on the ministry, life, and spirituality of the Dominican Order. Intended for any Dominican and those interested in the Dominican Charism.

Ecclesial History List

ecchst-l@bgu.edu

To subscribe, write to: listproc2@bgu.edu
Discussions for those interested in Church history, history of Christianity, and/or historical Theology.

Franciscan Mailing List

assisi-l@american.edu

To subscribe, write to: listserv@american.edu
A mailing list that is for and about Franciscans worldwide. It is open to all who love the spirit of St. Francis (d. 1226) and St. Clare (d. 1253).

History of American Catholicism

amercath@ukcc.uky.edu

To subscribe, write to: listserv@ukcc.uky.edu
Self-evident.

History and Concerns of Catholic Women Religious

sister-l@suvm.acs.syr.edu

To subscribe, write to: listserv@suvm.acs.syr.edu
Focus is on the history and contemporary concerns of Catholic women religious.
One need not be Catholic or a member of a religious congregation to participate.

Jesuit General Discussion List

Jesuit@maple.lemoyne.edu

To subscribe, write to: listserv@maple.lemoyne.edu
Discussion revolves around Jesuit ministries.

Liturgy

Liturgy@mailbase.ac.uk

To subscribe, write to: mailbase@mailbase.ac.uk
Discusses Christian liturgy.

Merton Research Institute List

merton-l@byd.mu.wvnet.edu

To subscribe, write to: listserv@byd.mu.wvnet.edu
This list is for discussion of the works of Thomas Merton, as well as the activities of The Merton Research Institute (TMRI) at Marshall University.

Medieval Discussion List

Mediev-L@ukanvm.cc.ukans.edu

To subscribe, write to: listserv@ukanvm.cc.ukans.edu
For those interested in the Middle Ages (allows topics between A.D. 283–1500)

"One Bread, One Body" Distribution List

obob-l@mintir.new-orleans.la.us

To subscribe, write to: obob-l-request@mintir.new-orleans.la.us
A distribution of reflections on the readings from daily Mass.

Order of St. Benedict Discussion List

osb-l@vm.marist.edu

To subscribe, write to: listserv@vm.marist.edu
This is an unmoderated list for a discussion of the values, ideals, and traditions of the Benedictine way of life, and on the relation of this way of life to various forms of work undertaken by Benedictines in the modern world. The list is open to members of the Order of St. Benedict and to members of religious houses, communities, and congregations whose way of life is based on, or derived from, the Rule of Benedict of Nursia (d.c. 547).

Roman Catholic Information Request List

romcathl-request Majordomo@astro.ufl.edu

To subscribe, write to: romcathl-request@astro.ufl.edu
Self-evident.

Secular Franciscan Documents and News

ciofs-l@american.edu

To subscribe, write to: listserv@listserv.american.edu
Distribution list of Secular Franciscan documents and news from the International Fraternity in Rome.

Vocation Directors' List

vocdir-l@pwa.acusd.edu

To subscribe, write to: listproc@pwa.acusd.edu
List for vocation directors.

Water Mailing List

water@his.com

To subscribe, write to: water-request@his.com

A mailing list sponsored by Women's Alliance for Theology, Ethics, and Ritual.

CatholiCity Mailing Lists

CatholiCity Crosstalk lists are monitored daily by full-time CatholiCity workers. They read every posted message but do not screen messages before posting them. To subscribe, just select "Crosstalk" on their homepage located at:

http://www.catholicity.com/cityhall/

Public Crosstalk Groups

CatholiCity Talk	Discusses a broad variety of Catholic topics, including current events, liturgy, the Internet, family issues, books, and Church teachings.
Marian Apparitions	Discusses historical and current Marian apparitions. This is CatholiCity's biggest group.
Prayer and Devotion	Discuss devotions, prayers, prayer movements, and liturgical practices.
Holy Scriptures	Obviously, participants discuss the Bible here. You do not have to be a scholar to participate.
Catholic Events	This is actually more like a news service than a discussion group. Postings concern local or national Catholic conferences, talks, Papal declarations, retreats, or any other Church-related announcements.
Catholic Home Schooling	Both for home-schooling parents and older home-schooled children. Topics include curriculum, books, advice, Internet sites, and parenting.
Knights of Immaculata	This list is for members of Saint Maximilian Kolbe's worldwide lay association or those considering membership. Discussion centers around entrustment to Mary, Saint Maximilian Kolbe, Marian spirituality, the Rosary, and use of technology to evangelize the world.

Private Crosstalk Groups

You cannot directly subscribe to these groups. You must contact them by the e-mail address supplied on their homepage to apply.

Spiritual Warfare	Discussions, questions, and sharing of experiences about spiritual warfare issues, the occult, the New Age, and related topics. A moderator reads and approves all messages before they are posted.
Coming Home Network	A private discussion group for members of Marcus Grodi's Coming Home Network. His ministry is dedicated to helping Protestant pastors and ministers who have returned or are considering returning to the Catholic Church.
Catholic Webmasters	This group is open to Catholic Webmasters of religious and secular sites who maintain them as an apostolic work. Technical and spiritual topics are discussed.

CATHOLIC ANSWERS

I wish to stress one point about conversations by e-mail on the Internet. If someone asks you questions about the Catholic faith, I beg you, please do not begin your answer with, "Well, I think . . ." or "In my opinion. . . ." I have witnessed some very poor answers given to non-Catholics on matters of Faith, morals, and other topics. When someone asks, "What does the Church teach about such and such?" Tell them what the Church teaches. You can look in the Catechism of the Catholic Church for the answer. (See the Introduction about obtaining the Catechism.) If you still feel you cannot answer someone's question adequately, tell him or her that you are not able to answer the question or refer him or her to someone who can.

START YOUR OWN MAILING LIST

If you really have some free time on your hands, you may want to start your own mailing list. All e-mail computer programs come with an *address book* much like the one you have at home listing people and their locations, except in this one, you type a person's name and e-mail address. Now as you build up your address book, you could start a mailing list by asking people in it if they want to be on your mailing list. Then, your e-mail address becomes the center from which people have conversations on the subject you choose for the list. When someone responds to someone else, you receive the e-mail and send it on to everyone on your list. That is the bare bones way to have a mailing list.

If you receive an e-mail with a long list of names before the message, the sender has done exactly this. If you reply to this e-mail, everyone on the list will see your response. Keep that in mind when you respond. A better way to set up a mailing list is to buy computer programs on the market designed for this. You can ask those who have lists to recommend the best programs for creating them. One such program can be found at:

http://tile.net/lists/

If you already have a mailing list, make sure you submit it to the directories for mailing lists I've already mentioned to gather more interest in it.

Bulk Mailing

There are computer programs that allow you to do a bulk mailing (e-mailing) to many people at once. These programs also compile e-mail lists of people for you. On CompuServe I am frequently bombarded by e-mail advertising for such programs so they should not be hard to find. Be sensitive to those who may not want to receive advertising they did not request. Usually bulk advertising will give people the option to either receive more information about their product or to be removed from their bulk mailing list.

Mailing lists and bulk mailings are both ways of spreading the Word of God and meeting new friends. As I mentioned, you will want to be sensitive to people who do not want to be on your mailing or bulk-mailing list. If you irritate people enough, you may get nasty e-mail responses, possibly even containing *viruses*.

VIRUSES

This looks like as good a place as any to talk about viruses. The first time I saw an anti-virus computer program, I thought it was a joke. How can a computer get a virus? I wondered. Will my computer sneeze at me one day? Will I have to take it to the doctor or veterinarian? Unfortunately, we live in a world where people can do things to hurt their neighbors. Some people who know computers very well have written little computer programs that hide themselves on floppy disks, in other computer programs, and even in e-mail messages.

Once these little programs get into your computer, they can make it do some funny (and some not-so-funny) things. Some are harmless; for example, "Hello" may come up on your computer screen. Others are written to destroy your computer. They can scramble all the files on your hard drive or keep your computer from starting at all by destroying basic information it needs in order to run.

Now that I have scared you to death talking about viruses getting into the $3,000 computer system you just bought, let me tell you the good news: You can buy relatively inexpensive anti-virus computer programs that can protect your computer. The bad news is that people keep writing new viruses all the time so you will have to pay for upgrades to your anti-virus program. (I wouldn't be surprised if some of the people who write anti-virus programs are the same ones who wrote some of the viruses!) My advice is "Protect your computer system and sleep better at night."

3

▼▼▼

Homepages

As I mentioned before, viewing a homepage is like looking at the table of contents in a book. The difference is, when you select one of the items on an index on a homepage, it will bring up your selection on your computer screen. At times it will send you to the index of someone else's homepage. This is normally referred to as a *hyperlink*. The address of a homepage is referred to as its *URL* or Uniform Resource Locator. Many homepages—besides having text—now have pictures, sound, video clips, and interactive (and even three-dimensional) graphics. You need to have the correct software program to view these homepages. Most access providers will give you these programs free.

WEB-BROWSING SOFTWARE

The two most popular Internet Browser computer programs are Netscape Navigator and Microsoft's Internet Explorer. Both of these can be downloaded from the Catholic Information Network's homepage (see Chapter 5). If you do not have a very fast computer or connection to the Internet, you will soon discover that some homepages take forever to come up on your screen. One way to speed things up is to turn off the graphics and sound in your Internet Browser program. You will usually find these features under either "Options" or "Preferences" on the title bar (for more details, see Chapter 4). If you still have problems with a homepage, you can get information off that page by using e-mail (as described in Chapter 4). Some unfortunate Catholic missionary in Papua New Guinea may have to resort to this method.

CREATE A HOMEPAGE

If you are served by a major access provider, they will furnish you with a free software program to make your own homepage. I was talking to someone who thought that he would get only one page on which to put his material. You can usually have as many pages as you want, starting with a main page that indexes all your other pages. We have over 200 pages hyperlinked from our main page. The number of pages you can have is limited by how much Internet space your access provider is willing to give to display it. Usually they will give you a set amount, such as 5 megabytes of space. This is calculated the same way you calculate space on the hard drive of your computer. The programs you receive to create your homepage are designed for easy use so don't be afraid to take advantage of your free homepage spot. It can be used for evangelization, or you can put hyperlinks on your homepage that lead to good Catholic homepages already on the Internet.

Design Tips

I would refrain from using too many pictures or graphics on your homepage. These will be slow in coming up on the screens of those whose computers are slow. If these users are like me, they won't wait to see your homepage. Your main homepage should be like a table of contents to your subpages. These should not contain too much information; if they do, subdivide them. This way someone can get the information from your homepage quickly. If you really want to do some fancy things on your homepage give people the option of viewing either the stripped-down version or the fancy version.

Another tip for designing your homepage is to remember that some people go directly to the inside of a book without looking at the table of contents; people may skip your main page as well. By using *Internet directories* or *search engines* (as they are sometimes called), users can go directly to one of your subpages without first viewing your main page. This is possible because such directories categorize almost all the pages on the Internet so users can search for something by name or phrase. Now that isn't bad except that you might want people to see your main page. To encourage this, you should put a selection on each of your pages that enables the user to return to the main page. That way people can quickly access other things you want to show them instead of getting stuck on one of your pages.

Creating a Homepage on the Big Two

If you are on America Online, the KEYWORD for going to the place where you can create your own homepage is HOMEPAGE (isn't that original?). If you are on CompuServe, select the "Internet" button and then select "Create a homepage". You will then be instructed on how to download the free computer program for constructing and publishing your homepage on the Internet. Don't be shy about constructing one. I knew absolutely nothing about constructing a homepage when I downloaded CompuServe's program on my notebook computer.

Free Homepage Sites and More

If your access provider will not give you a spot for your homepage, some Catholic groups on the Internet will do it free. RCNet (the host of our homepage) hosts homepages free of charge to Catholic parishes, schools, and organizations. You just create your homepage and then e-mail it to Peter Wagner at: webmaster@rc.net. Also, you can call him at 313-572-0640. He promises to put the pages up right away.

Ecclesia Web Service offers free homepage space to Catholic organizations. For more information about setting up a spot, e-mail them at: sfabian@usbusiness.com.

Catholic Online hosts homepages for free. To find out how to do it, see their homepage at http://www.catholic.org.

CatholiCity, a division of the Mary Foundation, designs and builds homepages for national organizations free of charge. If you operate (or work for) a national or international Catholic organization that is completely loyal to the Holy Father and to the infallible teachings of the Magisterium of the Roman Catholic Church, contact Dan Davidson, Director of Internet Services. You can call 216-333-9827 or write to: CatholiCity, Box 26101, Fairview Park, Ohio 44126. Or leave them a message at CatholiCity: http://www.catholicity.com.

If your organization already has an Internet homepage somewhere other than CatholiCity, and you meet CatholiCity's qualifications, you can establish a link in CatholiCity or set up a secondary site there. Some of the organizations in CatholiCity have their own site on another server, but choose to have a second site in CatholiCity for the increased exposure it provides them.

Liturgical Publications of Saint Louis, which has been involved in Church communications for the past 25 years, also offers free homepages to Catholic churches. This is great for parishes as they can offer easy access parish information to parishioners and prospective parishioners. Liturgical Publications will design, set up, and host the homepage. Further, they will maintain and update the page so that the information will stay current. Information on the page could include the Sunday bulletin, parish newsletter, parish worship and event schedules, parish regulations, registration information, and pastor messages. This same offer is extended to seminaries, dioceses, convents, Catholic organizations, and Catholic newspapers. They can be reached at their homepage: http://www.liturgical.com, by e-mail: Webmaster atggregd@liturgical.com, by phone: 314-394-7000, or by mail: 160 Old State Road, Ballwin, MO 63021-5915.

If your organization does not own a computer or know the first thing about the Internet or building a homepage, Liturgical Publications will work with you to design and build your page free of charge. Just send them electronic files, or even flyers and brochures, and they'll have you up soon. Electronic information must be in a format they can use. Send electronic files on 3.5-inch floppies, or on an Iomega Zip disk. Files should come in one of the following formats: plain text, MS-DOS text, Microsoft Word for Windows, Microsoft Word for Mac, Adobe Pagemaker, or WordPerfect 5.1 for DOS.

Design Volunteers

Computer Ministry Foundation (http://www.catholic.net/RCC/Catholic Media/free help.html) is a non-profit organization for the Archdiocese of Newark. The foundation is a good source of help for Catholics seeking to use computers to aid their parishes, dioceses, and other ministries. For example, Computer Ministry was involved in the Newark Archdiocese hookup of computer terminals to a local retirement home for sisters. These sisters are now able to reach out through the Internet, giving Catholics the benefit of their training and years of experience in the field of education. Christine Maggio of the Computer Ministry Foundation may be contacted at: chris.mac@applelink.apple.com.

The Illuminated Web has an apostolate to create Web pages and sites for orthodox Catholic organizations, including dioceses, schools, parishes, religious orders, publications, and other organizations. This service is totally free, depending on availability, and they provide:

- Professionally designed and developed homepages.
- Assistance in finding service providers and locations for homepages.
- Maintenance of new or existing homepages.
- Search engine registration (they advertise the homepage on Internet directories).

The Illuminated Web service specializes in creating homepages to convey an organization's mission and message. They work with Catholic organizations all over the United States, Canada, and throughout the world. You can work with them by mail, phone, or the Internet.

Their offer is limited to the number of pages that can be done in the available time. If, due to demand for their services, they cannot provide you with help right away, they will do their best to give you approximate dates when the work can be completed.

You can reach Janet Perry for help with homepages by mail: The Illuminated Web, 3354 Brittany Circle, Napa, CA 94558; by phone: 707-257-6957; by e-mail: janetp@napanet.net, or by going to their homepage: http://www.napanet.net/~janetp/illuminate/index.html.

Other Free Places for Homepages

- Eternal Word Television Network, http://www.ewtn.com
- Best Internet Services, http://www.best.com
- All Faiths Press—pages for religious organizations, http://www.achiever.com/design/freehmpg.html
- Angelfire—general free Web pages, http://www.angelfire.com
- Geocities—general free Web pages, http://www.geocities.com
- Lighthouse Business Services—free pages for Christian churches, missions, and non-profit organizations, http://www.lhbs.com/free.htm
- SpiderCity—free homepages, http://www.spidercity.com

Directories of Sites Offering Free Web Pages

- Home on the Web, http://www.vivanet.com/~woodj/money-mart/freeway/homepages.html
- Free Homepage Directory, http://www.california.com/~sgeler/main.htm

Free Homepage Software and More

The following software programs to create homepages are offered free of charge. The only thing you have to do is get them!

For IBM Compatibles:

- "HotMetal Pro" http://www.sq.com/products/hotmetal/hmp-org.htm
- "HTML Assistant Pro" http://www.brooknorth.com
- "Internet Assistant" http://www.microsoft.com/OfficeFreeStuff/Word/

(Note: You must have Microsoft Word to use "Internet Assistant".)

For Macintosh:

- "World Wide Web Weaver" http://www.MiracleInc.com

Other computer programs that are also good for constructing homepages are out there for a minimal price. Upgrading to Microsoft Word 97 will help you construct a homepage. Other programs you may already have can be upgraded to versions that can build homepages.

Learn from Others

You can learn HTML from other homepages as well. Many Internet homepage browsers will store the homepages you view on your computer disk. Under FILE on the title bar, select SAVE when viewing a homepage you like. Pick the name and directory where you want to save the homepage with its extension of "htm" or "html." If you look at these homepages with a regular word-processing program, you will see the HTML language commands in the homepage and can use them in your own homepage. Normally, you will have to tell your word processor to display ALL FILES when you open the directory of the saved homepage. Otherwise it may just display text files or Word document files.

If you are using either Internet Explorer or Netscape Navigator, there is an easier way to look at a homepage's HTML code. First, get the homepage. On the Netscape Navigator's menu, select "View" and either "Document Source" or "Frame Source." On the Internet Explorer's menu, select "View" and "Source." You will then be looking at the HTML code. If you have Windows, you can copy code from the homepage to a file by highlighting what you want with the mouse. Then press CTRL+C to copy it to the clipboard. Paste it wherever you want.

Here is what the HTML on our main homepage on the RCNet would look like with a word processor. You will find it at http://www.rc.net/org/monks/.

HTML Example

```
<html>
<!— The following HTML tags are the header and title tags. These tags allow you
to specify a title for this page. —>
<head><title>The Monks of Adoration</title></head>

<!— The following HTML tag is the body tag. This defines the body portion of this
page or document. —>
<body bgcolor="#3299cc" background="natr_bak.gif">

<!— The following is an HTML headline tag. Values for this tag range from H1
(largest) to H6 (smallest). —>
<center><h1>The Monks of Adoration</h1></center>

<center><h1>A Catholic Community</h1></center>

<center><h4>Interested in downloading our free publication called THE TABER-
NACLE? Select Download Magazine below and then page down to the selection
for the magazine.</h4></center>

<!— The following HTML tag is the external link tag. This tag is a hot link to the
specific URL (or location). —>
<br><center><UL><Ll><a href="http://ourworld.compuserve.com/homepages/
catholic_monks_of_adoration/">Download Magazine</a></UL></center>

<center><h4>Interested in becoming a Monk of Adoration? Select Vocational In-
formation below.</h4></center>

<br><center><UL><Ll><a href="http://www.catholic.org/vocation/monks.html
">Vocational Information</a></UL></center>

<center><h4>Pray along with us every day. Besides praying the Liturgy of the
Hours (contains hymns, readings from the Old Testament, New Testament, and
Saints; Psalms, Canticles, Intercessions, etc.), we pray the Holy Rosary and some
devotional prayers. Select Devotional Prayers below to see them.</h4></center>
```

```
<!— The following HTML tag is the internal link tag. This is a hot link to another page in your project. —>
<br><center><UL><LI><a href="ourprays.htm">Devotional Prayers</a></UL></center>

<center><h4>Do you have any prayer requests you would like us to pray for? We will present them to Our Lord during Eucharistic Adoration. E-Mail it to us.</h4></center>
<br><center><UL><LI><a href="mailto:102634.1754@compuserve.com">E-Mail</a></UL></center>

<center><h4>Like a monk to speak to your parish or prayer group? Select Monk Speaker below.</h4></center>
<br><center><UL><LI><a href="monkspk.htm">Monk Speaker</a></UL></center>

<center><h4>Help the homeless and poor! Select Poor below.</h4></center>
<br><center><UL><LI><a href="poor.htm">Poor</a></UL></center>

<center><h4>We have some items from our Gift Shop you may be interested in. Select Gift Shop below.</h4></center>
<br><center><UL><LI><a href="giftshop.htm">Gift Shop</a></UL></center>

<center><h4>Did you know that in every Catholic Church Jesus Christ, the Son of God, is present Body, Blood, Soul, and Divinity? For more information select Real Presence below.</h4></center>
<br><center><UL><LI><a href="realpres.htm">Real Presence</a></UL></center>

<center><h4>Would you like to start Perpetual Eucharistic Adoration in your parish? For more information select Parish below.</h4></center>
<br><center><UL><LI><a href="parishad.htm">Parish</a></UL></center>

<center><h4>Learn about God's Mercy. Select Divine Mercy below.</h4></center>
<br><center><UL><LI><a href="divmercy.htm">Divine Mercy</a></UL></center>

<center><h4>Learn about a heavenly visit from the mother of Jesus and the miracle that 100,000 people witnessed. Select Fatima below.</h4></center>
<br><center><UL><LI><a href="fatima.htm">Fatima</a></UL></center>
```

```
<center><h4>Choose from many wonderful religious written articles for children.
Select Children below.</h4></center>
<br><center><UL><LI><a href="childint.htm">Children</a></UL></center>

<center><h4>Choose from over one-hundred fifty articles on prayer by Brother
John Raymond. Select Prayer Column below.</h4></center>
<br><center><UL><LI><a href="prayart.htm">Prayer Column</a></UL>
</center>

<!— The following HTML is just plain text. —>
<p><center><pre>There will be more on this page so come back and visit
us!</pre></center></p>

<!— The following is an HTML horizontal rule tag (or line). —>
<hr align=center width=80% size=3>
<hr align=center width=90% size=3>
<hr align=center width=90% size=3>
<hr align=center width=80% size=3>
<hr align=center size=1>
<hr align=center>

</body>
</html>
```

More HTML

You can alter the wording on the downloaded homepage and the hyperlinks also. Or you may just want to learn how somebody did a certain thing on their homepage so you can incorporate it into yours. If you really want to get into this, why not buy one of Prima's Web books such as, *Create Your First Web Page in a Weekend, Create Front Page Web Pages in a Weekend,* or *Jazz Up Your Web Site in a Weekend.* You can also learn about creating homepages by looking under "Help" on Netscape Navigator's menu and selecting "How to Create Web Services." You may also find some useful information under "Help" on Internet Explorer's menu and its "Web Tutorial."

Homepage Counter

There are people on the Internet who can provide you with a free homepage counter. What's that? It counts how many people have looked at your homepage.

Why would you want to know how many people have viewed your homepage? Well, it can boost your ego, tell you how your advertising is doing, tell you how well your design is attracting people, and perhaps get you listed in magazines for having a popular homepage. You can get a free counter from http:websidestory.com/wc.world.html. One benefit of putting this counter on your page is that, if you get enough "hits" (people who have looked at your homepage), you will be listed on the Websidestory homepage as one of the top 1,000 homepages in the world in your particular category.

Chat Area?

How about putting a chat area on your homepage? You can have an area for people to get together, with or without you, on your homepage and discuss whatever you want—live. To set up a free chat area, go to http://parachat.web page.com. The only stipulation (there is always a catch) is that you allow them to advertise in your chat room. However, for a monthly fee, you can bypass this.

Another place that contains counters, guest books (that people who visit your homepage can sign in), and more is http://www.pergatory.com/. (Don't get that confused with Purgatory!) The guest book will cost you a one-time fee.

ADVERTISING YOUR HOMEPAGE

So now you have your homepage software, have created your homepage, and put it up on the Internet. How is anyone going to find it with the millions of homepages out there? In Chapters 5 through 13 I have listed some big Catholic directories that are available on the Internet. If you tell them about your homepage, they probably will add it to their directory.

A mailing list has been created for those interested in receiving notification of new Catholic homepages and for those interested in submitting their own pages. The CATH-URL was created in the beginning of October 1995 by R. Paul Gordon, who maintains The Catholic Connection homepage.

Now CATH-URL is called the "Catholic Web Announcement" mailing list or "Cath-web." The following commands can be sent to Cath-web's mailing list (cath-web@press.smp.org.) in the SUBJECT area of your e-mail message: subscribe, unsubscribe, subscribe digest, digests (returns a list of digests for the past 30 days, along with instructions for retrieving them via e-mail), and help. Unlike other mail-

A SIMPLE BEGINNING

Just to show you how things can develop on the Internet: Paul began creating The Catholic Connection in June of 1995 because a friend sent him a list of several Catholic sites that he thought he would enjoy. Paul decided to turn those sites into an index directory of Catholic sites. Soon he was flooded with e-mail of new Catholic sites to add to his Catholic Connection directory.

Because there are several other directories similar to The Catholic Connection directory on the Internet, Paul thought it would be nice if the suggestions he was receiving for new Catholic sites were distributed to everyone interested. So he started the CATH-URL mailing list.

ing lists, these commands and any e-mail posts to the mailing list go to the same e-mail address. To correspond directly with a person, write to khoogheem@smp.org.

Reach Out

We should not limit our advertising of Catholic homepages to Catholic directories. One way to get your homepage well known is to spend time submitting it to Internet Directories. The best way to submit your page is through Yahoo. To do this, first go to http://www.yahoo.com. You will see different categories listed. Select the one you think best applies to your homepage. You will now see a button that says ADD URL; select this to add your homepage to this category. After you do that, you will see at the bottom of the Yahoo homepage a button for more places to submit your homepage. You will find a long, long list. With a little patience, you can submit your homepage to numerous directories. Avoid selecting any special deals claiming to submit your homepage to 200 directories for some specified amount of money. You can just as easily do it yourself.

Some other places to consider for submitting your homepage are:

"What's New" at http://www.ncsa.uiuc.edu/SDG/Software/Mosaic/Docs/
    whats-new.html
"Open Market's Commercial Sites Index" at http://www.directory.net
"PostMaster" at http://www.netcreations.com/postmaster/
"Alta Vista" at http://www.altavista.digital.com

"Yellow Pages of the U.S." at http://www.telephonebook.com

"Webaholics Top 50 Links" at http://www.ohiou.edu/~rbarrett/webaholics/favlinks/entries.html

Reference Books

If you go into a bookstore or library, you will see Internet Directories or Yellow Pages. Look under Religion and you may find some Catholic homepages, mailing lists, and Usenet groups. You can contact them and find out how they were able to get into these books. They may have paid for it, just as people pay to be included in the Yellow Pages of a phone book.

WebCrawlers

There are computer programs that do nothing but search the Internet night and day to compile directories like the ones I've listed. They are sometimes referred to as "WebCrawlers." To get a complete list of the active WebCrawlers on the Internet (so you can advertise your homepage) look at http://info.webcrawler.com/mak/projects robots/active.html.

Online Malls

You should also consider getting listed in online malls, many of which consist largely of pointers to other sites and provide pointers for free. I managed to get my homepage advertised free in an Internet Mall. It is like a regular mall, but on the Internet you don't have to walk! You can do your shopping directly from your computer. The Internet Mall put me in the "Tent City," sort of like having a shop outside a mall under a tent. (This is getting scary, isn't it? You can lose track of what's real.)

Usenet

I talked about Usenet in the Introduction. You can post your homepage to the Catholic group. There is also a group for general announcements of new homepages at: comp.infosystems.www.announce.

Mailing Lists

Remember the mailing lists? In Chapter 2 you can find out how to get a list of mailing lists. Then you can announce your homepage address on those lists that would be interested.

Online Publications

Finally, if you have a really good homepage, you might consider telling online publications about it. They may review it in their publication. Many of them reside at the Electronic Newsstand at http://www.enews.com.

4

Useful Information for People on a Low Budget

HOW TO DO EVERYTHING BY E-MAIL

You can access almost any Internet resource using e-mail. Perhaps you can't afford the latest and greatest computer and modem. If you want information, you can still get it on the Internet. Maybe you've heard of FTP, Gopher, Archie, Veronica, Finger, Usenet, Whois, Netfind, WAIS, and the World Wide Web. You can use simple e-mail commands to access all of these, and much more, on the Internet. Using e-mail services can save you time and money. Dr. Bob Rankin has put together all the information you will need to take advantage of e-mail services. You can get his document easily. It is available from several automated mail servers. To get the latest edition, send e-mail to one of the following:

For the U.S., Canada, and South America: mail-server@rtfm.mit.edu. Enter only this line in the body of the note: send usenet/news.answers/internet-services/access-via-email.

For Europe, Asia, etc.: mailbase@mailbase.ac.uk. Enter only this line in the body of the note: send lis-iis e-access-inet.txt.

You can also the file by anonymous FTP at one of these sites:

rtfm.mit.edu: pub/usenet/news.answers/internet-services/access-via-email or ftp. mailbase.ac.uk: get pub/lists/lis-iis/files/e-access-inet.txt

On the Web, in HTML format, you can find it at: http://www.activesol.com/www/dbobfram.htm.

Finally, you can download it off Bob's homepage at: http://www1.mhv.net/~bobrankin.

If you'd like to keep up with the latest updates and announcements of new versions, send the command SUBSCRIBE ACCMAIL Firstname Lastname in the BODY of a message to the address: Listserv@listserv.aol.com. The ACCMAIL list is a great place to ask questions you have about this document. You're likely to get a quicker response from one of the list subscribers because the author gets several hundred messages per week.

Homepages by E-mail

For me the greatest advantage of Dr. Rankin's techniques has been getting homepages by e-mail. Almost all the Catholic resource information found in Part II has been retrieved from homepages this way.

How would you like to get 50 different homepages off the Internet in about eight minutes? That's how fast you can get the information by e-mail. Even the best computer programs on the market for viewing homepages cannot come close to this speed. How do you do it? First, you need the URL (or address) of the homepage you want to look at. Let's say I wanted to look at my homepage on Catholic Online. I would send an e-mail to one of the following addresses: agora@dna.affrc.go.jp (Japan), agora@kamakura.mss.co.jp (Japan), getweb@info.lanic.utexas.edu (USA—alias for above address), agora@picard.tec.mn.us (USA), or agora@mx.nsu.nsk.su (Russian users only).

In the body of the e-mail message, I would put: SEND http://www.Catholic.org/Vocation/monks.html.

That's all there is to it! Sometimes the homepage can come back to you within five minutes.

More Commands

You can put up to 10 lines of SEND commands in one e-mail, so you can retrieve up to 10 homepages with one e-mail. If you put the command DEEP followed by the URL of a homepage, you will get the homepage plus everything it references. This may sound easier, except you may get a lot of useless information. In addition, the information obtained by e-mail from a homepage is limited to only 5,000 lines.

Amazingly enough, you can even retrieve the HTML code for a homepage. Instead of the SEND command mentioned, type SOURCE and you will receive the homepage in a file on your hard drive that you can examine with your browser.

If you want to learn more about the commands you can use to retrieve e-mail, send an e-mail to: agora@kamakura.mss.co.jp. In the body of the mail, write: SEND-http://www.w3.org/hypertext/WWW/Agora/Help.txt.

Possible Problems

Sometimes you may get back an error message about a particular homepage. This happens because the e-mail addresses for getting homepages are temporarily not working. Simply retry the address the next day or try another address from those listed previously. Another option is to use The WebMail Server at: webmail@eolas.ucc.ie. This will also retrieve homepages by e-mail. Send your e-mail to the address listed previously and in the body type only GO URL, replacing URL with the homepage address you want. Unlike the other e-mail servers, you can place only one request per e-mail message. Further you are limited to 50 messages per day and a homepage cannot exceed a file size limit of 65,535 bytes.

If worse comes to worst, you can use your Internet browser program as discussed in Chapter 3 to get homepages. If you select "source" from the browser menu you can see the homepage HTML code with its referenced URLs. Or you can save the homepage to your hard drive and then look at it with a word-processing program. Using either technique, you will find the URLs that you want to look at and can then retrieve them by using the e-mail procedure explained above.

Please consider, the e-mail servers listed in this guide are, for the most part, operated by kind-hearted volunteers at companies or universities. If you abuse (or overuse) the servers, there's a good chance they will be shut down permanently. This actually happened to several of the most useful e-mail servers in 1995. Try to limit your data transfers to one megabyte per day. Don't swamp the servers with many requests at a time.

How to Access the Internet Search Engines

Search engines are useful tools for finding things on the Internet. For a detailed listing of what you can do with them, see Chapter 14. Let's begin with an example using the popular search engine called Lycos. Imagine that I want to find the homepage called "The Catholic Goldmine." Using the aforementioned technique for getting homepages, I might choose to send the e-mail to the address: agora@kamakura. mss.co.jp. In the body of the mail message, I would input the following command: source http://lycos11.lycos.cs.cmu.edu/cgi-bin/flpursuit?The+Catholic+Goldmine. In response, I would receive a file I can look at with my browser for all the homepages that mention these words. I can also use the "send" command mentioned already. Make sure you do not put any carriage returns or line feeds in your command line. Of course, you can substitute anything you want for "The Catholic Goldmine" after the "?". The "+" is used so that the search engine will look for all three words.

Another popular search engine is WebCrawler. You would use the same technique described for Lycos except that your command line for the previous example would look like this: source http://www.webcrawler.com/cgi-bin/WebQuery?The+ Catholic+Goldmine.

Directory Assistance by E-mail

"Whois" is a service that queries a database of Internet names and addresses. If you're looking for someone, send an e-mail to: mailserv@internic.net. Put the following in the subject area: whois <name>. This is not a comprehensive listing of all Internet users. It contains mostly network administrators and some "notable" Internet figures.

You can search for someone using a database at MIT that keeps tabs on everyone who has posted a message on Usenet. Send an e-mail to: mail-server@rtfm.mit. edu. Include this command in the body of the mail: send usenet-addresses/<name> (substitute the person's name for <name>). For example, to search for John Smith you would put in the body: send usenet-addresses/John Smith.

You still haven't found the person you are looking for? Don't give up. Netfind is another search tool that uses a person's name and keywords describing a physical location to return a lot of information about the person. Let's say John Smith happens to live in Detroit, Michigan. To find him, I would address an e-mail to one of the addresses previously mentioned for retrieving homepages. In the body of the message I would type: gopher://ds.internic.net:4320/7netfind%20dblookup?john+ smith+detroit+michigan. You will receive a list of domain names (for example: ud.detroit.edu) where this person may possibly be found. Pick the most likely one and send an e-mail to the same address you used for the last one. This time the body of your message would read: gopher://ds.internic.net:4320/0netfind%20netfind%20 John%20Smith%20ud.detroit.edu. With luck you would receive enough information about John Smith to make the identification.

FOR THOSE LONG-DISTANCE CALLS

Why pay for long-distance phone service to surf the Net? There may be a local Internet service provider to your home or business that you are not aware of. Further, once you find a local provider, you can use that phone number to connect to other popular services such as America Online or CompuServe. To find out more, look at Chapter 14 under "Searching for Internet Service Providers."

BROWSING THE WEB WITH AN OLD COMPUTER

Like me, you may have an old 286 DOS personal computer with 1MB of RAM and a 40MB hard drive. I still use mine for word processing. What about the Internet? Yes, even an old clunker like this can send and receive e-mail over the Internet. And as I have shown, you can do a lot with e-mail. You will, however, need a modem. Normally, when you buy a modem, you will receive software that lets your computer talk with other computers. With both a modem and software, you are ready to check with your local Internet service provider to get information about connecting.

DOSLynx

Perhaps you want to do more than just use e-mail for everything. The text-based Web browser called "DOSLynx" will work on a 286 or even an 8086 PC with either SLIP or PPP Internet connections. You will, however, need 512K of RAM, DOS 3.0 or higher, and a monochrome monitor. This browser is free and you can download it at http://lynx.browser.org/. However, you have to download the correct driver for your Internet Provider, which you can get at: ftp://ftp2.cc.ukans.edu/pub/WWW/Dos Lynx/support/. You will also need to download a dialer or use a terminal program to call your Internet service. You will also have to learn the commands to get into SLIP or PPP mode. So you will first dial up the Internet provider, then exit the dialing program, load the SLIP or PPP driver, then run your DOSLynx program.

Net-Tamer

A shareware program called Net-Tamer automates access to the Internet from computers as old as a 286 XT with a Hercules graphics card. This program offers e-mail, FTP, Telnet, and a Web browser. Net-Tamer will only display graphics, however, on a 386 machine or better. Also, it supports only PPP connections. You can download it at: http://people.delphi.com/davidcolston/.

Minuet

If you have a DOS 386 PC without Windows, you can get homepage graphics on your computer, but not as many or as quickly as with Windows. To do this, the popular shareware browser Minuet is available. Minuet requires at least 512K of RAM, DOS 2.1, and a hard disk. Although this Web browser is text based, it can still display GIF and JPEG images on a computer with VGA graphics. You can't, however, click on the images that are hyperlinked to other homepages. Minuet also has e-mail, Gopher, Telnet, FTP, and Usenet news. By default, this program uses a SLIP connection. You can configure it to run with a PPP connection, but there will be glitches. To download this program, try these addresses:

http://www.cesnet.cz/pub/gopher/minnesota/minuet/,
ftp://minuet.micro.umn.edu/pub/minuet/latest/minuarc.exe, or
http://www.cren.net/www/minuet/overview.html

Mosaic or Netscape Navigator

Now if you have a 386 PC with 4MB of RAM, a VGA monitor, and Windows 3.1 running in enhanced mode, you can browse the Web in Technicolor. You will need at least a 14.4 Kbps modem. These features meet the minimum requirements for Web browsing software such as Mosaic or Netscape. You can connect to the Internet through America Online, CompuServe, or Prodigy. To speed things up a bit, you might want to get a 16550x UART chip. You can buy this chip yourself and plug it into the motherboard or purchase a high-speed serial card such as Hayes ESP.

DOS User's Guide

Another place to look for help with your old computer is *The DOS User's Guide to the Internet* at: http://www.palms.4kz.com.au/dos.html. Here you can find out about other Internet utilities such as mail or FTP programs.

Give Your Internet Browser a Tune-Up

Many people get their Web browsing software such as Internet Explorer or Netscape Navigator and never adjust their settings. With the proper adjustments, pages that take a minute or more can be displayed in 10 seconds! The default settings under "Options" in these programs favor graphics, plug-ins, Java, and JavaScript. These are time-consuming downloads that you may not care to see. By turning off these features, you will get the no-frills text of the homepage with markers showing you where graphic images are. You can actually click on any of these graphic markers to download the graphic that goes there. If for some reason you are having trouble or want to see the pictures, hear the sounds, or watch the animation, you can just recheck these options and reload the page. If you see a button labeled "Images," you can push it and the browser will load the images while your setting stays the same.

Stripping Down the Browser

Let's examine these programs. Starting with Netscape Navigator 3.0 under the menu items, select "Options." Uncheck "Auto Load Images." Now select "Network Preferences" and the "Languages" tab. Uncheck the boxes that mention Java. Next, get rid of annoying alert warnings that pop up. Under "Options," you will see "Security Preferences." Select the "General" tab. Clear all the check-boxes under "Show an Alert Before." There are more alerts to remove. Under "Options" select "Network Preferences" and then "Protocols." Again, uncheck the boxes under "Show an Alert Before."

If you have Internet Explorer 3.0, you will find "Options" under the "View" menu. Select the "General" tab and uncheck "Show Pictures" along with sounds and videos. To eliminate the Java features, select "Options" and the "Security" tab; uncheck all the elements under "Active Content"; then clear out those useless warning messages. To do this, choose "Options" once again along with the "Advanced" tab and clear all the boxes under "Warnings."

Give Your Computer a Tune-Up

Sometimes the traffic jams that slow down your surfing speed are not out on the Internet but in your own computer. Typical fixes may involve fine-tuning Windows communications settings and serial port settings or buying a new modem, more RAM, a video card, and a CPU. Because fine-tuning can double your surfing speed without any expense, let's start there.

Adjusting Port Speeds

Windows 3.1 communications' driver software cannot support port speeds over 56 Kbps. To remedy this, download Cybercom.drv replacement from any Sim Tel file archive such as: ftp.digital.com/pub/micro/pc/simtelnet/win3/drivers/cybercom.zip.

Follow the instructions for doubling your potential speed.

If you have Windows 95 and are thinking, "Good thing I upgraded," I'm sorry, but you have to fiddle around too. Your communications driver already supports 115 Kbps, but the modem setup wizard often defaults to 56 Kbps. If you have a 28.8 Kbps modem, you are going to want to change the setting. Under "Start," choose "Settings" and then "Control Panel." Open the "Modems" window and adjust the port speed to 115 Kbps.

Serial Ports

Let's now look at the serial port. Older PCs may contain unbuffered serial ports. This means that they can only pass data at a rate of 56 Kbps. You can buy a buffered serial port card for as little as $15 and double your surfing speed. Still, you may have software in your computer that turns off these buffers. You will need to download the CTS Serial Port Utilities to learn what kind of port you have and how to configure it. You can get this information from http://www.comminfo.com.

New Modem?

Your next option for increased speeds would be to buy a new modem. If you already have a 28.8 Kbps modem, you won't notice much difference by upgrading to a 33.6 Kbps modem. And if you go for a 56 Kbps modem, you may find that your Internet provider does not support this speed yet. Your phone line may not support this speed either. Check with your Internet provider before upgrading your modem.

More Memory?

Increasing your computer memory is probably an investment you will appreciate both on and off the Net. First, more memory typically means your computer will run faster. Second, once your browser program runs out of memory, it begins to use your hard drive. The browser works faster with your computer memory. So the more memory, the less hard drive caching, and the faster you can surf. Finally, with more memory, you can run more than one program at a time. Before upgrading your computer's memory, make sure you have open slots for more memory and determine what memory configurations will fit in your computer.

Video Cards

If you really enjoy viewing pictures or graphics on homepages, your video card could be slowing down the display. Adding inexpensive video memory, especially if you currently have only 512K of video RAM, can significantly increase surfing speed. You may also want to consider buying a video accelerator card.

New CPU?

Now as a last resort (because of the expense), you may want to upgrade your computer's central processing unit (CPU). This may require upgrading other components in your system as well to avoid bottlenecking the new CPU. So, if you are thinking about upgrading the CPU, you will want to compare the total costs against buying a new computer.

PART II

▲▲▲

What's on
the Internet
for Catholics?

5

Brother John's Top 20 Catholic Homepages and Internet Directories

Finding a good homepage amid the vast amount of information on the worldwide Internet can be like finding a needle in a haystack! If you have ever flipped through Internet magazines, at some point you usually find a list of recommended Internet sites, which can be very useful. Reviews of recommended sites help you find interesting information, much like TV guides that list what's on different channels so you don't have to switch from channel to channel. (Of course, TV remote controls mean you don't have to expend too much energy channel surfing these days!)

To give you some idea where to begin, I will recommend 20 Catholic sites on the Internet. Of course, everybody thinks his or her own homepage is the best, and each human being has different likes and dislikes based on personal opinions. Even though I have selected 20 recommended sites, this does not mean other homepages are not just as good or better. I selected these homepages because I believe they provide interesting Catholic information or services. Also, some are impressive because of the effort put into designing them. It is great to see people using their talents for the glory of God. The recommended homepages will hyperlink you to other Catholic places as well. So check them out!

THE VATICAN HOMEPAGE

http://www.vatican.va

How could I not recommend this one? My 75-year-old mother, who is not very familiar with computers, was visiting the monastery not long ago. While she was visiting, curiosity got the best of her. She stepped out in faith to see what all this Internet stuff her son was working on was all about. So I showed her the Vatican homepage. The next week she called me and said she just had to get on the Internet again to see the Vatican site!

The Vatican has guarded its homepage well by putting it under the protection of three archangels: Raphael, Michael, and Gabriel. These are the names of the three computers used for the Vatican's Internet and e-mail service. The Vatican has plans to put up some 1,200 papal and Vatican documents. Sister Judith Zoebelein, a member of the Franciscan Sisters of the Eucharist in the United States, is the technical director of the Vatican's new Internet office. She says the computers were named after the archangels because "A little protection always helps." Raphael will store texts and graphics from the Vatican museums as well as sound clips from Vatican radio. Michael, known as the great archangel protector against the devil, has been assigned to the computer that regulates access and protects the system against hackers (people who try to damage other computers). Gabriel, known for being the messenger of God, is the name assigned to the computer that communicates with the outside world. This computer also holds the programs that help people access documents they want.

The temporary homepage for the Vatican was first put on the Internet on Christmas Day 1995. Once revised, the new site received 2.9 million visitors in its first three days! Now that is a lot of traffic!

Because the Church is made up of people from every continent, you can expect information to be given in more than one language. In fact, some of the Vatican's homepage information is available in Italian, Latin, French, English, Spanish, Portuguese, German, and Dutch. Although these language headings may all appear under a document, only certain ones will be functional. This means that if a document hasn't been translated into a given language, you will not find the language button hyperlinked to anything.

The Vatican homepage uses frames, sort of like having two or more different windows open at the same time. Personally, I don't find frames very helpful because not all the windows will fit on my 15" computer screen. This happened with the main menu for the Vatican site. For those who would prefer to bypass frames and to learn in more detail what is on the Vatican homepage, see Chapter 8.

I was happy to see the "Vatican Radio" page, which has real audio broadcasts that you can listen to, featured in a secular computer magazine that reviews homepages on the Internet. Fancy effects on your homepage can attract the attention of even the secular world.

INFO CATHOLIC CONNECT!

http://www.cathconnect.org

Already mentioned as a stand-alone Catholic access provider in Chapter 1, Catholic Connect! allows guests to visit their online service through their homepage. Here you will find a totally Catholic atmosphere. The main menu lets you select a list of users online, help about the BBS, a list of recent callers, message areas, community chat, details on membership, an e-mail menu, library files, and wall links (hyperlinks to Catholic homepages). Also, you can "page a user." This simply means you can correspond with anyone currently accessing this site.

I encourage you to look at the forum and information areas. Although not everything found there is strictly about Catholicism, these areas certainly can be viewed as providing a wonderful service. How about "Ask the Accountant" or "Ask the Public Relations Professional"? Or if you want to visit Rockford, Illinois, the "Food and Restaurant Guide" forum area might be for you. Are you planning a vacation? Look into the "Travel in North America," "Travel in Europe," and "Latin America Travel" forums.

There are also plenty of forums concerning issues related to the Catholic Faith in Catholic Connect! Prospective college students and their parents will want to look into the forum about information and data concerning Catholic colleges. Also of related interest would be the "College Admissions" forum and the "College Financial Aid" forum. On a more local note, you might want to find out about the Catholic education in the Rockford Diocese.

There are many discussion areas. You might want to check out these sections: Catholic family guide, Catholic Press Association, Catholic book reviews, Catholic travel, daily inspirational thoughts and prayers, daily news for Catholics, family life and living for Catholics, discussions on a consistent ethic of life, Catholic origins, parish life and information, movie ratings and discussions, prayer intentions, television programs and ratings discussions, the third millennium, television and media coverage, and an open discussion/review of videos.

For Catholic news, you'll want to see the Rockford Vine, the Rockford Observer, and Rockford Diocese News & Events. If you are looking for a job, check out the Diocesan job postings.

Local interest discussions include Catholic schools in Illinois, Catholic charities in Illinois, Illinois legislative alert discussions, and items of interest to Illinois members.

If that is not enough for you, how about looking in their library? Most of the titles for library sections are self-explanatory. Perhaps there is something here you always wanted to know. Check out files on the following: the third millennium, an advertiser's index, the Catholic review of books, business-related files, Bishop Doran of the Rockford diocese, Catholic education file library, children's stories, classified ads, the CNS calendar, CNS news briefs, communications, a general-purpose file area, ITN daily news files, Rockford diocesan directory, education, electronic publishing, reviews from EWTN, games, graphics files, Gutenberg Bible-texts, electronic books from the Gutenberg Project, home and house files/programs, files from LifeLine, selections from the CFM, Catholic media guide, media library, movie reviews & ratings, NCCB-USCC statistics, NCCB-USCC articles, odyssey TV, the Pope Speaks, printing, religious files and programs, files for the Rockford diocese, run times for Windows programs, articles about television, disk and file utilities, DOS system utilities, articles relating to the Vatican, video information and reviews, the Vatican Information Service, and the weekly readings of the Mass.

INFO THE CATHOLIC INFORMATION NETWORK (CIN)

http://www.cin.org

CIN was founded in 1987 for evangelization through electronic messaging and text retrieval media. One of the largest Catholic networks in the world, CIN is carried through BBS (Bulletin Board System). Electronic bulletin board systems provide online services, generally on a small scale, and often with a particular focus. CIN hosts nodes (connections to their online service) to four continents and now reaches out to the world through their homepage on the Internet.

CIN's mission is to offer free information on the Catholic Faith to all, including the texts of papal addresses and encyclicals, news, and other articles as well as to facilitate open discussion on all matters of Catholic life. It is their intent to adhere to the Magisterium of the Church, the Holy Father, and the Bishops of the world united with him as pastors of the Church, while remaining open to dialogue with everyone.

The opening homepage for CIN gives you the opportunity to view their site with or without frames. They even have something to click on to test if your browser supports frames. They also provide you with a link to download either of the two most popular browsers. If you choose to view their site without frames, you will see a hyperlinked index of what you can find on their site. Also, for your convenience, they have provided a search engine for their site. Select "Search CIN" for this option. If you choose to see their site with frames, your computer screen will be divided into four of them. You can get rid of some of these frames by placing your mouse over the dividing lines and dragging them up, down, right, or left. I highly recommend closing some of the frames.

Once you have set up the screen the way you want, you will see that CIN has much to offer. You might want to look into their frequently asked questions, mailing lists, message board, Church documents, Bible study guide, Catholic calendar, daily Mass readings, and the Apostleship of Prayer.

Besides all this, there is much more. See CIN information and links concerning Pope John Paul II, Our Lady, prayer and liturgy, doctrine, Catholic education, Catholic home study, the Good News ministries, the Eastern Church, natural family planning, Pro-life, charismatic (an art gallery), saints, vocations, art and culture, poetry and literature.

If that's not enough for you, how about hearing what priests such as Father Chrysostomos, Father Hal Stockert, Father Pat Gaffney, and Father Mateo have to say.

Other interesting links include lay organizations, parishes, dioceses, and Internet resources. The *CIN Digest* is available online and includes a listing of CIN host node BBS numbers and an extensive CIN file list of free text documents that are available via the Internet.

You will also want to see the CIN mailing lists—16 popular mailing lists that range from Eastern Catholics to home schooling—or view the valuable read-only lists with papal texts (*Totus Tuus*), Catholic news, life information, and much more. (See Chapter 2 for more details.) Mike and Sharon Mollerus of CIN may be contacted at: sysop@catinfo.cts.com.

http://www.catholic.org

Catholic Online, already mentioned in Chapter 1, has a homepage with many selections of interest. From their homepage, if you are already a CompuServe member, you can enter the Catholic Online forum mentioned in Chapter 1.

The homepage opens with a beautiful picture of the Pieta, sculpted by the great artist Michelangelo. Next to the picture, you can choose their main menu, Catholic news, saints and angels, radio, the marketplace, or, you can find out what's new.

The main menu will take you to a hyperlinked table of contents running down the left side of the page. Some of the links here are to pages either hosted or put together by Catholic Online. They have so much here that if you don't see what you are looking for in the table of contents, you can choose their "Catholic Search Engine" and search their site either by a keyword, a topic, or a concept. In addition to all this, you can submit your homepage to them.

To give you some idea of what you'll find in the table of contents, here's some of what Catholic Online has put together or hosted: the Catholic education network, the U.S. Catholic Bishops database search, Our Blessed Mother, prayers, Catholic publications, Catholic organizations, parishes, dioceses, Catholic vocations, Catholic Online news releases, Catholic Online Foundation, the Catholic Catalog Company, youth apostles, the African-American Catholic communication task force, De La Salle Christian Brothers, New Zealand Catholic Conference, the Pilgrim Guide to educational media and media literacy, Fr. Kenneth Roberts, the Catholic historical society, and Catholic engaged encounter.

If you select "Catholic Online Media" to the right of the table of contents, you will find Catholic news, multimedia, and publications. For news, you can choose from the Catholic World News or the Vatican Daily News. Choosing Catholic Online Broadcasting will take you to a variety of live and pre-recorded broadcasts, both audio and video. Choosing publications will take you to an index of Catholic publications.

The table of contents also lists the Catholic Web Directory. Like the yellow pages of a phone book, this directory is designed so that all Catholics, dioceses, churches, schools, clergy, and others can locate and use the resources available to Catholics on the Internet. I will discuss these Catholic Internet directories in more detail.

Catholic Online has plans for what is called "Mass Intransit." This will be a database of all United States Catholic churches, including Mass schedules. The database will be searchable by location, allowing travelers to cite their destination and receive information about the closest Catholic church. Michael Galloway, the president of Catholic Online, may be contacted directly at: 70007.4674@compuserve.com.

ETERNAL WORD TELEVISION NETWORK (EWTN)

http://www.ewtn.com/

I have already mentioned EWTN in Chapter 1. This homepage has a library on it with over 10,000 Catholic files to look at. Of course, they couldn't list them all so they provide a search engine to aid you in finding what you want. EWTN screens what they put on their homepage for correct teaching according to the Catholic Church. I offered some articles I had written for their library and I was told that the librarian would have to look at them first.

Mother Angelica, a Poor Clare Nun of Perpetual Adoration, started the EWTN. This Catholic TV network broadcasts 24 hours a day, every day of the week. I would say that the most popular show on the network is "Mother Angelica Live." She interviews guests in a talk-show format and is continually expanding the network. From satellite broadcasting around the world, Mother has moved into short-wave radio, creating a station called WEWN. Finally, Mother bought the Catholic Resource Network on the Internet to expand in that direction.

Now, as can be expected, you will find information about their television and radio networks, including program schedules for both, on the homepage. You can find a list of guests for the "Mother Angelica Live" show and descriptions of special programs. Besides this, you can read and post messages in the "Information Conference" (announcements and prayer requests), ask questions of their panel of online Catholic experts, or browse through the vital questions and answers that have already been posted.

Because EWTN realizes that many people, like me, enjoy seeing pictures, there is an online gallery of religious artwork and photos. They also cater to those who have to keep up with the news: You can read daily Catholic news stories from Catholic World News and the Vatican Information Service and use the news search engine to find previous stories. The system operator for the page may be contacted at: sysop@ewtn.com.

UNIVERSITY OF ST. THOMAS– ARCHBISHOP IRELAND MEMORIAL LIBRARY

http://www.lib.stthomas.edu/ireland/

Here is a great source for theological resources on the Internet with around 100 sites to visit. Each subject category listed takes users to further subcategories where they will find abstracts and links to actual theological resources on the Internet. If a resource covers more than one subject, it may appear in more than one category.

All bibliographies here are copyrighted. They may be copied or downloaded for personal use only. If you send the reference librarian a theologically related reference question, you will receive a response within three business days. Send questions to Jan Malcheski: j9malcheski@a1.stthomas.edu.

At the Ireland Library and UST Resources you can find research help and question forms, their online databases, and library catalogs.

Of much more interest is their listing of theological resources on the Internet. You can find information in the following categories:

Catholic Church: directories, sites, and information
Moral Theology: ethics, and issues
Liturgy, religious music, and the arts
Church history and documents
The Bible
The biblical and medieval world
Pastoral ministry and Canon Law
Theological libraries, bibliographies, and special collections
The Christian denominations
Non-Christian religions
Professional organizations, e-journals, and religious publishers
An HTML tutorial for theologians
Search the Internet with Infoseek, Alta Vista, Yahoo, and Lycos.

♫ CHRISTUS REX ET REDEMPTOR MUNDI

http://christusrex.org/www1/icons/index.html

Michael Olteanu, the Webmaster of this site, received an M.S. in Computer Engineering in 1970 and has been designing and engineering data networks for 27 years (five years in Europe and 22 years in California). He is a lay member of The Marian Movement of Priests.

Michael joined the Anti-Soviet underground movement in 1954 and became a leader in 1958. He was captured by the KGB in May 1959, tortured for months, then sentenced by a military tribunal to a prison term of 23 years (since he was 17 at the time of his capture, the court could not impose the standard death penalty). He spent five years in the death camps of the Romanian Gulag.

Michael owes his life and freedom to various Congressmen and to President Gerald Ford, who all spent much time interceding on his behalf with Ceausescu, the Romanian dictator at the time. Michael and his family were authorized to leave Romania for the United States in December 1975 and became U.S. citizens in May 1985.

Michael began Christus Rex (Christ the King) as a private, nonprofit organization dedicated to the dissemination of information on works of art preserved in churches, cathedrals, and monasteries all over the world.

Christus Rex is working on assembling a collection of images that will constitute a visual representation of the Bible. Also, they have started building the database for a worldwide tour of churches and monasteries, comprising in excess of 5,000 images. If you would like to participate in this project, send them your favorite color photographs and they will process and present them with appropriate credits.

When you go to his homepage, you will find some picture tours that will occupy you for awhile. You can see Vatican city (255 images); the Sistine chapel (325 images); the Vatican museums (596 images); the Raphael Stanze and Loggia (226 images); Nazareth, Bethlehem, and Capharnaum; the Way of the Cross in Jerusalem (223 images); the Basilica of the Holy Sepulchre in Jerusalem (155 images); a worldwide tour of churches; and Tiananmen: a pictorial history (273 images).

This site isn't all images; they have more, including the Our Father in 30 languages, Church documents, writings of and about Pope John Paul II, a history of the general councils of the Church from A.D. 325–A.D. 1870, meeting Christ in the Liturgy, weekly reflections on the Sunday Gospels, and the Catechism of the Catholic Church.

There is more. For those who have to have the news, they provide an information service (C.R.I.S.) that publishes news bulletins in many languages. They also have news from the Holy See, world news, and news from the Holy Land. Send your comments to Michael Olteanu at: root@christusrex.org.

`INFO` NEW ADVENT CATHOLIC WEBSITE

http://www.csn.net/advent

New Advent is a Colorado-based nonprofit organization, organized for the purpose of using new media to spread the Catholic Faith. They have dedicated their Web site to the Immaculate Heart of Mary.

I am told that the authors of this directory of Catholic information screens whatever it considers placing on their homepage. This screening ensures that all the information on the homepage is in accord with Catholic teaching. This homepage claims to be one of the largest Catholic sites in the world, with over 2,400 Catholic files. (With EWTN's homepage claiming 10,000, perhaps New Advent is only the second largest.) Many files are part of their project to put the entire edition of the Catholic Encyclopedia online—currently 1,662 articles and still growing. The volumes of the Catholic Encyclopedia take up a whole shelf in our library!

New Advent also has St. Thomas Aquinas's *Summa Theologica* online. This summary of Catholic theology produced in the Middle Ages is still considered an awesome work.

You still want more? Perhaps you'll want to check out the Church Fathers (hundreds of books, sermons, letters, and other works from the first eight centuries of the Church). You can look things up on their site using their alphabetical table of contents. Comments can be e-mailed to them at: knight@knight.org.

`INFO` CATHOLICITY

http://www.CatholiCity.com/Airport/Arrivals.html

CatholiCity is a complete, freestanding Internet site available free-of-charge to "surfers" on the World Wide Web. The site is subsidized and managed by the Mary Foundation, a tax exempt, nonprofit organization founded by Bud Macfarlane, Jr., and based just outside of Cleveland, Ohio. Visitors to CatholiCity virtually see an overview of a city: There are streets, a cathedral, a school, a post office, a market-place, a grotto, and even a city hall. There are chat rooms (named Village Green, Cathedral Catacombs, Market Square, and SchoolYard), e-mail lists (see Chapter 2 for more details), e-mail drops, and all the other services available in cyberspace. There is even an airport for travel to other major Catholic Internet sites or "cities." The CatholiCity homepage represents an interesting approach, and it is evident that much work has gone into its design.

Catholic organizations of every kind can be found in CatholiCity: publishers, pro-life groups, magazines, homeschool organizations, stores, apostolates, Marian groups, and so on. Most organizations are now national, but eventually, the site hopes to have regional and local organizations.

CatholiCity went online in May of 1996, and the "city" is growing every day! Check it out.

INFO CATHOLIC INFORMATION CENTER ON THE INTERNET (CICI)

http://www.catholic.net

I had the pleasure of talking on the phone with James S. Mulholland, Jr., president and founder of CICI and Catholic Telecom, an Internet access service. Mr. Mulholland told me about his plans to create a Catholic directory of Internet sites that will be the world's most extensive database of dioceses, parishes, clergy, schools, resources, organizations, and e-mail addresses. He has recruited some help for his massive project. (He was thinking of recruiting me, but I was deep into my studies for my Masters in Theology so it wasn't possible at the time.)

CICI's present Catholic Internet Directory off their main page has the following categories: online books, commercial webs, Church councils, early Church writings, history, culture and exhibits, liturgy and worship, news bits, Catholic organizations, Papal writings, the Pope, saints, Scripture, the Vatican, and other related information sources.

Some of the topics off the main page include teachings of the Church, Catholic periodicals, issues and fact forums (addressing topics that frequently trouble Catholics and non-Catholics alike), Pope John Paul II, and the Holy See's Mission to the United Nations. You will also find a Catholic media directory, pro-life directory, and a directory of dioceses online. They are constructing a Mass time and church locator that will search for the parish and Mass times nearest you.

CICI wants to be a valuable resource to scholars, journalists, lay people, and clergy seeking information or forums that reflect the genuine teachings of the Church. CICI is willing to assist dioceses and Catholic institutions in getting online.

If you are interested in seeing what Catholic Telecom offers for Internet access, you can contact them at 216-528-0059, toll free 888-729-2426, or by e-mail sales@cathtel.com.

`INFO` CATHOLIC ANSWERS

http://www.catholic.com/cgi-shl/index.pl

Catholic apologetics and evangelization are two very important issues in the Church, especially as we approach the third millennium. Apologetics deals with defending what we believe as Catholics. Evangelization involves spreading the Faith and hopefully gaining new members to the Church. As Catholics we have been given the fullness of truth. It is up to us to share this with others. Otherwise, we become like the worthless servant in the Gospel parable who buried his master's money instead of investing it wisely to make more money.

Given the importance of knowing our Faith, this homepage has many valuable things to offer. Catholic Answers is the largest Catholic apologetics and evangelization organization in North America. It is run by lay people devoted full time to promoting the Catholic Faith through books, booklets, tracts, *This Rock* magazine, tapes, and television and radio appearances. Some of the members always have been Catholics, some have returned to the practice of their Faith after having lapsed, and some are converts from other faiths. Their staff of apologists answers questions about the Faith and also give parish seminars.

Regarding their beliefs and goals: They believe the Catholic Church was established by Jesus Christ and teaches the fullness of Christian truth. They believe all Catholics, not just the clergy and those in the religious life, are called to evangelize. They want to spread the Catholic Faith by helping good Catholics become better Catholics, by bringing former Catholics "home," and by resolving misconceptions non-Catholics may have about the Church and what she teaches. Their work has the approval of many Bishops in the United States and in other countries.

Of special interest, for me, on this homepage is the section titled "Answers." In this area you will find answers to your questions about the Catholic Faith and much more. When I viewed this page they had two booklets and more than 100 tracts online. Under "tracts" you will find the following index: Evangelism and conversion;

God: Father, Son, and Holy Spirit; Creation and science; Scripture; Tradition; Magisterium; The Church; The Pope; Sin and salvation; The Sacraments; The Virgin Mary; The Saints; The Last Things; Anti-Catholic Charges; Churches, Sects, Movements, and Moral Issues.

Catholic Answers will be adding new titles regularly. Soon they will have a database of thousands of questions and answers about the Faith. You can read articles from their magazine *This Rock*. To make life a little easier for you, they have a search engine on their page that allows you to find what you want to know. You can also ask them questions directly if you can't find the answer on their page.

 ## THE CATECHISM OF THE CATHOLIC CHURCH

http://christusrex.org/www1/CDHN/ccc.html

What better way is there to learn about your Faith than by studying the Catechism of the Catholic Church? When I was visiting the Vatican homepage, I noticed that they were in the process of putting the Catechism online but that it wasn't ready yet. So until you can find it there, the Christus Rex et Redemptor Mundi homepage has the entire Catechism on their site. Technically speaking, this is not a separate recommendation for the Top 20, but I thought it was important enough to include here.

When you go to this page, you will see the prologue and can click your mouse on "Contents" to see the table of contents for the Catechism. By clicking your mouse on any part of the table of contents, you can read what is in that section. The author of this homepage would be wise to add a search engine. It would be extremely helpful to be able to search the Catechism by a word or phrase. I have the actual book and find the index fails me at times.

INFO THE CATHOLIC CALENDAR PAGE

http:www.easterbrooks.com/personal/calendar/index.html

The liturgical year is very important in the Church. "Christian liturgy not only recalls the events that saved us but actualizes them, makes them present. . . . The whole liturgical life of the Church revolves around the Eucharistic sacrifice and the sacraments" (Catechism of the Catholic Church #1104, #1113). Given the importance of the seasons and days of the liturgical year to our living a life of grace, I selected this homepage as an aid to us in following it. For any day you choose, this page will tell you the liturgical vestment color, what is being celebrated, the season you are in, and the Mass readings for that day. If you don't understand some of the terms, a glossary defines them for you.

When I say you can view any day, I do mean any day! You can go backward or forward by calendar day, by month, or by year. If you prefer, you can look at the calendar for the whole year one month at a time. Clicking your mouse on any day in the calendar will give you that day's liturgical information.

One needs to remember when viewing this page that celebrations are given according to the General Roman Calendar, which is the general Church calendar. There can be exceptions according to observances of individual dioceses and decisions of the Bishops' Conference in a country; this calendar even notes variations according to those approved in the United States.

On this same page you can find out which Mysteries of the Rosary are prayed on any particular day, along with general Rosary information. Of course, one should realize that the Rosary is not part of the Church's liturgy, but can help in many ways—for example, in our recalling the great Mysteries of our Faith for pious meditation.

INFO THE ULTIMATE PRO-LIFE RESOURCE LIST

http://www.prolife.org/ultimate/

This list certainly lives up to its name as the "ultimate" resource list. Abortion is a terrible tragedy in our modern world. The number of children killed each year is staggering. I wrote an article about abortion for the prayer column I write for the Catholic Twin Circle. I called the pro-life office of our diocese for some information. In the course of the conversation I asked how many abortions had taken place in the United States during the current year. The person didn't know but told me how many abortions had taken place in past years. My reaction was total shock.

Given the fact that I believe this to be one of the worst evils in our era, any effort to stop it or to discourage those considering having one from doing so is well worth the effort. Richard Cormier, a friend of the monastery, participated in a peaceful prayer protest outside an abortion clinic. He was able to persuade one woman to give birth to her child. From that moment on, he dedicated his entire life to the pro-life movement.

This page is worth going to so you can learn how to help or where to refer others for help. You can learn about pregnancy assistance, post-abortion problems, adoption, politics, health and educational information, along with much more. This page has received many glowing reviews from those who rate homepages on the Internet.

SAINT PATRICK'S PARISH IN DUBLIN, IRELAND

http://users.homenet.ie/~aduffy/

You may wonder why I picked this one. (It is not because I am Irish—I don't have even a small percentage of Irish blood in my ancestry!) It is because Father Aquinas Duffy from this parish has put together an extensive site that took almost a year to make. I don't want that to scare you into thinking a homepage is extremely difficult to construct. Father Duffy included a few fancy features along with much text that he apparently wrote himself. It started with a simple homepage that contained a brief description of the three churches in the parish, a list of clergy, and the times of the Masses. Since then it has grown into a large site restricted in size only by space limitations. Fr. Aquinas not only designed the site but maintains it at his own expense. Father says, "I hope that it [his homepage] will encourage other parishioners around the globe to do the same for their parishes. Don't be put off. Remember that God works through the network of people of good will. All I learned about web design I learned from others."

St. Patrick's is a rural/urban parish in the Archdiocese of Dublin, Ireland. It comprises 1,200 Catholic families and is situated on the northeast, in north county Dublin. They are about 15 miles north of Dublin city. The parish consists of three churches: St. Patrick's Donabate, St. Ita's Portrane, and Balheary Church. The parish is 10 miles from one end to the other and comprises three very different communities. Donabate has many members who work in the city. Portrane has a large hospital and many of the staff live in the area. Balheary is a rural farming area. You can imagine Father has a challenge following St. Paul's advice to be all things to all men, given the diversity of his parish!

Father has arranged his opening page with an easy-to-understand table of contents. On the left of the table are the titles for various pages to which he has hyperlinks. On the right side of the table are short descriptions of what you will find there. He has the word "new" next to those pages that he has recently constructed or that are new links to other homepages. While you figure out what to look at first, you can listen to the nice organ music in the background.

Plenty of photos with descriptive commentaries can be found on his homepage, including a few monastic photos. Imagine, Father even uses animation to show you all the panes in a circular stained-glass window in the church. For aspiring homepage designers, whether pastor or parishioner, Father Duffy has some tips for how to start. I would tell you more, but having piqued your curiosity I expect you will visit the page to check it out!

SAINTS' LIVES

http://www.pitt.edu/~eflst4/saint_bios.html

Here is a little quiz question for you: Does the Church proclaim everyone in Heaven a saint? The answer is no. The Church canonizes a person because he or she lived a life of heroic virtue and lived in fidelity to God's grace. But that's not all. Saints are chosen because their lives are examples that show us how to live the Christian life. If we do not read the lives of the saints, we will not benefit much from their examples, will we? I have therefore chosen this homepage so you can learn more about them.

There is nothing fancy about this homepage. It is as straightforward as they come, with an alphabetical list of saints and hyperlinks to information about them. There isn't even a single graphic or image. This illustrates that homepages need not be fancy in order to provide useful information to their visitors.

Besides the saints listed, there is a pretty good set of links to related saints' information. There are also links to lives of saints from the Orthodox Church. (Note: The Orthodox Church may recognize some individuals as saints that the Catholic Church does not.)

It's a good idea to get to know the saints in Heaven, as they are great intercessors for us before the throne of God. Look, I dedicated this book to St. Albert the Great and see how it turned out? (Okay, so that wasn't the best of examples!) Saints have come from all walks of life and backgrounds so there's no excuse for not becoming a saint.

FRANCISCAN CUSTODY OF THE HOLY LAND

http://www.christusrex.org/www1/ofm/TSmain.html

The Franciscans sure are lucky. They are the ones who have the joy of taking care of the Catholic churches in the Holy Land. Some of these churches have great significance to our Catholic heritage. For instance, they take care of the Church of the

Annunciation in Nazareth and the Church of the Beatitudes. I had the great grace of making a pilgrimage to the Holy Land and spending about a week there. Once you've been there you want to go back. While I was visiting, there was one couple in my group who was returning for the tenth time! When Brother Craig (my superior) was there, he met a woman from Spain who had visited 18 times!

For Catholics, or for that matter, any Christian, Moslem, or Jew, the Holy Land is where they claim their origins. Not all of us can make a pilgrimage to the Holy Land, but the Internet opens up the possibility of at least taking a virtual trip there. By the way, we owe the Franciscans credit for establishing the wonderful devotion called the "Way of the Cross." This devotion was spread around the world by the Franciscans so that those who couldn't go to the Holy Land could make a "spiritual pilgrimage."

I chose this homepage because the Franciscans let you "share their experience of the Holy Land." On their homepage, you can access a lot of information and even some pictures. I recommend you start by clicking on "Christian Sanctuaries of the Holy Land," where you can find information and pictures concerning the Nativity site at Bethlehem, the Shepherd's fields, the Annunciation site at Nazareth, Capharnaum, the Holy Sepulchre, the Holy Cenacle, Dominus Flevit (where Our Lord wept over Jerusalem), the tomb of Mary, the Way of the Cross (pictures and reflections), and the Kidron Valley (pictures). There is so much to see that I will leave it up to you to explore.

INFO THE REAL PRESENCE OF CHRIST IN THE EUCHARIST

http://www.pitt.edu/~aagst8/a.html

I have to admit I am totally biased in this choice. As a Monk of Adoration, how can I not like a well-put-together homepage on the Real Presence? This topic is not only close to my heart but one that should interest all Catholics. After all, the Holy Eucharist is Jesus—really and truly living among us Body, Blood, Soul, and Divinity. The Holy Eucharist should be everything to us because Jesus should be everything to us. Pope John Paul II said, "The Church and the world have a great need of Eucharistic worship. Jesus waits for us in this Sacrament of Love. May our adoration never cease."

My bias has not totally clouded my judgment though. This homepage is put together very well. The opening page depicts the Holy Father raising a chalice. Next to Him are the words taken directly from the Gospel of Saint Matthew, where Our

Lord says at the Last Supper that the bread and wine are His Body and Blood. Also, this page tells us the Catechism of the Catholic Church's teaching on the Real Presence of Jesus.

You can find out about Perpetual Eucharistic Adoration. Many parishes now have people taking turns spending time with Our Lord 24 hours a day, seven days a week, with the Sacred Host in a monstrance. There is a link on the page for Eucharistic miracles. Sometimes it takes such a miracle to bring a doubting Thomas around to belief. For those who already believe, these miracles will bolster their faith. The author of this page covers Biblical texts concerning the Holy Eucharist and early Christian belief in the Real Presence. Also, this page will give you excerpts from the Second Vatican Council on the Holy Eucharist, personal testimonies, periodicals, and prayers for Holy Hours. Besides all this, there is a mailing list on the Holy Eucharist and links to relevant sites.

 THE MARY PAGE

http://www.udayton.edu/mary/

As Catholics, we have a special place in our hearts for Mary, the mother of Jesus. She has played a special role in our salvation by cooperating in God's plan of redemption. Even though Mary is now in Heaven, she continues her role as our spiritual mother. She intercedes for us with her Son and guides us to Him. And her Son wishes us to honor her for what she has done for us. So given all this, my Top 20 list would just not be complete without a homepage on Mary.

The Mary Page is maintained by The Marian Library/International Marian Research Institute at the University of Dayton in Ohio. They are an international center of research and study on the role of Mary in Christian life. The Marianists founded the University of Dayton in 1850. Since 1943 it has been a home to the Marian Library, which holds the world's largest collection of printed information on Mary. The goal of the page is to present information about the mother of Jesus and to lead people to a loving knowledge of her, the first and most holy of the faithful. They believe that by learning more about Mary, we develop a more complete knowledge of Christ, who is the fulfillment of our human existence.

As you can imagine, this page is full of information about Mary. You will want to see the gallery first. Here you can view exhibits of contemporary Marian art from around the world with some commentary. After that you can select "Resources" from the main menu in order to look at the institute's data files on Marian topics. Then you might want to select "Meditations" that will take you to several online reflections on Marian topics that may aid in your spiritual growth. Next follow the "News" link to a variety of items that includes the myriad ways people honor Our Lady. Finally, you might have a question about Mary or want to learn more about her through their "FAQ" (Frequently Asked Questions) link.

▼▼▼

CATHOLIC NET REVIEW

Fortunately, you do not have to rely only on my opinion of the top 20 Catholic sites on the Internet. Not far from me in Boston, Massachusetts, Troubadour Information Systems has launched its new online publication, *Catholic Net Review,* available at http://www.bettnet.com/cnr/. *Catholic Net Review,* edited and written by Domenico Bettinelli, Jr., is a periodical review of Internet sites related to Catholic and Christian themes. This publication is intended to be a critical review of what's available as a service to Catholic Net users who feel overwhelmed by the astounding number of sites available. Mr. Bettinelli believes CNR will help you by providing detailed reviews of what's great, merely good, and not worth seeing. CNR updates its reviews on a biweekly basis.

As I said, opinions are great but there must be some criteria behind them. What is the basis of Mr. Bettinelli's judgment? He says that to receive a good review, a site must include pleasing and logical site design, compelling content, and doctrinal fidelity to the principles of Catholicism and Christianity.

Catholic Net Review officially launched its first reviews on May 1, 1997. They chose to evaluate EWTN Online and the New Advent Catholic Supersite. Both, I might add, are among my Top 20 picks. Catholic Net's review offered a critical analysis of each site highlighting the good and the bad.

Who is Domenico Bettinelli, Jr.? He is an employee of Catholic World News at: http://www.cwnews.com/. He works simultaneously as a reporter, assistant editor, and Web site designer. A graduate of Franciscan University of Steubenville, located in Ohio, Domenico earned a B.A. and is working toward an M.A. in theology. He currently lives in Salem, Massachusetts. Because Domenico lives so close, I hope to meet him some day and perhaps share "opinions."

OFFICE FOR VOCATIONS, ARCHDIOCESE OF LOS ANGELES

http://www.catholic-church.org/vocation/

Priestly and religious vocations are important in the Church. Marriage is the vocation of most people but God does call certain individuals to serve His people as a priest, deacon, or religious. This page, designed for those who feel God's call, is inviting and simple to maneuver through. Perhaps other dioceses would consider putting up such a page on their site.

The first bit of useful information you will find here is descriptions of various vocations in the Church: diocesan priest, sister, deacon, religious order priest, and brothers. There is also information for those interested in serving, for a time, in other countries in a lay ministry. Those interested in the priesthood can find out about the qualities that are necessary for a priestly candidate. Anyone unsure if he or she has a vocation can look at the "Signs of a Vocation" or take the "Vocations Anonymous Test." If someone is still not sure, he or she can always talk to a member of the site's vocation team by e-mail. There is also a link to "Discernment Programs," that includes a mailing list. To find vocation directors, look under "Vocation Team" for a mailing list.

The monks of the Monastery of Christ in the Desert in New Mexico designed this particular site. You may have read about them, as they have been featured in several major magazines, both secular and Catholic. You see, these Benedictine monks design homepages as their work. What makes them unique is that they are physically located in the middle of nowhere! They have neither electricity nor telephone lines. You are probably wondering how they could possibly do homepage design without these necessities. I would like to say it's a miracle—a miracle of technology. You see, the monks use solar cells to produce the electricity and a cellular phone to connect to the Internet—I wouldn't want to pay their phone bill!

6

Catholic Internet Directories

To select the Top 20 sites listed in Chapter 5, I used Catholic Internet directories that linked me to thousands of Catholic sites. Some of the sites I mentioned in Chapter 5 have Catholic Internet directories on them as well.

What Are Catholic Directories?

You may wonder: What exactly is a Catholic Internet directory? These directories usually consist of a hyperlinked list of Catholic Internet homepages. Somebody has taken time to compile such a list for the convenience of Catholics who are looking for certain Catholic information or people. There are various approaches for the layout of such directories. Homepage titles can be listed alphabetically or they can be by topic. Some directories give only the titles of homepages while others have a short commentary on each. Catholic homepages may be grouped under the following headings: parishes, dioceses, organizations, publishers, or doctrine.

Directories can be compiled by actually searching the Internet for a particular topic or by having people submit their homepage to the directory. In the latter case, usually a person will be required to fill out a form specifying the address of their homepage and the category into which it fits. Some directory compilers take time to look at each homepage before including it in their directory. This is a good idea as homepages can have erroneous Catholic doctrine on them. In addition others may be submitted by people who want to play a joke.

Because some Catholic information can be found on non-Catholic homepages, some directories may point you to such non-Catholic sites. Other Catholic directories may have extraneous links to homepages that have nothing to do with the Catholic Faith. But, for some reason, the compiler may have thought a Catholic would be interested in that site.

Why Catholic Directories?

With the search engines or Internet directories I have mentioned in previous chapters, you may wonder why we would need Catholic directories. The problem with using search engines is that, depending on what you're looking for and how you look for it, they can return too much information. For example, if you search for homepages with the word "Catholic" in the title, you will probably find about 200,000 matches. Even if you narrowed the search, you could still come up with a list of thousands. And just because the homepage has your particular phrase in it doesn't mean it really contains what you are looking for. For example, I might search for "Fathers of the Church" and end up on another religion's homepage that talks about their founding fathers. So, as you can see, Catholic directories can indeed be helpful.

In this chapter, I list directories for finding Catholic places and people. I have included their topics so you will have an idea of what's there and where to look for particular information. These directories may also lead you to other Catholic directories.

INFO **THE CATHOLIC INTERNET DIRECTORY**

http://www.catholic-church.org/cid/

This directory file is an extensive index of Catholic Internet information put together by Timothy DeRyan. When you go to this homepage, you can download his whole directory for free, or if you prefer, you can download it by individual chapters. If you select "Search the Database," you can look for specific listings. Mr. DeRyan verifies all the listings in this directory by e-mail, phone, or through the Official Catholic Directory and has updated it monthly from April 1995.

For those interested in downloading the directory from the homepage, here are its chapters:

- The Top 25 Catholic Sites on the Internet
- UCCB/USCC Directory
- Catholic Diocesan Web Sites
- Diocesan E-mail Directories
- Catholic Publications
- Catholic Organizations on the Web
- Christian Service, Volunteer Organizations
- The Main Catholic Directories on the Internet
- Religious Orders, Vocation Information
- Catholic High Schools on the Web
- Catholic Colleges and Universities
- Catholic Campus Ministries, Newman Centers
- Catholic Resources
- Ecumenical Resources
- Catholic Internet Newsgroups
- Catholic Internet Mailing Lists
- Catholic Online Communications Services
- The Catholic Information Network Nodes

This directory is the limited edition release of the Catholic Networking Directory, which was created as an aid to interdiocesan and general Church communications.

If you must have the most recent edition of this directory, you will have to pay for it. The most recent Catholic Internet Directory can be ordered only in book form. See their homepage for details.

You can send additions or corrections for his directory to: tim@deryan.com.

INFO CATHOLIC MEDIA DIRECTORY

http://www.nd.edu/~theo/RCD/Directory5.html

Kern Trembath, Assistant Chairman of the Theology Department at Notre Dame University, maintains this directory. His wife, Sally, is a doctoral student in systematic theology at the same university. They have four children—Calvin (6), Mark (11), Alex (6), and Emily (11). I would think the children know their Catechism, having parents with such qualifications! Anyway, as an aid to diocesan and Church communications, Kern has put together a directory.

On this homepage you will find links to 13 chapters concerning the media. Here's what they are:

- Catholic News Services/Outlets
- Catholic Television Stations (U.S.)
- Catholic Radio Stations (U.S.)
- Religious Broadcasting Satellite Networks (U.S.)
- Prominent National Radio Outlets, Secular
- Prominent National Radio Outlets, Christian
- Catholic Communications Organizations (U.S.)
- National Media Literacy Organizations
- National Catholic Magazines/Newspapers
- Catholic Online Communications Services (U.S.)
- National News Services
- E-mail Directory for Catholic Publishers/Organizations (29K file)
- E-mail Directory for General U.S. Media (31K file)

Besides this, you will find a chapter on Catholic health care associations. Also, you can find free help on this homepage if you are a Catholic organization thinking of going online. If you need to update any entries, Kern has a form that you can complete and submit.

If you want to find out more about Kern and his family, click on his name found at the bottom of his homepage. He can also be reached at: ~Ktrembat@www.nd.edu.

ALL IN ONE CHRISTIAN INDEX—CATHOLIC INDICES

http://www.interlog.com/~mkoehler/allinone/catholic.html

The All in One Christian Index wants to help you find the right directory for what you need. In other words, this index gives you the table of contents of various Catholic directories on the Internet so you can see what each offers.

In addition, the Index provides a rating system for each directory. Ratings from zero to four stars appear next to the directory name and the ratings are based on the following factors:

- Number of sites indexed
- Organization of the index
- How current the index is
- Usefulness of the descriptions
- Overall ease of use of the index

The URL I have given you is for Catholic directories. This site also has indexed Christian directories as well. Here you will also find an easy way to submit to numerous Christian indices at the same time. You can enter the information about your homepage once and automatically submit it to Christian directories without having to retype the relevant information with each submission. Also, for those directories that require an e-mail submission, you can send it to a number of relevant addresses with a single e-mail message. To do this, click on "All In One Christian Submit All" found at the top of their page and follow the directions.

If you maintain a Catholic directory and would like to be included on this homepage, select "Submit/Update Index" found on the top of their page. Then fill out the form they provide.

Michael Koehler, who maintains this index, can be reached at: ~mkoehler@ www.interlog.com.

INFO THE CATHOLIC GOLDMINE

http://www.cris.com/~stambros/catholic.html

This directory is maintained by Chris Miller, who recently graduated from St. Ambrose University with a degree in Business Administration and a double minor in economics and philosophy. He is 22 and from a small town in Iowa. Chris started working on this directory in 1995. After two years of being up on the Internet, the directory has been visited over 100,000 times and contains almost 1,000 Catholic links. Perhaps this is because he dedicated this homepage to the Sacred Heart of Jesus and the Immaculate Heart of Mary. It truly is amazing how things can develop on the Internet. What started out as something fun to do has developed into a truly useful index of Catholic homepages.

When you go to his homepage, you will find that it uses two frames, both of which contain his index of categories. The one on the right, however, gives short descriptions of the categories. You can get rid of the frames by clicking "Exit Frames" in the left-hand frame. You will notice that Chris has his own chat room. He lets you know when he will be there so you can chat with him.

You will find around fifty-six links or categories in this index. Since it keeps growing all the time, you will want to click on "What's new this week" to get the most recent additions to this directory. Here are the categories or links I found in this index:

- Really Good Links/What's Hot!
- Apparitions
- Church Documents
- Prayers and Devotions
- The Brown Scapular of Our Lady of Mt. Carmel
- Pro-life Information
- Priesthood
- The Mass/Liturgy
- Women's Religious Orders
- Men's Religious Orders
- Vocations
- Pope John Paul II
- Mary
- Eternal Word Television Network
- WEWN—Catholic Shortwave Radio
- Catholic Apologetics
- World Youth Day 1997—Paris
- People in the Church
- Saints
- The Prayer Chapel
- Retreat Centers and Catholic Tours
- Catholic Shrines
- Catholic Chat Links
- Catholic Radio and Television
- Catholic Church/Dioceses Online
- Churches Online
- Byzantine Links
- Other Catholic Pages
- Priests with a Homepage
- Papal Visit '95
- The Vatican

- Catholic Organizations/Groups
- Catholic Schools
- Catholic Education
- Catholic Homeschool Links/Information
- Catholic College Links
- RCIA/Convert Links
- Catholic Penpals/Catholic Singles
- Catholic History Links
- Natural Family Planning Links
- Catholic Mailing Lists
- Catholic Youth
- Catholic Books Online
- Catholic Bookstores and Giftshops
- Catholic News, Newspapers, and Magazines
- Catholics and Political Issues
- Catholic Publishers
- Catholic Video Producers
- Catholic Businesses
- Knights of Columbus
- Foreign Language Catholic links
- Music Links
- Religious Art
- Ways to Block Out the Garbage on the Internet
- Learn How to Create Your Own Page
- Miscellaneous links

As you can see, Chris Miller has a good-sized Catholic directory. If you would like to contact him, he can be reached at: stambros@cris.com.

INFO DIOCESENET

http://www.diocesenet.com/index.html

DioceseNet provides a U.S. dioceses image map with links to the more than 50 United States Catholic diocesan Web sites. You can choose your state on the map provided or use the pop-up state-listing menu to view dioceses' listings by state. They have put together some of these homepages, in a standard format they use for their diocesan pages. You can push any of a set of eight buttons to see diocesan information in the following categories:

- The Diocesan Newspaper
- Marketplace
- Parish Web Pages
- Diocesan Services
- Information Center
- Diocesan Policies
- Diocesan Ministries
- Other Ministries

Add your parish or diocese to DioceseNet by sending an e-mail to: helpdesk @diocesenet.com. Webmaster Jeff Pearring, who created the Web sites for the dioceses of Colorado Springs and Pueblo, is willing to help others. DioceseNet wants to help people find diocesan and Catholic information and also is willing to offer advertising from diocesan newspapers on their Web site. Project leader John F. Pearring may be contacted at textpros@usa.net.

 ## CATHOLIC COMMUNITY ON AMERICA ONLINE

http://members.aol.com/cpolmin/html/index.htm

Strictly speaking this would really not qualify as an Internet directory. They say every rule has an exception. I figured that since I talked so much about this place in Chapter 1, it would be good to tell you about their Internet site as well. Internet surfers who come across this homepage should start with the description of what they are about. Then you might want to read the descriptions of their many discussion groups provided within their Catholic community. You can download various issues of Catholic Community newsletters including ones for youth.

Of special interest is the "Ask a Catholic Priest" selection. Questions are e-mailed to priests at: cpolmin@aol.com. Questions can also be asked in Spanish, French, Italian, and German. You can even send your prayer intentions.

Most of what you'll find here will benefit only America Online users. They can see the Catholic Community schedule, message boards, and file libraries. There is an area for nonmembers to have a Catholic chat. Send all comments or suggestions regarding this site, including postings, to: cpolmin@aol.com.

CATHOLIC DIRECTORY DETAILED LISTINGS

What Have I Done?

In Chapters 7 through 13, I present much of what is contained in certain Catholic Internet directories not previously listed. If you are still unable to find what you are looking for, see the end of Chapter 14. There I provide tips on how to search the Internet for people or places using general Internet searching tools.

I have chosen particular directories that others have put a lot of time and effort into compiling. Certain people have been gracious enough to give me permission to use the information from their directories in this book. AlaPadre's Catholic Corner directory in Chapter 7, created by a parish priest, uses an alphabetical approach for organization. The other directories are organized by topic. In Chapter 8, you will find John Mark Ockerbloom's Catholic Resources on the Net; in Chapter 9, Tad Book's Catholic Resources on the Net; Chapter 10 presents Catholic Cincinnati; Chapter 11 contains Ecclesia; Chapter 12 conains RCNet; and in Chapter 13 you'll find Catholic and Christian Resources on the Internet.

My Organization

Remember that the directories I selected to show you are on the Internet. The authors of these directories have organized Catholic homepages under their own particular categories.

I have given the URLs or addresses for everything mentioned in these directories. If you see something you like in these chapters, you can go to your Internet browser program, type in the URL, and go visit the site. To do this for either Microsoft's Internet Explorer or Netscape Navigator, look under "File" on their menu selections. Then choose "Open" on Microsoft Explorer or "Open Location" on Netscape Navigator. Simply type in the address for the homepage you want to view.

Alternatives

Remember that these directories on the Internet have hyperlinks to the homepage titles you see in this book. So you can type in the URL or address for the directory in your browser and go to the title of the homepage that interests you, click on it, and presto—you are there!

If that's not enough, I have given you addresses for the categories. So if you want to look around for a particular category, put its URL in your Internet browser and you're ready to go!

Other References from the Index

I hope you're with me so far. This book is intended to help you make sense of confusing material! At the end of each directory, you will see "Other References from the Index." When you actually use your browser to go to any directory's opening page, you are likely to see items listed that I have not discussed. You'll find these items under "Other References from the Index."

Comments

You will notice comments next to the homepages listed in these directories. Some of them I relate to the homepage as it appears on the Internet. At times, I threw in tidbits relating to the title of the homepage. Other times I went off on a tangent—what do you expect after looking at around 2,500 homepages?

Edited Directories

I have edited these directory lists to avoid unnecessary repetition and to omit irrelevant sites. You may find a homepage title on the Internet directory that is not in this book or vise versa. This could mean either that I removed it from their directory, or the directory changed or added new listings since this book was published. I also removed some homepages that did not relate to Catholicism.

Given that Internet directories can change or even cease to exist on the Internet, you may benefit from having the URLs provided in this book.

False Error Messages

Problems can occur at times that make you think a homepage is not there. Once, when I tried to connect to the big Internet directory or search engine called Yahoo (mentioned in Chapter 3), I was told it couldn't be found. Now I knew that this Internet directory did not move or just disappear. I discovered that because the access lines were so busy, the computer was unable to connect and told me it couldn't find or connect to Yahoo. When I tried connecting to some homepages from directories presented in Chapters 7 through 13, I encountered the same problem: I would be told the homepage did not exist or could not be found; then when I tried later, I found it. I put an asterisk next to links that gave me trouble and wish you better luck. If you run into similar problems accessing a homepage with an asterisk next to it, you can always search for it. (You have its name, which is a big help.) See Chapter 14 for more information on how to conduct such a search.

Submit it!

I plan to construct a form on my homepage that will allow you to submit your own Catholic homepage (with its description) for my next book. So many movies have sequels that I thought, why not this book? (Miracles do happen!) If you want to get in the Top 20 in my next book—or just plain get listed—fill out the form on our homepage at http://www.rc.net/org/monks/ and submit it!

7

▥ AlaPadre's Catholic Corner

http://www.wsnet.com/~alapadre/

In late 1994, Fr. John Stryjewski began to post hyperlinked directories and search devices on his World Wide Web site in order to help Catholics locate resources and people throughout the world. It has become a megalink compendium of Catholic reference and research interest items. Fr. John is a priest for the Archdiocese of Mobile, Alabama. To add your e-mail address or Web site to this directory, send it to Fr. Stryjewski at: alapadre@maf.mobile.al.us.

When you enter the opening page of this directory, you may notice that some of the headings I list do not correspond to his headings. If this occurs, it is because he has changed his directory format since the publication of this book. But you will not find this a problem. Just use his alphabetical listing to find headings you don't see, or type in their URL directly from this book. You will want to see "AlaPadre Spotlites" for the sites that he currently recommends. If you can't find what you want here, he has included some links to popular search engines for your convenience.

You will notice that Father mentions *bookmarks*. What are they? If you are using Netscape Navigator, you should see "Bookmarks" on the menu bar on your Internet browser. By selecting it, you will be given an option to either add a bookmark or go to a bookmark. They chose the word "bookmark" because Internet bookmarks work much like those that help readers remember where they left off reading. If you

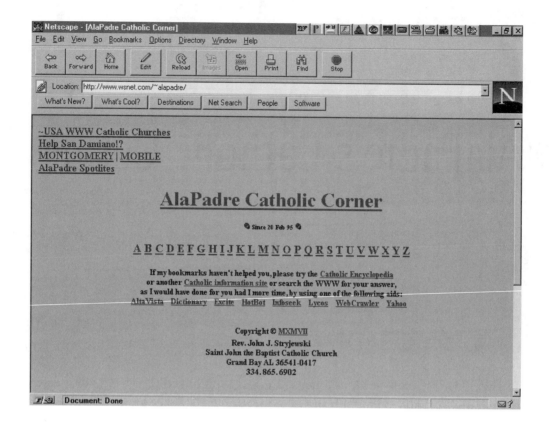

like the homepage you are looking at, choose "Add Bookmark" on Netscape Navigator or "Add to Favorites" under "Favorites" on Microsoft's Internet Explorer. Once you do that, you can easily return there by selecting the title of that homepage under "Favorites" or "Bookmarks." I think you will want to bookmark this directory.

INFO BOOKMARK A

http://wsnet.com:80/~alapadre/indexa.html

As I mentioned before, I have deleted some miscellaneous or inappropriate material. So when you see "Alabama Saltwater Fishing" under "A" on the Internet, you will not find it in my book. As fun as fishing may be, I can't see what it has to do with a Catholic directory! In the upper and lower left-hand corners of all his pages, you will see "MGM|MOB." If you click on "MGM," it will return you to Father's main page.

You can also use the "Back" function on your Internet browser to accomplish the same thing.

Ace
http://www.nd.edu/~ace/

The Alliance for Catholic Education. See their homepage links on spiritual development, becoming professional educators, the (arch) dioceses they serve, and community life.

Adoremus: Society for the Renewal of the Sacred Liturgy
http://www.erinet.com/aquinas/arch/adoremus.html

A nonprofit organization whose sole purpose is promoting authentic reforms of the liturgy of the Roman Rite according to the intention of the Second Vatican Council as expressed in its decree on the liturgy, Sacrosanctum Concilium.

Alabama Churches
http://cpfc.baynet.net/churches/north_america/united_states/alabama/

An extensive link to parishes in this fine southern state. This is the easy way to do some church hopping!

Alliance for Children
http://www.adoption.com/alliance

A nonprofit adoption agency with related links. Surely anything that helps people adopt children in need of a good home is a great blessing.

*Angelicum
http://www.informedia.it/dipiu96/st/st_eng.htm

The Pontifical University of St. Thomas Aquinas in Rome is the Holy Father's Alma Mater. This Dominican school of philosophy and theology attracts students from all over the world, especially because it offers its theology courses not only in Italian but also in English. This is also where Brother Craig, my superior, studied philosophy and theology.

Angelus Organ
http://wsnet.com/~alapadre/tkoerner.html

The Organ Design Guild. Although I have no musical ability and can play only a couple of lines of chant music on the organ at the monastery, I do like to hear nice organ music in church. The organ is still the favored instrument for church music.

Anointing of the Sick
http://christusrex.org/www1/CDHN/heal2.html#SICK

The Catechism of the Catholic Church on this sacrament. It is important for all of us to understand when this sacrament can be given so we will know when it is appropriate to call a priest for our sick loved ones and friends.

Apologetics Homepage
http://transporter.com/apologia/index.htm

This homepage includes a defense of the Catholic Faith and a very interesting section on how other Christian churches or denominations compare to the Catholic Church, which historically goes back to Jesus and the Apostles.

Apologetics: Catholic Apologetics Toolkit
http://www.columbia.edu/cu/augustine/a/

Defense of Catholic Faith approached from The Way, The Truth, and The Life.

Apologetics: NABT Page
http://www.primenet.com/~jakin/

James Akin, Ed.
jakin@primenet.com

A straightforward homepage that will help you understand what Catholics believe, from where they received these beliefs, and what they do with them.

Apostles: Shields of the Twelve Apostles
http://www.nwu.edu/chaplain/office_staffdocs/shield.html

Discusses shields that symbolize the twelve apostles.

*Apostles' Creed
http://listserv.american.edu/catholic/catholic/other/creed-a.txt

Here's a subject that is not only the *basics* of our Faith but one could almost say is the *basis* of our Faith!

Apostolic Fathers: Search the Apostolic Fathers
gopher://ccat.sas.upenn.edu:3333/77/.index/Apostolic/indx

A search engine to find what you want to know about these early witnesses to the Catholic Faith.

Apostolic Fathers, Writings of
ftp://iclnet93.iclnet.org/pub/resources/christian-history.html#fathers

Look at the writings of those who tradition says were disciples of the Apostles!

APS Research Guide—Catholic
http://www.utoronto.ca/stmikes/theobook.htm#CATHOLIC

A guide to resources for theological and religious studies. If you have some time for this study, this is the place.

Art: Religious Images, Icons, and Art
http://osiris.colorado.edu/~brumbaug/CHURCH/RES/images.html#clip

1,227 sites, 76 categories, grouped into eight broad areas. This homepage is dedicated to religious resources on the Internet covering: Bible resources, publications, reference, religious art and images, religious organizations, youth and young adult, and commercial religious services.

Aquinas: Loughlin's Aquinas Webpage
http://www.epas.utoronto.ca:8080/~loughlin/index.html

Everything you wanted to know about St. Thomas Aquinas (d. 1274) and Thomism. St. Thomas was not only a very intelligent scholar and theologian, but he is a Doctor of the Church. He is known more specifically as the Common Doctor of the Church because he is the one for everybody! He is also the patron saint of Catholic schools.

Aquinas: Summa Theologica
http://www.knight.org/advent/summa/summa.htm

The great theological synthesis of St. Thomas Aquinas can be found here. Don't expect to read it in one night!

Athanasius
ftp://iclnet93.iclnet.org/pub/resources/christian-history.html#Cyprian

His writing on the Incarnation. This Father of the Church (A.D. 270–336) was the Bishop of Alexandria. He wrote several theological treatises and was the chief defender of the Nicene Creed. This poor bishop was exiled five times because of the Arian heretics.

Augustine
ftp://iclnet93.iclnet.org/pub/resources/christian-history.html#Cyprian

He was Bishop of the church at Hippo, North Africa, and is considered by many to be one of the greatest fathers of the Church (d. 430). You will find some of his writings here, especially "The Confessions" along with links to more of his writings. He is a doctor of the Church and is known more specifically as the Doctor of Grace because of his profound writings on grace. He is buried in Pavia, Italy.

Augustine Club at Columbia University
http://www.columbia.edu/cu/augustine/

A student organization dedicated to the study of Christian intellectual approaches to the ideas underlying the issues of our day.

INFO BOOKMARK B

http://wsnet.com:80/~alapadre/indexb.html

Baltimore Catechism
http://128.235.249.100/RCC/Catechism/1/Welcome.html

The older question-and-answer catechism can be found here, along with a tool to search for what you want to know. Many, can I say, older Catholics will remember learning about the Faith using the Baltimore Catechism.

Baptism
http://christusrex.org/www1/CDHN/baptism.html#BAPTISM

The catechism on the sacrament of Baptism. It's very important to have a good and solid understanding of this sacrament that begins it all!

Bible: ARTFL Project—Bibles
http://humanities.uchicago.edu/homes/BIBLES.html

A multi-version and language guide to Bibles.

Bible: Douay-Rheims Version
http://www.cybercomm.net/~dcon/drbible.html

Older English translation from the Latin Vulgate of St. Jerome (d. 420). Older Catholics will fondly remember this translation. You will find Old Testament books here that are still being worked on. You won't, however, find the Catholic commentaries here that are part of this Catholic Bible.

Bible: Search Engines
http://www.gospelcom.net/bible

A multi-version and language tool.

Bible: Search the Bible (Septuagint-Morph)
gopher://ccat.sas.upenn.edu:3333/77/.index/MLXX/indx

Yet another aid to learning more about (and understanding better) the Holy Bible.

Bible: Search the Bible (Vulgate)
gopher://ccat.sas.upenn.edu:3333/77/.index/Vulgate/indx

Since the Vulgate was translated by St. Jerome, it reminds me of his saying, "Ignorance of the Bible is ignorance of Christ."

Biography: Saints'
http://www.contrib.andrew.cmu.edu/usr/el28/st_index.html

Great place to look for saints this side of Heaven! Few things are more inspiring than reading the lives of the saints.

Boarding School: Saint Bernard Prep (Cullman AL)
http://iquest.com/~deesqrd/saint/SBP.html

This school is blessed to have such a patron as the great St. Bernard (d. 1153) who was a holy Cistercian monk, great preacher, advisor to the leaders of Europe, and someone who truly loved Jesus and Mary. It is believed that St. Bernard was the first to call the mother of God "Our Lady," and tradition tells us he wrote the prayer to Mary we call the "Memore."

Books Online: Alex
http://www.lib.ncsu.edu/stacks/alex-index.html

A catalog of electronic texts on the Internet. Contains roughly 2,000 entries, mostly on gopher servers. You can look for Catholic books.

Books Online: CMU Libraries/Library Catalogs
http://www.library.cmu.edu/bySubject/CS+ECE/lib/libraries.html

Need a book to read? If so this is your place. Imagine, a library online. You don't need to leave your home to go to the library anymore!

Books Online: CMU Online Books Page
http://www.cs.cmu.edu/Web/books.html

An index of thousands of online books. Another place to look for Catholic books.

Books Online: Internet Book Information Center
http://sunsite.unc.edu/ibic/IBIC-homepage.html

Links to book-related information. If you can't find the Catholic book you are looking for, follow these links.

Books: Classic Catholic-related Books
http://www.cs.cmu.edu/web/people/spok/catholic.html#books

John Mark Ockerbloom's links that you will find in the next chapter. There are so many great classic Catholic books to read. I hope I live long enough to read them all!

BOOKMARK C

http://wsnet.com:80/~alapadre/indexc.html

 Calendar: Calculation of the Ecclesiastical Calendar
http://cssa.stanford.edu/~marcos/ec-cal.html

A lot of calendar information here as well as a tool for finding the calendar for a particular year.

 Calendar: General Roman Calendar of Solemnities, Feasts, Memorials
http://www.cwo.com/~pentrack/catholic/romcal.html

Don't have a Church calendar? You can get it here with each day of the year's information.

 *Campus Ministry: Catholic Christian Outreach
http://www.dlcwest.com/~cco/

I know of some people who take offense to the phrase "Catholic Christian." I think they have good reason for this since to be Catholic means to be Christian. It's a bit redundant.

 Campus Ministry: Newman Centers/Catholic Chaplaincies
http://www.cco.caltech.edu/~newman/OtherNC.html

Here you will find extensive links to Newman centers. You will find this home-page spelled out in Chapter 9. This one reminds me that we should all remember to pray for those involved in campus ministry. They can really make the difference in the lives of these students.

Campus Ministry: University of Dayton
http://www.udayton.edu/~campmin/

A fun page to visit with bright color to perk you up and links to other Catholic information.

Canadian Retreat Center
http://www.rc.net/maranatha/

This would be especially beneficial for any northern readers or those who wish to make a retreat up in beautiful Canada.

Canon Law of Western Rite
http://198.62.75.12/www1/CDHN/canonlaw.zip

Downloadable zip file. Deals with canon law of the Latin Rite Catholic Church. If you want to know the laws of the Church in depth, this site is for you. Otherwise, just listen to your Bishop!

Canon: New Testament Canonical Information
ftp://iclnet93.iclnet.org/pub/resources/christian-history.html#canon

Presents the canons of the Council of Orange (A.D. 529). Remember that Bishops are the successors of the Apostles and what they say is important.

Creeds
ftp://iclnet93.iclnet.org/pub/resources/christian-history.html#creeds

These are summaries of what we believe as Catholics. Sometimes they are referred to as "symbols" because this word comes from the Greek *symbolon,* which can mean gathering, collection, or summary.

Cantus at CUA
gopher://vmsgopher.cua.edu/11gopher_root_music%3a%5b_cantus%5d

This is a database made up of indices of chants from sources of the Divine Office. If you like music, this will be of interest to you.

Capital Punishment:
http://search.onramp.net/ns.cgi?query=capital+punishment&delay=10&
results=100&a2z=1&altavista=1&infoseek=1&inktomi=1&lycos=1&we-
bcrawler=1&
yahoo=1

Abolition Now
http://www.abolition-now.com/

*Catholic Bishops of Illinois
http://www.archdiocese-chgo.org/cci.html

*Death Penalty Facts & Figures (Amnesty Intl)
http://www.igc.apc.org/prisons/issues/dpdocs/dpfacts.html

*Death Penalty: The Ultimate Revenge
http://www.bruderhof.org/issues/deathpen/menu.htm

I'm praying every day that capital punishment is done away with. Let's be merciful. These people can change if we pray and offer sacrifices for them.

*Catechesis
http://webzone1.co.uk/www/jcrawley/prologue.htm#HANDING

According to *The Maryknoll Catholic Dictionary,* "Catechesis" means "instruction given to Christian catechumens preparing for baptism, especially those in the early Church." The word was also used for the books containing such instruction, of which the most celebrated is that of St. Cyril of Jerusalem (d. 386).

Catechetical Studies: International Institute of Catechetical and Pastoral Studies
http://www.luc.edu/or/sj/lumen/index.html

An international institute has the advantage of learning from broad experience in various countries.

Catholic Alumni Clubs International: Single—Catholic—Professional
http://www.clark.net/pub/cac/

An organization of single Catholic professional men and women. Its purpose is to provide a friendly setting for single Catholics to meet and develop friendships with people who share their faith. And it could lead to "happily-ever-after" romance!

Catholic Charismatic Center
http://www.garg.com/ccc/

This will keep you up-to-date about charismatic renewal in the Roman Catholic Church—everything you want to know about it including upcoming events.

Catholic Church in Singapore
http://www.veritas.org.sg/index.html

Singapore's Catholic Archdiocese Internet homepage has news, announcements, what's new and what's hot, a Church directory, and a fair number of Catholic Web links.

Catholic Church: FAQ (90K)
http://www.columbia.edu/cu/augustine/a/faq-cc.html

A downloadable file. Remember FAQ means Frequently Asked Questions, in this case about the Catholic Faith.

Catholic Churches on the WWW
http://wsnet.com/~alapadre/churches.html

AlaPadre's list. You will see a detailed breakdown of this later on.

Catholic Colleges, WWW List of
http://wsnet.com/~alapadre/cathcoll.html

AlaPadre's list. If you are looking for a Catholic college, you will want to look here. The listings on this homepage can be found further on in this chapter.

Catholic Documents by Subject
http://www.cs.cmu.edu/Web/People/spok/catholic/by-subject.html

John Mark Okerbloom's list. This is very well done. You will find it in Chapter 8.

Catholic Education
http://www.avenue.com/v/cef/cef.html

You will find here a discussion forum for teachers, parents, and students, along with Catholic education links and content.

Catholic Elementary Schools, WWW List of
http://wsnet.com/~alapadre/indexe.html#ELEMENTARY

AlaPadre's list. Looking for a Catholic elementary school in your area? Check out his list later under Bookmark E.

Catholic Encyclopedia Online
http://www.knight.org/advent/cathen/cathen.htm

The 1917 version with everything you want to know about the Faith literally from A to Z.

Catholic Health Association of Wisconsin (CHA-W)
http://www.execpc.com/~chaw/index.html

Here you'll find their public policy, ethics, educational programs and events, newsletters, and links to health-care information.

Catholic High Schools, WWW List of
http://wsnet.com/~alapadre/indexh.html#HIGHSCHOOL

AlaPadre's list. This will link you to Bookmark H. You will only find home-schooling there.

*Catholic "Mailto:" Links
http://pwa.acusd.edu/~rpgordon/pages/diocesan/section1.html

Get in touch with other Catholics through this e-mail directory.

*Catholic Mothers' Internet Connection
http://www.sunflower.org/~catholic/mom.htm

Where would we be without good Catholic mothers?! I have one and I'll take this opportunity to say "Hi Mom" as people interviewed on TV do. Anyway, check out this homepage.

Catholic Publishers
http://wsnet.com/~alapadre/indexc.html#PUBLISHER

Those who publish good Catholic books are doing a great service to the Church.

*Catholic Relief Services
http://www.charity.com/crs.html

This is the American Catholic bishops' organization, which helps the poor, the sick, and the hungry throughout the world. They have given more to help the poor than any other Catholic charity in our country. Please look at this homepage (and perhaps send them a donation?).

Catholic Research Forum
http://www.execpc.com/~mcieslak/crf/

This site is composed of researchers and planners, most of whom are employed by Catholic dioceses and are members of the Conference for Pastoral Planning and Council Development.

Catholic Resource List at Carnegie Mellon
http://www.cs.cmu.edu/Web/People/spok/catholic.html

John Mark Ockerbloom's list. You can see it in Chapter 8.

Catholic Student Organization at UNH
http://www.unh.edu/catholic-student-center

Visit with the Catholic students at the University of New Hampshire.

Catholic Student Organization (Chinese) at Queen's University
http://www.ams.queensu.ca/qccc

Some of the students may come from mainland China—a country that has suffered much and continues to suffer under Communism. A Chinese Cardinal who had spent many years in prison in China for the Faith was finally released and was living near the seminary I went to in Connecticut.

Catholic Universities, List of
http://wsnet.com/~alapadre/cathuniv.html

AlaPadre's list. Perhaps you or someone you know is looking for a Catholic university. Skip a few pages ahead to see them listed later in this chapter.

Catholic Worker Bibliography
http://www.cais.com/agf/daybib.htm

Information about Dorothy Day (d. 1980) and the lay movement she and Peter Maurin started. A useful list of sources for this group that has done so much over the years to help feed and house the poor and to promote peace and pacifism.

Catholic Youth Ministry Directory
http://www.microserve.net/~fabian/files/ymdir.html

Scott Fabian's list. Do you work with young people or know someone who does? See Scott's directory in Chapter 11.

Catholicism
http://web.sau.edu/~cmiller/religion.html

Usually an "ism" after a name indicates it is a heresy. This isn't the case this time!

Centering Prayer
http://www.io.com/~lefty/Centering_Prayer.html

The Trappist monk and author Father Thomas Keating, O.C.S.O., has traveled the world teaching this form of prayer. I was at a conference on prayer in Manila where he gave a talk on Centering Prayer.

*Charlene, Saint from Louisiana?
http://lute.qnet.com/~oditch/charlene.html

You've really got to visit this homepage. It's about a very holy young girl and the graces that have been received at her much-visited grave.

Christian Classics Ethereal Library
http://ccel.wheaton.edu/

Here you will find a large selection of classic Christian books in electronic format from A to Z. Of course, you will find Catholic classics here.

Christian Resource Database: Catholic Resources
http://www.christianity.net/search/

You will find some Catholic information on this Christian database. Select "Churches and Denominations" and then "Catholic Resources."

*Christian Resource List
http://saturn.colorado.edu:8080/Christian/list.html

You might wish to look for Catholic resources here, too.

*Christian Resources on the Internet (1 of 3)
http://www.calvin.edu/Christian/christian-resources.html

This is a mega-list of Christian stuff. If you fish around you will find some Catholic information also.

*Church Calendar
http://listserv.american.edu/catholic/catholic/other/church.calendar

Did you know that each rite of the Church has its own calendar and each country has its own special feast days?

Church History: Encyclopedia of Early Church History
http://www.evansville.edu/~ecoleweb/

Translations of Judæo-Christian and Islamic primary sources to A.D. 1500, short essays on numerous topics, long essays on major topics and figures, Christian iconography and religious art, and timeline with geographical cross-index.

College: Spring Hill College in Mobile, Alabama
http://www.shc.edu/

College of Cardinals
http://www.erinet.com/aquinas/arch/cards.html

This is not about birds going to college! Here you will find everything you ever wanted to know about Catholic Cardinals, including who they are. This is an honorary title. Cardinals are chosen by the Holy Father to serve as his principal assistants and advisers in the central administration of Church affairs. Also, the Cardinals under 80 years old vote for a new Pope.

Computers for Christ
http://www.cforc.com/

This is a Christian ministry dedicated to using computer technology to expand God's kingdom and share the Gospel of Christ. Again you will have to look around for Catholic stuff.

Confessions, Saint Augustine
http://ccel.wheaton.edu/augustine/confessions/confessions.html

A fourth-century Father of the Church who recorded his spiritual struggles as a young man. It has been a bestseller for more than 1,500 years.

Confirmation
http://christusrex.org/www1/CDHN/confirm.html#CONFIRMATION

Learn what the Catechism of the Catholic Church has to say about this sacrament. If you haven't been confirmed yet, now is the time!

Contemplation: Merton Research Institute
http://140.190.128.190/merton/merton.html
http://www.marshall.edu/~stepp/vri/merton/merton.html

The purpose of TMRI is to foster, encourage, advance, and communicate research on contemplative life.

*Council Documents: Trent
http://listserv.american.edu/catholic/church/trent/trent.html

Take a trip through Church history by looking at the documents of this famous council.

Council Documents: Vatican II
http://www.rc.net/rcchurch/vatican2/index.html

These documents are just about a "must-read" for Catholics today. The first Church Council took place in Jerusalem when the Apostles gathered to discuss the issue of non-Jews being received into the Church.

Couple to Couple League Int'l
http://www.missionnet.com/ccl

This is a nonprofit, tax-exempt organization founded in 1971 to provide natural family planning services throughout the world.

*Creed: Apostles'
http://listserv.american.edu/catholic/catholic/other/creed-a.txt

Can you recite it by heart? Tradition tells us this goes back to the Apostles and that each one contributed to it.

*Creed: Nicene
http://listserv.american.edu/catholic/catholic/other/creed-n.txt

This one is named after the early Church Council from which it takes its origin. In those days, defining more clearly what we believe about the Trinity was the issue of the day.

Cremation
http://wsnet.com/~alapadre/cremation.html

Do you know what the Church says about it? If not, this is the place to find out.

Cross Fire
http://www.crossfire.org

Youth Ministry Magazine is committed to the spread of the Gospel throughout the world, with an emphasis on the concerns and needs of young people and those who are dedicated to a ministry to youth.

Cursillo ala Alta Vista
http://www.altavista.digital.com/cgi-bin/query?pg=q&what=web&fmt=.&q=cursillo

Here you will come across 600 links using a search engine. Having made a Cursillo weekend before becoming a monk and benefiting from it, I highly recommend looking into this ministry.

INFO | BOOKMARK D

http://wsnet.com:80/~alapadre/indexd.html

*Date of Easter
http://www.ast.cam.ac.uk/RGO/leaflets/easter/easter.html

Maybe someday there will be a fixed day for Easter Sunday. I heard there has been some discussion about this.

Daughters of Saint Paul
http://bay.netrover.com/~pauline/

An international congregation of Catholic sisters communicating God's love through media technology such as books, magazines, radio, TV, videos, cassettes, CDs, software, and music.

Day, Dorothy: Bibliography
http://www.cais.com/agf/daybib.htm

A saintly woman who strove to live Gospel poverty herself as well as starting a lay movement called the Catholic Worker. Dorothy Day was also an extraordinarily gifted writer and journalist.

Dead Sea Scrolls
http://sunsite.unc.edu/expo/deadsea.scrolls.exhibit/intro.html

They are older than any other surviving biblical manuscripts by almost 1,000 years. Here you will learn about this great discovery of our century.

*Definitions of Over 400 Terms for Beginning Study of Scriptures and Ancient Texts

http://www.nd.edu/~jvanderw/theo100/glossary/complete.htm

Keep in mind that the Bible and ancient texts were written in other languages and within other cultures. There is an expression that says the translator is a traitor. That is because one loses something whenever one translates a work into another language.

Didache

gopher://ccat.sas.upenn.edu:3333/00/Religious/ChurchWriters/Apostolic Fathers/Didache

This work's other title is "The Teaching of the Lord to the Gentiles by the Twelve Apostles." It is estimated to have been written in A.D. 140.

Divine Mercy Homepage

http://www.cais.com/npacheco/mercy/faustina.html

Here you will find information about this devotion that is based on the revelations about God's infinite Mercy given to Blessed Faustina Kowalska (d. 1938), a Polish nun and a member of the Sisters of Our Lady of Mercy.

Divine Office

http://wsnet.com/~alapadre/indexl.html#DIVINEOFFICE

The Divine Office is also called the Liturgy of the Hours and is the official Prayer of the Church. It is one way that the Church follows St. Paul's injunction to "pray always."

Docetism

http://www.evansville.edu/~ecoleweb/articles/docetism.html

Find out about this early Church heresy that claimed Jesus only seemed to have a human body.

Doctors of the Church

http://www.knight.org/advent/cathen/05075a.htm

Certain Church writers have received this title due to the great advantage the whole Church has derived from their doctrine. See this homepage to learn more about the Doctors of the Church.

*Documentary Sources on Catholic Teaching
http://listserv.american.edu/catholic/catholic/church/catholic.sources.html

Back to the sources! If someone asks you "Where did you get that?" this is the place to find out.

Dogma
http://www.knight.org/advent/cathen/05089a.htm

Dogma might be described briefly as a revealed truth defined by the Church as most certain of belief. Normally these are proclaimed when people are calling something we believe into question. For the longer definition, see this homepage.

Dominican Homepage
http://www.op.org/op/

The Order of Preachers was started by the great St. Dominic (d. 1221). Here you can learn about this order around the world as well as browse their library. You can even search for a Dominican by name.

 # BOOKMARK E

http://wsnet.com:80/~alapadre/indexe.html

Early Church History: Saint Pachomius Library
http://www.ocf.org/OrthodoxPage/reading/St.Pachomius/index.html

Archives of uncopyrighted English translations of the Church Fathers, the acts of the Christian martyrs, the proceedings of the Councils, the lives of the early saints, and so on.

Sunrise/Sunset/Twilight and Moonrise/Moonset/Phase Computation
http://tycho.usno.navy.mil/srss.html

Why does the date of Easter keep moving from year to year? If you are interested in how the date of Easter is chosen, this is the place to look.

*Ecclesiology: Yuri Josef Koszarycz
http://honey.acu.edu.au/~yuri/ecc/

Ecclesiology is the science or study of the Church in any or all of its aspects. If you are interested in this, you will definitely want to read the Vatican II document "Dogmatic Constitution on the Church."

Encyclicals
http://listserv.american.edu/catholic/church/papal/papal.html

Encyclicals are letters written by the Pope that are usually addressed to Bishops of the whole Church, a particular region or country. Here you will find letters by 13 Popes: Boniface VIII (d. 1303), Paul III (d. 1549), Benedict XIV (d. 1758), Gregory XVI (d. 1846), Pius IX (d. 1878), Leo XIII (d. 1829), Pius X (d. 1914), Benedict XV (d. 1922), Pius XI (d. 1939), Pius XII (d. 1958), John XXIII (d. 1963), Paul VI (d. 1978), and John Paul II.

Encyclopedia of Early Church History
http://www.evansville.edu/~ecoleweb/

Did you know that the Church was under persecution until the Edict of Milan in the early part of the fourth century? Then the Emperor Constantine proclaimed Christianity the state religion.

*Ethics and Medics Subject Index 1976–1994
http://www.lanic.utexas.edu/pjcenter.org/pjc/

A homepage dealing with very important and literally vital information.

Ethics Updates:
http://www.acusd.edu/ethics/

Abortion
http://www.acusd.edu/abortion.html

Animal Rights
http://www.acusd.edu/animal.html

We should be kind to animals. In the Book of Proverbs in the Old Testament, it talks about how the evil man is cruel toward his animals. We have to be concerned about God's creation, which has been entrusted to us, including animals.

Environmental Ethics
http://www.acusd.edu/environmental_ethics.html

We shouldn't be ruining and destroying the wonderful world God created. Living near the edge of the woods as I do, you cannot help but marvel at nature. An atheist was visiting with me one time, and while we were walking and talking in the woods, he told me that he experienced the presence of God. We relate to God through what he has created, so let's not destroy it.

Ethical Theory
http://www.acusd.edu/theory.html

Ethics is perhaps the most important branch of study nowadays. It deals with moral conduct.

Euthanasia
http://www.acusd.edu/euthanasia.html

Gender and Sexism
http://www.acusd.edu/gender.html

Poverty and Welfare
http://www.acusd.edu/poverty.html

Punishment and the Death Penalty
http://www.acusd.edu/death_penalty.html

Race and Ethnicity
http://www.acusd.edu/race.html

Reproductive Technologies
http://www.acusd.edu/reproductive_technologies.html

*Sexual Orientation and Gay Rights
http://www.acusd.edu/sexual_orientation.html

Virtues and Vices
http://www.acusd.edu/virtue.html

World Hunger
http://www.acusd.edu/world_hunger.html

A lot of Catholic ethical teaching here—dealing with topics under hot debate in our modern world.

Ethics: Catholic Resources on Medical Ethics
http://www.usc.edu/hsc/info/newman/resources/ethics.html

A very helpful homepage. This is not just for doctors and nurses. We need to know how to make proper medical decisions both for ourselves and for those we love.

Ethics: Formal and Material Cooperation
http://www.execpc.com/~chaw/FormalandMaterial.html

Learn about these ethical concepts concerning cooperation.

Ethics: Nutrition and Hydration Guidelines
http://www.execpc.com/~chaw/NutritionandHydration.html

This homepage deals with a very important issue concerning people who are starved to death or killed because they are refused water and food. This is incorrectly called "letting people die"; it is more correctly called "murder."

Ethics: Physician-Assisted Suicide
http://www.execpc.com/~chaw/Suicide.html

An urgent issue. Learn all you can about it. I am sorry to say that a doctor in my home state of Michigan has been pushing for this to be made legal and has assisted in a number of suicides.

Eucharist
http://christusrex.org/www1/CDHN/euch1.html

The Catechism of the Catholic Church on the Real Presence of Jesus. Know your Faith! A survey was conducted on Catholics' understanding of the Holy Eucharist and over two-thirds failed the test in the United States.

*Evangelization: John J. Myers
http://serviam.ncsa.uiuc.edu/St_Johns/bishop.html

To evangelize or to spread the Gospel is really everyone's responsibility.

*Evangelization: 12 Painless Ways to Evangelize
http://198.5.212.8/~edit/12ways.html

This title is catchy, isn't it? We seem shy about spreading the Faith here in the United States. This is not true in some other countries. So check out this page to find out how you can bear fruit for the Lord.

Evangelization: Apologetics Homepage
http://transporter.com/apologia/index.htm

The more you learn about the Faith, the better you can explain it to others. And believe me, some people have a lot of questions.

*Evangelization: Catholic Christian Outreach
http://www.dlcwest.com/~cco/

Still more helpful information for evangelization. We have the fullness of the truth and means to salvation. Let's not hoard it; let's share it!

Evangelization: Fides et Scientia
http://francis.veritas.org.sg/~nuscss/

Homepage of the Catholic Students' Society at the National University Of Singapore. Their goal is to foster a spirit of good fellowship among all students and understanding of the Catholic Faith through the members living this Faith.

*Evangelization: Pillar of Fire, Pillar of Truth
http://198.5.212.8/~edit/pillar.html

Just as the pillar of fire guided the Hebrew people through the darkness of night in the desert so the truth is the pillar of fire that will guide us through any "darkness" in this life to Heaven in the next.

 Evangelization: RCIA Resources
http://wsnet.com/~alapadre/indexr.html#RCIA

This refers to the Rite of Christian Initiation for Adults, that is, the process for becoming a Roman Catholic. Just recently a young man e-mailed me that he wanted to join us. He came from a family who practiced no religion, but he had been going to a Catholic parish for the past six years. But guess what? He didn't know there was a process to go through for becoming Catholic. There is—and this rite of initiation is it.

 Evolution: Catholics & Evolution
http://128.235.249.100/cgi-bin/HyperNews/get/evolution.html

An essay that makes a critical examination of Darwin's theory and explains how, in the debate on origins, the Church takes a reasonable middle ground between the poles of scientific and Protestant fundamentalism.

BOOKMARK F

http://wsnet.com:80/~alapadre/indexf.html

 Faith Movement (UK)
http://www.compulink.co.uk/~faith/Welcome.html

The promotion of a new synthesis of Catholicism, a synthesis of science and religion that makes sense of the modern scientific world while remaining true to the Church's Magisterium.

 Fathers of the Church
http://www.knight.org/advent/fathers/fathers.htm

A 38-volume collection of writings from the first 800 years of the Church. Most of the Fathers were Bishops.

Fatima Homepage
http://www.cais.com/npacheco/fatima/fatima.html

Learn about the Church-approved apparitions of the Blessed Virgin Mary at Fatima, Portugal, in 1917.

Focolare Movement
http://www.global2000.net/users/unity/movement.html

Their spirituality is drawn straight from the Gospels. There are many ways to belong to the Movement, ranging from a more committed lifestyle in small communities to collaboration in its various activities. Find out more about the Focolare on this homepage.

Franciscan Files
http://listserv.american.edu/catholic/franciscan

Here you will find Franciscan resources, apostolates, and more. If you like Franciscan spirituality, this homepage is worth a visit.

Franciscan: Secular Franciscan Order
http://www.ofs.it/sfo.html

See information on the Secular Franciscan Order worldwide, its fraternities, and its presence in the Church and in the world.

Funerals
http://christusrex.org/www1/CDHN/others.html

The Catechism of the Catholic Church on Catholic funerals. Learn more about this important religious service. Someday each of us is going to be part of one!

http://wsnet.com:80/~alapadre/indexg.html

Galanti Organ
http://wsnet.com/~alapadre/tkoerner.html

Do you play the organ? I have tried playing the one in our chapel and find it very challenging. Not only are there two levels of piano keys, but there are even foot pedals and "stops" that you can pull in or out.

Georgetown WWW Server for Medieval Studies
http://www.georgetown.edu/labyrinth/labyrinth-home.html

A global information network providing free, organized access to electronic resources in medieval studies through a World Wide Web server at Georgetown University. If you want to know Catholic information about this period of history, search here.

German Language: International Bible and Theology Gateways
http://www.uni-passau.de/ktf/gateways.html

Practice your German and learn something at the same time here.

German Language: KathWeb—Ein Kathpress-dienst from Austria
http://www.austria.eu.net/kathweb/

If you know German, check out this homepage and let me know what it's about!

German Language: Vatican Radio
http://wsnet.com:80/~alapadre/vatradio.german.html

Tune in to this German homepage. Keep up with the latest news as well as browse through the archive.

Glossary: 100–200 Word Glosses on People and Words Relating to Early Church History
http://www.evansville.edu/~ecoleweb/glossary.html

Nicely arranged links for information on this period. You can learn about the leading people, schools, heresies, and so forth of this period.

Golden Rosaries
http://www.cais.com/npacheco/rosary/gold.html

The purpose of this page is to present several personal accounts of the phenomenon of rosaries turning to a gold color, to discuss some technical aspects and, most importantly, its spiritual aspect. You might want to read about it. By the way, the links of my Rosary turned gold!

*Government: United States Federal Government World Wide Web Locations
http://www.tc.umn.edu/nlhome/m586/buch0075/usgov.html

This is not a Catholic site, but many Catholics will find the information on it helpful—especially those involved with Pro-Life work.

Gregorian Chant Homepage
http://www.music.princeton.edu/chant_html/index.html

This homepage's purpose is to support advanced research on Gregorian chant, particularly in the graduate seminar "Problems in Early Christian Music" (Music 511) taught at Princeton. The scholarly study of Gregorian chant is a wide-ranging, multi-faceted venture that interacts with many other areas of study, just as the liturgy for which it was created influenced many other areas of individual and social life.

Gregorian Chant TrueType Fonts
http://wsnet.com/~alapadre/smeinrad.html

Gregorian chant is named after Pope St. Gregory the Great (d. 604). The Benedictine monks and nuns here in Petersham, Massachusetts do Gregorian Chant beautifully.

Guadalupe
http://web.sau.edu/~cmiller/image.html

Learn about Our Lady's apparitions in Mexico and the miraculous image of herself that she left. Millions visit the shrine each year.

Guide to Early Church Documents
ftp://iclnet93.iclnet.org/pub/resources/christian-history.html

Contains links to Internet-accessible files relating to the early Church, including canonical documents, creeds, the writings of the Apostolic Fathers, and other historical texts relevant to Church history.

BOOKMARK H

http://wsnet.com:80/~alapadre/indexh.html

 Heraldry: Ecclesiastical
http://128.220.1.164/heraldry/topics/ecclesia.htm

This is the science of devising distinguishing marks or emblems according to Church rank or office. To learn more about this, visit here.

 WWW Research Sites
http://www.evansville.edu/~ecoleweb/internet.html

You'll find more than enough links here.

 Holy Orders
http://christusrex.org/www1/CDHN/orders.html

The Catechism of the Catholic Church on this sacrament. Have you ever been to an ordination? It is truly a moving event. Don't miss the next one in your diocese.

 Homeschool: Apostolate of Roman Catholic Homeschoolers
http://www.rc.net/org/arch/

They are mainly based in Southeast Texas. Keeping the children home for education is growing popular.

 Homeschool: LPH Resource Center
http://www.netaxs.com/~rmk/lph.html

Our Lady of Perpetual Help Resource Center is a place where local home-schoolers who are Catholic can get together with other Catholic homeschoolers and have some fun together—and also learn some subjects that can be difficult for parents to teach.

Homily: Father John Sandell Homilies
http://rrnet.com/~sedaqah/frj.htm

For health reasons Fr. John had to give up his pastoral duties but is still reaching out to us through the Internet. A much bigger congregation for his homilies, don't you think? Let's remember Father's health in our prayers.

*Homily: Index of Dominican sermons
http://www.op.org/op/sermons.eng/

Since the official name of the Dominicans is the Order of Preachers, these should be good!

Human Life International
http://www.hli.org/

A group founded by Fr. Paul Marx, O.S.B., and dedicated to upholding life. Their map will help you find their office located nearest to you, even on different continents. Find out about the different life issues and morality. Learn more about their programs and services.

INFO BOOKMARK 1

http://wsnet.com:80/~alapadre/indexi.html

Ignatius of Loyola: Spiritual Exercises
http://ccel.wheaton.edu/ignatius/exercises/exercises.html

This book has been very helpful to many people for centuries. It also has been referred to as an Ignatian retreat. Learn about it here and make one. Who knows, it could be a life-transforming experience for you also.

Ignatius Press
http://www.ignatius.com/

They are a publisher of Catholic books and periodicals and have videos and audiocassettes as well. They publish some excellent theological works.

IHM Web
http://www.marywood.edu/www2/ihmpage/

A congregation of the Sisters, Servants of the Immaculate Heart of Mary. When we speak of Our Lady as Immaculate, we are saying that she was never stained with even the slightest sin, including Original Sin.

Imitation of Christ
http://ccel.wheaton.edu/kempis/imitation/imitation.html

Thomas à Kempis's (d. 1471) 500-year-old work that has touched the lives of many.

*Information & Resources Concerning the Roman Catholic Church
http://www.geopages.com/CapitolHill/1709/

Sometimes we think a grade-school education in the Faith is enough, but it is not. We need to continually deepen our knowledge of the Faith for our spiritual growth.

International Bible and Theology Gateways
http://www.uni-passau.de/ktf/gateways.html

Here you will find many valuable links both in English and German.

 # BOOKMARK J

http://wsnet.com:80/~alapadre/indexj.html

John Paul II
http://wsnet.com/~alapadre/indexp.html#JP2

I think it's great that so many people throughout the world, even non-Catholics and non-Christians, admire the Holy Father.

James Tucker Recommends

http://convex.cc.uky.edu/~jatuck00/Religion/Religion.html

A page of links to Catholic teachings, beliefs, prayer, practices, reflection, places of interest, and the Bible.

Joyful Noise Music Ministry

http://www.geocities.com/Vienna/1488

Resources for Catholic musicians and other Catholic links. Protestants have produced so many tapes. I'm glad to see Catholic music companies springing up. I hadn't heard of very many before.

*Jude: Shrine of St. Jude Thaddeus

http://www.ultranet.com/~bellvill/wpcs/stjude/stjude.html

Since St. Jude is the Patron of desperate needs, he is very popular. His many devotees throughout the world attest to the efficacy of his intercession with God.

BOOKMARK K

http://wsnet.com:80/~alapadre/indexk.html

Knights of Columbus Information

http://www.knightsite.com.kofc.htm

Consists of over 120 individual Web pages: One Council and Assembly Web page for each U.S. state and each Canadian Province; Squires Directory (young members); Supreme Council's Web site; and various other pages of interest to Brother Knights of Columbus. Gives homepage and e-mail information for many Councils. They also have the Knights' Real-Time Online Chat, the Knights' Discussion Group, and the *K of C Cookbook.* Those interested in joining will find the information for doing so here.

Knights of Columbus Website Directory

http://wsnet.com/~alapadre/kcdirect.html

This one is not nearly as extensive as the previous listing. The Knights paid for the cleaning of the statues at St. Peter's Basilica at the Vatican.

 BOOKMARK L

http://wsnet.com:80/~alapadre/indexl.html

 Latin Prayers, A Treasury of
http://www.cs.cmu.edu/Web/People/spok/catholic/latin-prayers/index.html

It pays to know some prayers in Latin. When I was in Korea, I was able to pray the Rosary with a seminarian because we shared the common language of Latin.

 Latin: Resources for the Study of Ecclesiastical Latin
http://sak.uky.edu/mdtuck0/Resources/el.html

Want to learn the Church's official language? The Church continues to write all its important documents first in Latin. Then they are translated into the languages of the world.

 Legion of Mary
http://transporter.com/lom/

A lay movement whose works include door-to-door evangelization, parishioner visitation, prison ministry, visitation of the sick or aged, religious education, visiting of newly baptized adults, Pilgrim Virgin Statue home visits, and meeting the other spiritual needs of the parish community. This colorful homepage catches the eye and will tell you everything you want to know about this wonderful group.

 Library: Australian Catholic University Victorian Libraries
http://jude.aquinas.acu.edu.au/

Here you can select campus libraries, catalogues and databases, Internet search, electronic reference, resources by subject, and library policies.

 *Library: Benedictine College
http://www.benedictine.edu/bcacadlib1.html

Doesn't it boggle your mind that you can browse through a college library from your home?

 Library: Canisius College
http://www.canisius.edu/canhp/canlib/index.html

Includes library catalogs for libraries worldwide; indexes and databases; links to a variety of reference resources on the Internet such as directories, dictionaries, area codes, quotations, and maps; links to sites organized by subject and supporting the curriculum at Canisius College; and electronic versions of books and journals. Libraries are good places to start when looking for specific Catholic material.

Library: CUA Library Web Service
http://www.cua.edu/www/mullen/welcome.html

The Catholic University of America library information and links.

Library: Saint Joseph County Public
http://sjcpl.lib.in.us/

Here you have access to their library's databases and leased databases.

Library: Yale Divinity School
http://www.library.yale.edu/div/overview.htm

Of special interest here is the ATLA Religion Database that provides electronic access by author, title, subject, or keyword to articles published in periodicals and journals, essays and articles published in multi-author monographs, and book reviews in the fields of religion and theology.

Life Teen Program
http://www.lifeteen.org/

The purpose of the Life Teen Program is to create an atmosphere that leads high-school teenagers into a relationship with God through the teachings of Jesus Christ and His Church. I'd like to join except I may be a little old. This is fun page to look at even if you are out of high school.

*List of Catholic Mailing Lists
http://edge.edge.net/~jhbryan/catholic/catholic_mailing_lists.html

List of Patron Saints
http://listserv.american.edu/catholic/catholic/other/patron.saints

Have a particular need? Look up the saint known for his intercession regarding that need.

List of Popes
http://www.knight.org/advent/Popes/ppindx.htm

Here you will find all 265 Popes along with biographical information and links to more information. This is a shortcut to learning Church history.

Liturgical Press
http://www.osb.org/litpress/index.html

Publishers of liturgical, scriptural, theological, and pastoral resources in English and Spanish.

Liturgy: An Electronic Mail Discussion Group
gopher://delphi.dur.ac.uk/ORO-2204-/Academic/P-T/Theology/Computing/Liturgy/liturgy.txt

The word "Liturgy" comes from the Greek word "leitourgia," meaning a public service.

Liturgy from osb.org
http://www.osb.org/osb/gen/topics/liturgy/

The Order of Saint Benedict here provides you with links to liturgical texts, commentaries, and sites.

Liturgy: Oregon Catholic Press
http://www.ocp.org/

Publishers of music (English and Spanish) for liturgy and more.

Liturgy: Society for the Renewal of the Sacred Liturgy (Adoremus)
http://www.erinet.com/aquinas/arch/adoremus.html

"Adoremus" is Latin for we adore.

http://wsnet.com:80/~alapadre/indexm.html

 Mary
http://wsnet.com/~dibbs.net/indexbvm.html

Mary is the mother of God. The Son she conceived by the Holy Spirit is the eternal Father's Son, the second person of the Holy Trinity.

 Music
http://wsnet.com/~alapadre/indexm.html#MUSIC

Please make a "note" of this homepage.

 Magazine, Catholic: Crisis
http://www.catholic.net/RCC/Periodicals/Crisis/index.html

This magazine gives lay Catholic opinion on contemporary and Church issues.

 Magazine, Catholic: Saint Augustine Catholic Magazine
http://128.227.164.224/sac.htm

This one is put out by the Diocese of St. Augustine to inspire, inform, and educate the Catholics of this diocese. You can read it even if you aren't from the diocese.

 Magazine, Catholic: Spirituality for Today
http://www.spirituality.org/

Here you will find short descriptions of various editions of the magazine along with the text of that edition.

 *Magazine, Catholic: This Rock
http://198.5.212.8/~answers/thisrock.html

This is an interesting apologetics magazine.

Magisterium
http://www.catholic.net/RCC/Catechism/Magisterium/definition.html

This homepage, which defines Magisterium, might even help you when you play Catholic trivia.

Maps for Your Webpages
http://tiger.census.gov/cgi-bin/mapbrowse

This may be an interesting feature to put on your homepage—that is, if you want visitors from around the world knocking on your door.

Marriage Encounter:
http://www.scri.fsu.edu/~sollohub/wwme/wwme.html

See Also Retrouvaille
http://www.vicnet.net.au/~retro

The emphasis of Marriage Encounter is on communication between husband and wife, who spend a weekend together away from the distractions and the tensions of everyday life, to concentrate on each other. I have heard of so many couples who have benefited from this group.

Mary's Garden
http://www.mgardens.org/

Here you will find hundreds of flowers named in medieval times as symbols of the life, mysteries, and privileges of the Blessed Virgin Mary, mother of Jesus—as recorded by botanists, folklorists, and lexicographers. You can also find assistance in the planting of Mary Gardens. We have a Mary Garden here at the monastery.

Mass from Saint Ann's Shrine in Scranton, Pennsylvania
http://www.themass.org/

Excellent place to visit for the Mass of the day. Includes the prayers and readings along with an audio homily, audio petitions, and more. I tried out the audio homily here but grew impatient waiting for it to download. Perhaps Father went on a little too long!

*Matrimony
http://webzone1.co.uk/www/jcrawley/matri.htm#MATRIMONY

Learn more about this beautiful sacrament. Did you know that the priest does not administer this sacrament? The couples themselves administer this sacrament to each other. The priest stands as the Church's witness to the marriage. Since the Church regulates sacraments, she has decided on a particular form for this sacrament. Catholics are bound to follow it. A civil marriage between two Catholics is not a sacrament, but there are exceptions under extraordinary circumstances when two people are allowed by the Church to marry each other without a representative of the Church present.

Medjugorje Homepage
http://www.medjugorje.org/

Since 1981, in a small village named Medjugorje in Bosnia-Herzegovina, the Blessed Virgin Mary has been reported to be appearing and giving messages to the world. Although still under investigation by the Church, you can find a lot of information about Medjugorje here. I was privileged to visit there in 1989. I saw many conversions and changed lives among pilgrims.

Medjugorje on the WWW (Alta Vista Index)
http://www.altavista.digital.com/cgi-bin/query?pg=q&what=web&fmt=.&q
=+Medjugorje

A search engine index of links to information about Medjugorje.

Merton (Thomas) Web Site
http://140.190.128.190/merton/merton.html

A homepage where you can learn more on this priest, Trappist monk, writer, and poet of the twentieth century.

Method of Centering Prayer
http://www.io.com/~lefty/Centering_Prayer.html

Methods in prayer are to help us like training wheels on a bicycle. They can take us so far, then grace takes over to guide us from there.

Missionary Efforts: Letter from Siberia
http://dcn.davis.ca.us/~feefhs/lfs/frg-lfs.html

Newsletter of the Catholic Apostolic Administration of Asian Russia—Siberia and the Russian Far East. Catholics there need your support. A friend from Boston learned of their needs and is sending them books, medals, Rosaries, and so on.

Mithraism
http://www.evansville.edu/~ag5/mithraism.html

This pagan religion spread from Persia through the Roman Empire starting in 68 B.C. It was especially popular among merchants and in the army. It became a serious rival to Christianity but declined in the fourth century.

*Modern Liturgy Magazine
http://www.rpinet.com/ml/ml.html

Christians right from the beginning gathered to praise God as a community. We read in the Acts of the Apostles that the first Christian community gathered for the Breaking of the Bread and the prayers. Obviously, not all prayers were spontaneous. Certain prayers were learned by the community and prayed together. The "Breaking of the Bread" has always been understood to refer to the Mass.

Monarchianism
http://cedar.evansville.edu/~ecoleweb/articles/monarch.html

Learn about this early Church heresy. I would tell you something about it but then this homepage would be unnecessary.

Music Provider: Ave Maria Music
http://members.aol.com/kapelle888/heaven.htm

See their religious recordings, free catalog, hymn stories, and hymn survey.

*Music Provider: Carolina Catholic Music Publishing
http://www.infi.net/~ccmp/

More great music! Good music can be so uplifting. St. Augustine said that when we sing to God, we pray twice.

Music Provider: Inspirational Music by The Lightbearers
http://www.ultranet.com/~livflame/lightbearers/

Even more great music! You can really touch or heal someone spiritually with good religious music. It is really a ministry.

 BOOKMARK N

http://wsnet.com:80/~alapadre/indexn.html

National Association of Catholic Families
http://homepage.interaccess.com/~dfroula/nacf.html

These Catholic families try to give one another mutual, moral, spiritual, and social support in a culture at war with its values. They do this by linking committed Catholic families locally, nationally, and internationally—but always with the simple intention of mutual support. They are answering Pope John Paul's call for families to be truly Catholic families. Definitely a good place for you to visit.

National Catholic Center for Holocaust Education
http://www.ushmm.org/organizations/70.html

This organization that was begun in 1987 is an educational and academic resource center. It is directed by a couple of nuns, one in the United States and the other in Israel. You will find contact information here.

National Evangelization Teams
http://www.powerup.com.au/~netaust/

A Catholic ministry sharing the Gospel with young people in schools and parishes through drama, song, personal sharing, and prayer.

Natural Family Planning: CCL
http://www.missionnet.com/~mission/cathlc/ccl/rain.html

Couple to Couple League International's discussion of the Church supported method of regulating family size. Remember that the decision to not have a child is based on prayerful reflection and a serious reason. The Church has always encouraged generosity among couples. Even though methods of Natural Family Planning are morally acceptable, that doesn't mean they are to be used indiscriminately.

 Natural Family Planning: Family of the Americas' Ovulation Method
http://www.upbeat.com/family/om.html

Here you can find information about this method, which is based on a woman's natural fertility cycle.

 Natural Family Planning: Primer on
http://www.familyweb.com/faqs/natfamplan.shtml

More information on natural family planning.

 Nazareth Resource Library
http://www.io-online.com/james

I am not much of a reader myself, but I do value libraries, even online ones.

 Newman Centers & Catholic Chaplaincies: Listed and Wanted
http://www.cco.caltech.edu/~newman/OtherNC.html

If you are looking for a job in this area, you can advertise here! You can see Chapter 9 for this listing if you want.

 News: NewsLink
http://www.newslink.org/menu.html

Some people just have to keep up on the latest. There is all kinds of news here—Catholic news as well.

 News, Catholic: Baystate Catholic Publications
http://www.interpath.net/~mdoyle/

Among other information, you will find links to *The Catholic Spirit,* (the newspaper of the Diocese of Wheeling—Charleston) and the *Southern Catholic Review*—(ten Catholic newspapers covering the southeast).

*News, Catholic: Criterion (Indianapolis Archdiocese)
http://wl.iglou.com/criterion/criterion.html

See what's happening in the archdiocese of Indianapolis. This is really for news freaks!

News, Catholic: Georgia Bulletin
http://www.archatl.com/bullnews.htm

These news articles are reprinted in their entirety from previous issues of the *Georgia Bulletin,* the official newspaper of the Archdiocese of Atlanta. With the advent of newswires, local papers now can carry both national and international news. So you may find more than Atlanta Catholic news here.

News, Catholic: Our Sunday Visitor
http://128.235.249.100/RCC/Periodicals/OSV/indexosv.html

National weekly news magazine. This is the largest weekly news magazine in the United States. I have submitted articles but they have never been accepted. So this must be a pretty good paper!

News, Catholic: Southern Catholic Review
http://www.interpath.net/~mdoyle/regnews/regnews.html

Ten Catholic newspapers covering the Southeast.

*News, Catholic: The West Texas Angelus
http://nshome01.web.aol.com/sanangelo/anglogo.htm

The title of this newspaper reminds me to remind you about praying the Angelus. When I was in the Philippines, they would pray the Angelus three times a day. Amazingly, all the workers would stop their work at that time for prayer, even the cashier at the checkout counter!

News, Catholic: Western Catholic Reporter
http://www.supernet.ab.ca/Mall/Religion/westerncath.html

The largest weekly religious newspaper in Canada.

Nicene Creed
http://www.dma.org/~thawes/nicene.html

This is the Profession of Faith that states the major truths of the Catholic Faith, composed by the Council Fathers at Nicaea in A.D. 325.

Notre Dame Archives
http://archives1.archives.nd.edu/

You won't find full-text copies of the documents in their collections. It is set up more like a library catalog in that it contains descriptions of their holdings.

 # BOOKMARK O

http://wsnet.com:80/~alapadre/indexo.html

OCF Icon Archive
http://www.mit.edu:8001/activities/ocf/icons.html

This is the start of what Constantine Christakos hopes to be an online archive of icons. This would certainly be a great place to visit. Icons can be so impressive and beautiful to look at and can raise our minds to heavenly things.

One Bread, One Body
http://www.veritas.org.sg/presentation_ministries/reflections/

A daily Mass reading reflection publication. It is a good idea to ponder the Mass readings. This is an aid to do this.

Opus Dei—Finding God in Ordinary Life
http://www.opusdei.org/

Opus Dei (Work of God) is a personal Prelature of the Catholic Church that seeks to spread the message that all men and women are called to the fullness of Christian life and the perfection of love and to bear witness to Jesus Christ in the fulfillment of their ordinary lives, especially through their work.

*Orders: Holy Orders
http://webzone1.co.uk/www/jcrawley/orders.htm#ORDERS

Visit this homepage to learn more about this sacrament. If you are in the seminary, I hope you already know about it!

Ordinatio Sacerdotalis: Responsum ad Dubium 28 Oct 95
http://www.knight.org/advent/docs/df95os.htm

The response of the Sacred Congregation for the Doctrine of the Faith to a doubt about whether the Church's statement about women's ordination is to be held definitively or not. The answer was yes.

Oregon Catholic Press
http://www.ocp.org/

A publisher of a wide variety of music and worship materials.

Original Sin
http://www.knight.org/advent/cathen/11312a.htm

The following information can be found on Original Sin: its nature, meaning, and principal adversaries of this doctrine; Original Sin in Scripture, tradition, and in face of the objections of human reason. If you don't think there is such a thing as Original Sin, look around!

BOOKMARK P

http://wsnet.com:80/~alapadre/indexp.html

Papal Documents
http://listserv.american.edu/catholic/church/papal/papal.html

I think it's good to read and study papal documents and thereby enrich one's faith. The profound depth in these writings always impresses me. Certainly the Holy Spirit inspires the Popes.

Papal Visit—October 1995

http://wsnet.com/~alapadre/jp2visit.html

The Pope's visit to the United States. If you didn't get a chance to be there, it's still not too late!

*Paraclete

http://199.172.191.10/~alapadre/paraclet.html

This name, "Paraclete," refers to the Holy Spirit. It comes from a Greek word meaning "advocate." Jesus applied this name to the Holy Spirit. (Cf. January 14,16).

Pastoral Studies: International Institute of Catechetical and Pastoral Studies

http://www.luc.edu/or/sj/lumen/index.html

This is run by the Jesuits.

*Patristic Studies

http://www.knight.org/advent/fathers/fathers.htm

If you want to learn about the Fathers of the Church, this is the homepage for you.

Patristic Texts

ftp://iclnet93.iclnet.org/pub/resources/christian-history.html#patristic

Written by the Fathers of the Church. The time span for the Patristic Age customarily places its beginning toward the end of the first century A.D. The end of the era of the Fathers can be debated, but some would place it around the middle of the fifth century.

*Paulist Directory

http://www.clark.net/pub/paulist/directory.html

The Paulist fathers were founded in the nineteenth century by Father Issac Hecker (d. 1888), an American convert who was a great friend of many New England Transcendentalist thinkers of Boston and Concord.

*Penance

http://webzone1.co.uk/www/jcrawley/healing.htm#RECONCILIATION

This homepage is about the sacrament of Reconciliation. Normally we associate this sacrament only with the forgiveness of sins. The idea of reconciliation takes on many facets: with God, our neighbor, the Church, and humanity.

*Pilgrimage: Pilgrims' Progress (UK Walk on Pilgrimage)

http://dialspace.dial.pipex.com/town/square/fk76/

Walking pilgrimages are still popular in the United Kingdom where they were a great tradition in the Middle Ages. People still walk the 90 miles from London to Our Lady of Walsingham's shrine in Norfolk.

Pipe Organ Sound

http://wsnet.com/~alapadre/tkoerner.html

I have never had a musical ear. A friend of mine who played the piano once pressed one foot pedal and played a note. He then pressed another and played another note. He turned to me and said, "Hear the difference?" I said, "No."

Pope John Center

http://www.pjcenter.org/pjc/

An institute faithful to the Magisterial teachings of the Catholic Church that engages in research and education in biomedical ethics and publishes ethical studies in health care. One of the priests at this center, Fr. Germain, OFM. Conv. was my undergraduate ethics professor at St. Hyacinth's Seminary in Granby, Massachusetts.

Pope John Paul II: American Speeches (4–8 Oct '95)

http://christusrex.org/www1/pope/speeches.html

Read what the Holy Father said when he was here. Sometimes with all the media hype his message gets lost.

Pope John Paul II: Archive

http://listserv.american.edu/catholic/church/papal/jp.ii/

Great source for Papal documents of this Pope. Some people's entire lives have been transformed by reading these documents.

Pope John Paul II: Crossing the Threshold of Hope
http://www.catholic.net/RCC/POPE/HopeBook/toc.html

His recent book, which is written in a question-and-answer format. An important lesson he mentions is "Have no fear." He certainly does not seem to have any as he travels regardless of death threats.

*Pope John Paul II: Evangelium Vitae
http://listserv.american.edu/catholic/catholic/church/papal/jp.ii/jp2evanv.html

This is about the evangelical life. Many times people associate only poverty, chastity, and obedience with religious life, but everyone should strive to have the spirit of these. They are opposed to the three obstacles to pure love of God and neighbor: covetousness, lust, and pride.

Pope John Paul II: Letter to Women
http://listserv.american.edu/catholic/church/papal/jp.ii/jp2wom95.html

The Church has not forgotten the role of women. Two of them, St. Teresa of Avila (d. 1502) and St. Catherine of Siena (d. 1380) are Doctors of the Church.

*Pope John Paul II: Ut Unum Sint
http://listserv.american.edu/catholic/catholic/church/papal/jp.ii/jp2utunu.html

Ut unum sint means "may all be one." This was certainly the prayer of Our Lord the night of His Passion. Unity is of the Holy Spirit. Division is always the fruit of sin and the devil.

*Prayer
http://webzone1.co.uk/www/jcrawley/pray1.htm#PRAYER

It seems we can always learn more about prayer!

Prayer: Method of Centering Prayer by Thomas Keating
http://www.io.com/~lefty/Centering_Prayer.html

Prayer: Veritas! Daily Reflection Page
http://www.veritas.org.sg/

Great for meditation.

Prayers
http://convex.cc.uky.edu/~jatuck00/Religion/Prayers.html

Premarital Sex
http://info.rutgers.edu/catholic-center/publish/FrRonStanley/p-m.sex.html

Ronald Stanley, O.P., discusses the value of Christian marriage against the backdrop of peer pressure on college students to have sex.

Pro-Life: Catholics United for Life
http://www.mich.com/~buffalo/

Pro-Life: Healing After Abortion
http://ivory.lm.com/~lou/rachel.html

*Pro-Life: National Students for Life
http://www.cencom.net/~jen/life/ertelt/nsl2.html

*Pro-Life: Natural Family Planning
http://ds1.gl.umbc.edu/~tcunni1/om.html

*Pro-Life: PLN Index of Pro-life Resources on the Web
http://jupiter.ee.pitt.edu/~frezza/PLresources.html

*Pro-Life: Priests for Life, Pro-Life Shopping Guide
http://www.crnet.org/antonin/listab.html

Protestant: Protestants & Sola Scriptura
http://128.235.249.100/cgi-bin/HyperNews/get/solascriptura.html

This is a response to the theory of *Sola Scriptura* (Scripture only), the cornerstone of Protestant belief.

Publisher: Catholic University of America Press
gopher://vmsgopher.cua.edu/11gopher_root_cupr

They publish scholarly works of interest to scholars and academic libraries, or for use in courses in the fields of philosophy, theology, language and literature, history, and political theory.

Publisher: Resource Publications, Inc

http://www.rpinet.com/

An interesting Catholic publisher. Catholic writers will want to check out this homepage.

Publisher: Saint Anthony Messenger Press

http://www.americancatholic.org/

Publishers of books and audiotapes on liturgy, sacraments, aids to prayer and spirituality, understanding Scripture, theology, Church history, and parish ministry resources.

Publisher: Saint Bede's Publications

http://www.stbedes.org/

Seeing that this publisher is our neighbor, only two miles up the road, I had better mention this one or I'll hear about it! Saint Bede's Publications is an excellent Catholic publisher and the work of the Benedictine Nuns of St. Scholastica's Priory here in our town of Petersham, Massachusetts. They publish theological and spiritual works, prayer, monasticism, and lives of the saints. They also translate foreign works to make them available in English.

Publisher: Saint Mary's Press

http://wwwsmp.smumn.edu/

Publishers of religious education materials for adolescents in Catholic schools and in parish settings. They also have youth ministry resources and prayer resources.

Publishers' Catalogs

http://www.lights.com/publisher/#us

Browse through catalogs from all over the world. If you are having a hard time finding something, don't give up; look here.

*Purgatory
http://198.5.212.8/~edit/cathfund.html

A place of purification after death for those who die in the state of grace but are not yet ready for Heaven. We can help those in Purgatory by our prayers and sacrifices so let's not forget to pray!

 # BOOKMARK Q

http://wsnet.com:80/~alapadre/indexq.html

Questions Answered: Fides et Scientia
http://francis.veritas.org.sg/~nuscss/

Here you will find questions and answers about Faith and science. Some people would like to paint Faith as an enemy to progress and science. This couldn't be further from the truth.

 # BOOKMARK R

http://wsnet.com:80/~alapadre/indexr.html

Radio: Catholic Radio (Fr. Paul Keenan @ WABC & WOR)
http://wsnet.com/~alapadre/catradny.html

Radio: Catholic Short-wave Radio
http://www.ewtn.com

Mother Angelica's radio station (WEWN). This is an amazing radio ministry. Brother Craig visited their headquarters and recorded programs for them. He was very impressed by their worldwide broadcasting.

RCIA at Alta Vista WWW Search
http://www.altavista.digital.com/cgi-bin/query?pg=q&what=web&fmt=.&q=rcia

This refers to the process for becoming a Roman Catholic. An index of links using a popular search engine.

RCIA at Infoseek WWW Search

http://guide-p.infoseek.com/WW/NS/Titles?qt=RCIA&col=WW

These search the Internet to find all the homepages about the Rite of Christian Initiation for Adults.

RCIA at Inktomi WWW Search

http://204.161.74.6:1234/query/?query=RCIA&hits=50+documents&disp=Text+Only

RCIA at Lycos 19 WWW Search

http://nineteen.srv.lycos.com/cgi-bin/pursuit?query=RCIA.&matchmode=or&minscore=.1&maxhits=40&terse=standard

RCIA at University of Dayton Campus Ministry

http://www.udayton.edu/~campmin/becoming-a-catholic.htm

Find out about becoming a Catholic.

Reach Out: Saint Francis House (Boston)

http://www.stfrancishouse.org/

New England's largest, most comprehensive day program, run by the Franciscans, for homeless poor men and women. This is putting the Gospel into practice.

*Reconciliation

http://webzone1.co.uk/www/jcrawley/healing.htm#RECONCILIATION

The sacrament for the forgiveness of sins. If you don't think the priest has the power in the name of Jesus to forgive sins, look at John 20:23.

Relics

http://www.umich.edu/Gateway/Catalog/Relics.html

Renaissance Liturgical Imprints: a Census (RELICS). This project serves to catalog over 9,300 Catholic and Protestant liturgy books published before A.D. 1601, which are held in libraries in the United States and Europe. Good luck!

Religious: Danish Cistercian Nuns
http://inet.uni-c.dk/~grant/kloster1.htm

A lot of interesting information here, including links around the world and mirror sites—the Vatican, the Cistercians, a photo album, and more. This is Brother Craig's favorite homepage.

Religious: Links to Religious Communities
http://www.marywood.edu/www2/ihmpage/Resources/rel-orders.html

Want to learn more about religious communities? Or perhaps you have a vocation but don't know where to go? Look at these links then.

Retreat Ministry: NET
http://www.powerup.com.au/~netaust/ministry.htm

Interested in retreats? Some spiritual writers say it is a good idea to make a retreat once a year. This will keep our spiritual life on track.

*Retreat Ministry: USA Retreat Centers
http://199.172.191.10/~alapadre/retreats.html

Are you looking for a place to make a retreat? If you are, I suggest you check this homepage. This is certainly a wonderful service.

*Roman Catholicism in 19th Century Great Britain
http://www.iris.brown.edu/iris/RIE/religions/Catholic.html

Learn about the "Second Spring," Cardinal Newman, and others in Great Britain in the last century.

*Rosary, Buy a
http://rosaries.com/roseplus.html

Need to buy a Rosary? I have heard of a man who has a Rosary museum in the Northwest United States.

Rosary, How to Say the
http://www-cgi.cs.cmu.edu/Web/People/spok/catholic/rosary.html

Here you will find a detailed guide to Our Lady's Rosary. There are people who do not know how to pray it. I instructed a young man how to do it when I was in Medjugorje.

 # BOOKMARK S

http://wsnet.com:80/~alapadre/indexs.html

Sacramentals
http://christusrex.org/www1/CDHN/others.html#LITURGICAL

This will point you to the Catechism of the Catholic Church's teaching on this subject. Learn the Church's teaching on Rosaries, scapulars, and other sacramentals. I would tell you what a sacramental is, but then you wouldn't follow this link.

Sacraments
http://christusrex.org/www1/CDHN/baptism.html#SEVEN

Learn what the Catechism of the Catholic Church teaches about the sacraments. The sacraments really form the foundation of our spiritual life. They are meetings with the living Lord Jesus.

*Sacred Scripture
http://webzone1.co.uk/www/jcrawley/profess4.htm#SCRIPTURE

Visit this homepage to increase your knowledge of the Holy Bible.

*Saint Alphonsus de Liguori
http://wsnet.com/~alapadre/indexs.html#AlphonsusdeLiguori

This saint (d. 1787) was a kind and gentle priest, the founder of the Redemptorist Order, and a Bishop. He is a Doctor of the Church and is known more specifically as the Doctor of Moral Theology.

*Saint Ignatius of Loyola

http://wsnet.com/~alapadre/indexs.html#IgnatiusofLoyola

He (d. 1556) was the founder of the Jesuits and author of the Spiritual Exercises.

*Saint John of the Cross

http://wsnet.com/~alapadre/indexs.html#JohnoftheCross

Doctor of the Church (d. 1591) and great Carmelite teacher on prayer and the Dark Nights of the spiritual life.

*Saint Thomas Aquinas

http://wsnet.com/~alapadre/indexs.html#ThomasAquinas

He is called the Angelic Doctor. This Dominican saint synthesized the theology up to his time into one great work: the *Summa Theologica.*

*Scriptures Glossary Project

http://www.nd.edu/~jvanderw/theo100/glossary.htm

A great aid to the study of Sacred Scripture. There are so many terms in the Bible that we need help to understand, as they were written in a different culture, history, and language.

*Secular Franciscan Order

http://www.iglou.com/members/wilmhoff.html

Learn about what used to be called the Franciscan Third Order. It's now called the Secular Franciscans. I know a few people who belong to it and they love it.

Sermon: Index of Dominican Sermons

http://www.op.org/op/sermons.eng/

Do you want to read an interesting sermon? There are actually books published of priests' sermons.

Shields of the Twelve Apostles

http://www.nwu.edu/chaplain/office_staffdocs/shield.html

Do you know the symbols for each of the twelve apostles yet? Bishops continue this custom by choosing, when they are appointed, certain symbols to be arranged on a shield as an expression of their interests or spirituality.

Shroud of Turin Homepage
http://www.cais.com/npacheco/shroud/turin.html

Learn about this fascinating Christian relic, which I believe is the burial cloth of Christ. Here is some of what you can choose here: frequently asked questions about the shroud, history, scientific research through 1976, current scientific research, literature, and centers.

*Sick: Anointing of the Sick
http://webzone1.co.uk/www/jcrawley/heal2.htm#SICK

A sacrament of the Church that sometimes brings physical healing but always gives spiritual strength to endure the trials and tribulations of illness.

Single Interest: CACI Single—Catholic—Professional
http://www.clark.net/pub/cac/

An interesting homepage. I hope they allow nonprofessionals to participate also.

*Single Interest: Catholic Singles Network
http://www.kaiwan.com/~prchoudh/

Single Catholics meeting other single Catholics. Some people feel called to the single life. Single Catholics do many good works for the Church.

Sistine Chapel
http://christusrex.org/www1/sistine/0-Tour.html

An informational and pictorial tour of this church known for its ceiling painting by Michelangelo.

Software of Catholic Interest: Daughters of Saint Paul
http://bay.netrover.com/~pauline/csoftwar.html

Yes, the Daughters have moved into software.

Special Ed Folks
http://wsnet.com/~alapadre/spedsand.html

If you are involved in special education, you will want to go here. We recently had a vocational visit from a man who worked in a school totally dedicated to special education. He told us about his interesting and very important work.

Stoicism
http://cedar.evansville.edu/~ecoleweb/articles/stoicism.html

This was one of the most important and influential traditions in the philosophy of the ancient Greek world. Some Christian thinkers have been influenced by it.

Storyfest
http://storyfest.inter.net/storyfest/welcome.html#anchor431551

Here you will find a school of sacred storytelling. This includes the art and wisdom of storytelling—storytelling for the spiritual formation of children, weekly Saturday storytelling for preachers and homilists, a weekly Lectionary-based storytelling for 9- to 13-year-old children, and much more.

Syriac Study Connection
http://www.cl.cam.ac.uk/users/gk105/

Everything you wanted to know about this language. It also includes links to the Concordance to the Syriac New Testament, a comparative edition of the Syriac Gospels, and the Holy Apostolic Catholic Assyrian Church of the East (U.S.).

 # BOOKMARK T

http://wsnet.com:80/~alapadre/indext.html

Teen Interest: Life Teen Program
http://www.lifeteen.org/

This is great for teens! And helping teens is a wonderful ministry. I met a teenager who was so on fire for Christ that I could hardly restrain him from answering every question I posed to the teenage group.

Television, Catholic: EWTN
http://www.ewtn.com

It's time for Mother Angelica and her Catholic television network. It is no accident that this Poor Clare Nun began a television network. St. Clare, the foundress of the Poor Clares, is the Patron of television.

Ten Commandments
http://christusrex.org/www1/CDHN/decalog.html#TEN

The Catechism of the Catholic Church on each and every one of the Commandments.

Theological Resources: Woodstock Theological Center
http://guweb.georgetown.edu/woodstock/web-theo.htm

You will find many links here to sites that provide useful places on the Web for beginning research on religious and theological questions.

*Theology 100 Online Glossary Project
http://www.nd.edu/~jvanderw/theo100/glossary.htm

This project was done, I believe, by a professor of Notre Dame University.

Thesaurus Precum Latinarum
http://www.cs.cmu.edu/Web/People/spok/catholic/latin-prayers/index.html

Here you will find a treasury of Latin prayers.

*Trent, Council of
http://listserv.american.edu/catholic/church/trent/trent.info.html

Learn about this important council that reaffirmed and defined various truths of the Faith.

INFO BOOKMARK U

http://wsnet.com:80/~alapadre/indexu.html

Universities, List of AlaPadre Top Catholic
http://wsnet.com/~alapadre/cathuniv.html

http://wsnet.com:80/~alapadre/indexv.html

Vatican Exhibit Rome Reborn
http://sunsite.unc.edu/expo/vatican.exhibit/Vatican.exhibit.html

This is the Library of Congress Vatican Exhibit. Among other things you will find the Vatican library, archaeology, humanism, mathematics, music, medicine, and biology, nature, the Orient to Rome and Rome to China—along with pictures.

Vatican II Council Documents
http://wsnet.com/~alapadre/catv2doc.html

They are: *Ad Gentes* (The Church's Missionary Activity), *Apostolicam Actuositatem* (The Apostolate of Lay People), *Christus Dominus* (The Pastoral Office of Bishops), *Dei Verbum* (Dogmatic Constitution on Divine Revelation), *Dignitatis Humanae* (Declaration on Religious Freedom), *Gaudium et Spes* (The Church in the Modern World), *Gravissimum Educationis* (Decree on Christian Education), *Inter Mirifica* (The Means of Social Communication), *Lumen Gentium* (Dogmatic Constitution on the Church), *Nostra Aetate* (The Church and Non-Christian Religions), *Optatam Totius* (Decree on Priestly Training), *Orientalium Ecclesiarum* (Eastern Rite Catholic Churches), *Perfectae Caritatis* (Renewal of Religious Life), *Presbyterorum Ordinis* (Ministry and Life of Priests), *Sacrosanctum Concilium* (Constitution on the Sacred Liturgy), *and Unitatis Redintegratio* (Decree on Ecumenism).

Vatican II Nostra Aetate, Dei Verbum, and Unitatis Redintegratio
http://www.iconovex.com/ANCHOR/DEMOS/VATICAN.HTM

Another look at just these three documents.

Vatican Museums
http://christusrex.org/www1/vaticano/0-Musei.html

Here's a way to visit the museums without going to Vatican City!

Vatican Radio auf Deutsch
http://wsnet.com/~alapadre/vatradio.german.html

Vatican WWW
http://www.vatican.va/

*Vatican WWW Plans
http://199.172.191.10/~alapadre/vatplans.html

 BOOKMARK W

http://wsnet.com:80/~alapadre/indexw.html

World Peace Day Homepage:
http://www.peaceday.org/

Here you will find: The Peace Days, World Peace 2000 Proclamation, Tateyah Topa's Peace Forces Registration, a chat area, a Web board, an events calendar, links, kids' pages, projects, and more.

See Also Retrouvaille
http://www.vicnet.net.au/vicnet/community/retro/retro.htm

This is a great opportunity for you to enrich your marriage.

 BOOKMARK Y

http://wsnet.com:80/~alapadre/indexy.html

Yahoo
http://www.yahoo.com/

This is a popular search engine. For details on it see Chapter 14.

Young Adult Ministry: L. I. G. H. T. (Daly City, CA)
http://www.hooked.net/users/amdg85/light3.html

This is about young adults of St. Andrew's parish who reach out to their peers, share their faith, empower each other, and serve their community in the name of Jesus Christ. Find out about their activities, service, newsletter, community, music, reflections, and photos.

Young Adult Ministry: Young Adult Planning & Advisory Council
http://members.aol.com/yapac/yapac.htm

Their purpose is to reach out in peer ministry to young adults throughout the Diocese of Trenton, New Jersey. See their calendar, constitutions, and links; find out about Youth 2000; and get advice about how to start a young adult group in your area.

Youth Apostles Institute
http://csugrad.c.s.vt.edu/~membree/ya/

Attention young people! You too can be an apostle for Christ. St. John the Apostle was probably a teenager when he first was called by Jesus.

Youth: Cross Fire—Youth Ministry Magazine
http://www.crossfire.org/crossfire/menu.htm

This is really an excellent page for both teens and adults alike. Adults will love reading the "Children's Letters to God." The monthly features for teens are: "Role Models," "Active Ministry," and "Questions of the Faith." With the last one, you can actively participate by submitting your answer to the question. Make sure you stop here.

Youth: Life Teen Program
http://www.lifeteen.org/

This apostolate began when Fr. Dale met a young man he hadn't seen in church for a while at the grocery store. In 1985, 150 teens gathered together for Mass and pizza afterward. Ten years later, this scene is replayed every Sunday night with approximately 30,000 young people attending a Life Teen Mass and Life Night all over the country! Visit here to get involved in this program.

Youth: Toronto Archdiocese Office of Catholic Youth
http://web.idirect.com/~youth/

See their events, links, ministry, and letter to youth. This is the place to be if you're at all interested in youth ministry and getting youth involved in your community.

Youth Ministry Network
http://www.ymnetwork.net/

This is an absolutely awesome homepage! It is based in Venice, Florida. Now in the highly unlikely event that you have picked up this book and don't have a computer, you will want to get in touch with them by calling 941-488-7477. Everything you wanted to know about youth ministry is here both for those in charge and those who would like to participate in it.

CATHOLIC COLLEGES

http://wsnet.com/~alapadre/cathcoll.html

Since Father removed this from a listing on his main page, you can still find a link to it under Bookmark C or you can just type in the URL for this page. Father lists these colleges alphabetically and by state. I have chosen the former here. These colleges are listed first by name and then by city and state separated by a slash.

Now you realize that colleges are going to have very specific information on them: curriculum, entrance requirements, college newspaper, and so forth. Sometimes they will give you a pictorial tour of the campus. The students put up homepages that can be interesting. I have tried to point out that "little extra" that might make a particular college homepage different. I hope that students will get connected to each other through these listings. Also, if you are thinking of attending a Catholic college, this is a good way to "shop around" for one with little expense.

You can nominate your favorite American Catholic College. Send its homepage to: malapadre@dibbs.net

See also:

Catholic Universities
http://wsnet.com/~alapadre/cathuniv.html

Allentown College of St. Francis de Sales/Allentown, PA
http://www.allencol.edu/general.html

I'm praying to St. Francis de Sales (d. 1622) for this book because he's the patron of writers.

Alverno College/Milwaukee, WI
http://www.alverno.edu/

This college is run by Franciscans. Mount Alverno was where St. Francis received the Stigmata or Wounds of Our Lord.

Assumption College/Worcester, MA
http://www.assumption.edu/

Here you'll find a virtual tour of the campus as well as views of the Chapel of the Holy Spirit from the outside and of the stained glass on the inside.

Benedictine College/Atchison, Kansas
http://www.benedictine.edu/bchome.html

Of special interest here is the Benedictine College library and government documents sites, the Benedictine College environmental conference, and search tools on the Internet. You can learn about the Net here also.

Canisius College/Buffalo, New York
http://gort.canisius.edu/ http://gort.canisius.edu/

See their library, information technology services, and Internet resources.

Clarke College/Dubuque, Iowa
http://www.clarke.edu/

Want to go to college near the Mississippi River?

*Emmanuel College/Boston, Massachusetts
http://emmanuel.edu/Catholic

This Catholic college is in the city of colleges! A lot of these colleges share resources, as I learned when checking out the theology program at the Weston School of Theology.

Felician College/Lodi, New Jersey
http://www.felician.edu/

This college is run by the Congregation of Sisters of St. Felix of Cantalice (d. 1587)—better known as the Felician Sisters.

Fontbonne College/Saint Louis, Missouri
http://gatekeeper.fontbonne.edu/

Looking for a Catholic college in the "Gateway to the West"? I saw the famous arch in St. Louis when I visited this city.

Holy Cross, College of the/Worcester, Maine
http://www.holycross.edu/

Take a virtual tour of the campus. They have an overhead picture of the campus with numbers marking the buildings you can tour. Brother Craig and I often go there by car, not by Internet, to use their library.

Incarnate Word College/San Antonio, Texas
http://www.uiw.edu/

This college is in Texas's historic city of San Antonio.

Le Moyne College/Syracuse, New York
http://maple.lemoyne.edu/

See Fr. Bucko's "Mighty Homepage." This is Father Bucko's personal gateway to the Web, of particular use to those interested in a full yet basic guide to the Internet. Also, pay a visit to Le Moyne students' Virtual Museums—students in Fr. Bucko's Museums and Social Science course created virtual museums on the Web. Look at their images, which they offer to spice up your homepage.

Loras College/Dubuque, Iowa
http://www.loras.edu/

Loras College, Iowa's oldest college, was founded in 1839.

Loyola College in Maryland/Baltimore, Maryland
http://www.loyola.edu/menu.html

I think St. Ignatius of Loyola is a good patron for a college. He himself went back to school to study for the priesthood when he wasn't so young.

Manhattan College/Riverdale, New York
http://www.manhattan.edu/

You can look at the Web and Internet resources including Web search engines here. You will find a glossary of Internet terms also.

Marist College/Poughkeepsie, New York
http://www.marist.edu/

Located in a really scenic part of New York state. The college is located right along the Hudson River.

*Mercyhurst College/Erie, Pennsylvania
http://utopia.mercy.edu/

This college was founded in 1926.

*Molloy College/Rockville Centre, New York
http://www.molloy.edu/

This college is run by the Dominican Sisters.

*Providence College/Providence, Rhode Island
http://www.providence.edu/pchome.htm

And this one's run by the Dominican Fathers and Brothers. The settlers named it Providence after Divine Providence.

Rockhurst College/Kansas City, Missouri
http://vax1.rockhurst.edu/

The Jesuits run this college in the heartland of America.

Saint Benedict, College of/Saint Joseph, Minnesota
http://www.csbsju.edu/

Get an aerial view of two colleges and a look at the Sacred Heart Chapel, and see selections from Michael Crouser's "Saint John's in Pictures." Hear Saint Benedict's

Monastery Schola and some longer sound files as well as Saint John's Abbey banner bells.

*Saint Francis College/Fort Wayne, Indiana
http://plan.educ.indiana.edu/~www/francis.html

This college was founded by the Franciscan Sisters way back in 1890.

Saint Francis College/Loretto, Pennsylvania
http://www.sfcpa.edu/

And this one was founded by the Franciscan Fathers and Brothers even further back in 1847.

Saint Joseph College/West Hartford, Connecticut
http://www.sjc.edu/

I like the name of this one. This college was founded by the Sisters of Mercy.

Saint Joseph's College/Rensselaer, Indiana
http://www.saintjoe.edu/

This page allows you to view any building on the Saint Joseph's College campus. Just click on the building that you would like to see, and a picture will load with a description and history of the building.

*Saint Joseph's College of Maine/North Windham, Maine
http://www.sjcme.edu/about.html

*Saint Mary-of-the-Woods College/Saint Mary-of-the-Woods, Indiana
http://onyx.indstate.edu/community/smwc/home.html

I think this college has a really nice name. This college was founded by the Sisters of Providence in 1840.

Saint Mary's College/Notre Dame, Indiana
http://www.saintmarys.edu/

Years ago the talented nun poet Sister Mary Madeleva, C.S.C., was president of this girls' college. It is run by the Sisters of the Holy Cross.

*Saint Michael's College/Colchester, Vermont
http://waldo.smcvt.edu/smcintro/index.html

This college in scenic Vermont has a good strong patron, St. Michael. This college is run by the Society of St. Edmund.

Saint Scholastica, College of/Duluth, Minnesota
http://www.css.edu/welcome.html

St. Scholastica (d. 543) was the twin sister of St. Benedict and the first Benedictine nun.

Saint Vincent's College/Latrobe, Pennsylvania
http://www.stvincent.edu/

*Spring Hill College/Mobile, Alabama
http://www.shc.edu/

This is another Jesuit-run school. They are involved in much higher education work.

Thomas More College/Crestview Hills, Kentucky
http://www.thomasmore.edu/about/contact.html

This college is run by the diocese of Covington. The saint this college is named after was martyred in England because he stood up for Papal authority.

Wheeling Jesuit College/Wheeling, West Virginia
http://ricci.wjc.edu/wjc.html

See the pictures of their buildings, athletics, and other images. Also, learn everything you ever wanted to know about the Jesuits through their links.

CATHOLIC UNIVERSITIES

http://wsnet.com/~alapadre/cathuniv.html

The priest Webmaster for this page has chosen to list the universities in alphabetical order. Also, you will find the name of the university first, followed by the city and the state separated by a slash.

The Internet really found its first practical use by hooking up universities around the country to each other. I would imagine that students at these schools are heavy Internet users. As can be expected, there will be a lot of Catholic information and links on these pages. You may even get the chance to browse the school library. Besides this, graduate and undergraduate students have their opportunity to "show off" their skills on these pages. Again, I hope students will get connected to one another. Also, if you are looking for a Catholic university to attend, this is an inexpensive way to tour the campus first before driving or flying there to check it out!

Like the college sites, you are going to find much information of a specific nature such as curriculum, requirements, and activities. So I have chosen, again, to spell out the things I considered special on these homepages. Of course, what I consider special may not be what you consider special. But since I can't know your opinion, you are stuck with mine!

Nominate your favorite American Catholic university. Send its homepage to: alapadre@dibbs.net

See also:

Catholic Colleges
http://wsnet.com/~alapadre/cathcoll.html

Barry University/Miami Shores, Florida
http://www.barry.edu/

Here you can take a pictorial tour with a lot of commentary regarding the main campus. Or go on a historical picture tour that includes the Cor Jesu (Heart of Jesus) Chapel.

Boston College/Chestnut Hill, Massachusetts
http://infoeagle.bc.edu/

See this university's electronic viewbook, which will give you a pictorial tour with a commentary, along with much more.

Catholic University of America/Washington, D.C.
http://www.cua.edu/

Take a virtual tour of the campus along with seeing their Virtual Student Union—what the students do for fun!

Chaminade University/Honolulu, Hawaii
http://www.pixi.com/~chaminad/

If you're interested in this university—everyone should be interested given the weather in Hawaii—they will send you a free diskette containing images and information about it, which they call a slideshow. Just fill out the form and they will send it to you.

Christian Brothers University/Memphis, Tennessee
http://www.cbu.edu/

You can view the student pages here and find FAQs and step-by-step guides to creating homepages. You will find links to institutions operated by the Brothers of the Christian Schools, founded by St. John Baptist De La Salle (d. 1719). Don't miss their Web search with lots of helpful links to finding things. If you want to find out about nonviolence, see the Gandhi center that includes a photo library and links.

Creighton University/Omaha, Nebraska
http://bluejay.creighton.edu/

Here you can see their short photographic tour of the campus. You will have to select "Campus Tour" and then "Tour."

Dallas, University of/Irving, Texas
http://www.udallas.edu/

This university has a European campus near Rome, Italy.

Dayton, University of/Dayton, Ohio
http://www.udayton.edu/

See their general virtual tour (a medium-length tour designed to capture the look and spirit of the university), the in-depth tour (for the person who doesn't want to miss a thing), and the student-life tour (a look at residential living and recreational activities of undergraduates).

DePaul University/Chicago, Illinois
http://www.depaul.edu/

This university is run by the Vincentians who were, of course, founded by St. Vincent de Paul.

Detroit Mercy, University of/Detroit Michigan
http://www.udmercy.edu/

Find links to other Jesuit schools here. My father went to school at this university.

Duquesne University/Pittsburgh, Pennsylvania
http://www.duq.edu/

Click on any object on the map they provide to get a photo and commentary on it.

*Fairfield University/Fairfield, Connecticut
http://192.160.243.26/fairnet.htm

Here's another school run by the Jesuits. It was begun in 1942.

Fordham University/New York City, New York
http://www.fordham.edu/

Under "Maps and Calendar," you can get a picture tour of the university.

Franciscan University/Steubenville, Ohio
http://www.franuniv.edu/

See their Catholic links arranged in alphabetical order with short commentaries. Many Catholic conferences open to the public are held at this university.

Gannon University/Erie, Pennsylvania
http://www.gannon.edu/

This university is run by the diocese of Erie. Not many universities are run by a diocese.

Georgetown University/Washington, D.C.
http://www.georgetown.edu/

This university is run by the Jesuits.

Gonzaga University/Spokane, Washington
http://www.gonzaga.edu/

Named after the Jesuit seminarian St. Aloysius Gonzaga (d. 1591), whose name was really Luigi but has been Latinized over the years. He died quite young as a result of caring for victims of a plague.

Great Falls, University of/Great Falls, Montana
http://www.ugf.edu/

This university is run by the Sisters of Providence and was founded in 1932.

LaSalle University/Philadelphia, Pennsylvania
http://www.lasalle.edu/

Their virtual tour takes about 5–10 minutes to complete. There is no place to exit out of the tour, so once you start it, you have to finish it.

Loyola Marymount University/Los Angeles, California
http://www.lmu.edu/

Did you know that the complete name of the city of Los Angeles is "Ciudad de Nuestra Señora de Los Angeles"? It is the city of Our Lady of the Angels.

Loyola University/Chicago, Illinois
http://www.luc.edu/

Under "University" and then under "Campus Photos," you will find campus photos of the lake shore, water tower, Mallinckrodt Campus, medical center, and campus maps.

Marquette University/Milwaukee, Wisconsin
http://www.mu.edu/

This university is named after the great Jesuit explorer, Father Marquette (d. 1675).

Marymount University/Arlington, Virginia
http://www.marymount.edu/

This university is run by Sisters called Religious of the Sacred Heart of Mary.

Niagara University/Niagara Falls, New York
http://www.niagara.edu/

They have a photo tour of the campus under "Campus, Information & Directories" that you will want to check out.

Notre Dame, University of/Notre Dame, Indiana
http://www.nd.edu/

Look under "Tourist" and "Sights and Sounds" to discover the sights and sounds of the university. The sights are arranged in a collage where you can click on an individual photo to get a blow-up of it. The sounds include the Notre Dame "Fight Song," the "Alma Mater," and "Notre Dame, Our Mother." If you want to be entertained, check out the "Notre Dame Bands." There you will find movies, pictures, and sounds of the band. See the "Notre Dame DomeCam" and the 'Notre Dame StadiumCam" for more special effects.

Portland, University of/Portland, Oregon
http://www.uofport.edu/

This university is run by the Holy Cross Fathers, as is Notre Dame.

Quincy University/Quincy, Illinois
http://www.quincy.edu/

Under the "Campus Tour Map," you will find a photo tour with a commentary on the campus. You move around by clicking on objects on the map or the index beside the map.

Saint Ambrose University/Davenport, Iowa
http://www.sau.edu/sau.html

Check out "Where the Wild Things Are," a librarian's guide to the best information on the Net.

Saint Bonaventure University/Olean, New York
http://www.cs.sbu.edu/

Tour this campus of 600 acres, 24 buildings, golf course, spacious lawns, and various indoor and outdoor recreational facilities. Select "Campus Profile" and then "Campus" to look at 33 photo sites. You can also listen to the campus radio.

Saint Edward's University/Austin, Texas
http://www.stedwards.edu/

Select the "Campus Map" to visit the various buildings on campus. By selecting a building, you will have access to services and departments housed within, as well as to images of the building.

Saint John's University/Collegeville, Minnesota
http://www.osb.org/index.html

St. John's University was founded in 1857 by the Benedictine monks.

*Saint John's University/New York City, New York
http://uits.stjohns.edu/

This university is run by the Vincentian Fathers and Brothers.

Saint Joseph's University/Philadelphia, Pennsylvania
http://www.sju.edu/

A year or so ago, I was in Philadelphia and I visited the shrine of St. John Neumann (d. 1860), which is definitely worth seeing.

Saint Louis University/Saint Louis, Missouri
http://www.slu.edu/

One saint for both the university and the city!

Saint Mary's University of Minnesota/Winona, Minnesota
http://140.190.128.190/SMC/HomePage.html

Select "Winona Campus" to go to their "Conferencing and Chat System." Here you can choose among 12 different characters to represent yourself in three chat rooms. This is a really wild interactive place where you can literally (almost!) walk around.

Saint Thomas, University of/Saint Paul & Minneapolis, Minnesota
http://www.stthomas.edu/

These people publish *Catholic Digest* magazine. I like their short humorous true stories.

Saint Xavier University/Chicago, Illinois
http://www.sxu.edu/

Look under "About Saint Xavier University" to see a chronology with pictures.

San Diego, University of/San Diego, California
http://www.acusd.edu/

Select "Community Web Picks" and then "Peter Lubczynski's Virtual Tour of USD." It contains a map of USD plus close-up pictures and descriptions of buildings, along with links to departments inside those places.

San Francisco, University of/San Francisco, California
http://www.usfca.edu/

This university is run by the Jesuits. I'm told the chapel is like a basilica in Europe and is very beautiful.

Santa Clara University/Santa Clara, California
http://www.scu.edu/

Under "General Information," you can select "Sights and Sounds" for a self-guided tour of the mission gardens or the undergraduate presentation of the university.

Scranton, University of/Scranton, Pennsylvania
http://www.uofs.edu/

Founded in 1888 as Saint Thomas College, the school received its University Charter in 1938. In 1942, Scranton became the 24th of 28 Jesuit schools in the United States.

*Seattle University/Seattle, Washington
http://www2.seattleu.edu/

Another Jesuit school. This one was founded in 1891.

Seton Hall University/South Orange, New Jersey
http://www.shu.edu/

Select "Virtual Open House" for Quicktime Virtual Reality (Apple computers' video format. Can be played using Macintosh or Windows) and Java Scripts.

Villanova University/Villanova, Pennsylvania
http://www.vill.edu/

Select "About Villanova" and then the "Campus Maps" to view illustrated maps of the campus. When you select one of the numbers on the map, you will see a photo of the object and a commentary.

Xavier University/Cincinnati, Ohio
http://www.xu.edu/

To get to the virtual tour, you'll have to go through a few steps on this page. Under "Admission" you will want to select "Campus Tour." Then you will want to click on "Tour of Xavier." Now you come to a crossroad. You can try the "Walking Tour" where you go from building to building or you can choose the "Tour Map." The latter will allow you to skip around to whatever you would like to look at in whatever order you want to look at it.

Xavier University of Louisiana/New Orleans, Louisiana
http://www.xula.edu/index.html

Select "Campus Tour" for a look around the campus by photos with commentaries. If you're new to the Internet you might want to visit their "Internet Start Shop" also.

MARY

http://wsnet.com/~alapadre/indexbvm.html

BVM: Golden Rosaries
http://www.cais.com/npacheco/rosary/gold.html

Many people have experienced that, at places such as Medjugorje, the links of their Rosaries have turned gold.

BVM: Guadalupe
http://web.sau.edu/~cmiller/image.html

Visit this homepage about Our Lady of Guadalupe, Patroness of the Americas.

BVM: Marian Hour
http://netpage.bc.ca/marianhr/

Radio Rosary in English and French. The format of their homepage is similar to that of their radio broadcasts. With each prayer is a link to recorded sound files from their radio program. Images relate to the Joyful, Sorrowful, and Glorious Mysteries. Text only versions of the prayers of the Rosary are available in Polish, French, Luganda, Tagalog, Hungarian, Portugese, and Latin.

CATHOLIC INFORMATION SITE

http://wsnet.com/~alapadre/megalink.html

*European Catholic News Web
http://communio.hcbc.hu/ecnwhome.html

New Advent Catholic Web Site
http://www.knight.org/advent

Saint Pachomius Library
http://www.ocf.org/OrthodoxPage/reading/St.Pachomius/globalindex.html

The patron saint (d.c. 346) of this library lived in the early part of the fourth century. He began a monastery on the banks of the Nile. By the time of his death, he had founded nine monasteries for 3,000 monks. He died May 15.

OTHER REFERENCES FROM THE INDEX

http://www.wsnet.com/~alapadre/

Pray!
http://www.veritas.org.sg/

Laugh!

http://www.gospelcom.net/rev-fun/rf.shtml

Put together by Dennis "Max" Hengeveld, a graphic designer for Gospel Films. You will find cartoons, the "Reverend Fun Book," the "Artchives," links, and you can join their mailing list.

Ask Father

http://members.aol.com/askfather/1.html

Father Michael Venditti's online apostolate started about five years ago when he began to answer questions about the Faith informally on America Online.

8

Catholic Resources on the Net– John Mark Ockerbloom

http://www.cs.cmu.edu/Web/People/spok/catholic.html

This directory is a comprehensive listing of Catholic resources on the Internet. John Mark Ockerbloom, a student at Carnegie-Mellon University, first compiled it in 1994.

I must give John credit. When I am in a bookstore and flip through secular or Christian "Yellow Pages" of Internet sites, I always see this directory listed. I give him credit because, unfortunately, I seldom see anything else Catholic listed, except possibly the Vatican homepage. Now I'm hoping you'll help to change this situation by following my homepage advertising tips found in Chapter 3.

This directory is organized according to topics. You won't find dazzling graphics or a fancy background here. You won't even find pictures. You will find on the opening page a simple, straightforward table of contents with hyperlinks (if you don't know what that is, you skipped Part I!). Those visiting this site will benefit because they want exactly what John provides—an index of Catholic-related resources. You

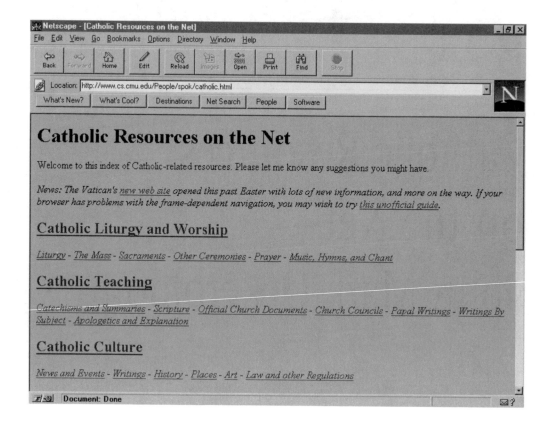

can click on the main headings on this page or subheadings to go to them. Once you are on these pages, you can always go back to his main index by clicking on "Back to Main Catholic Resources Page," found at the bottom of his pages.

The author of this page has provided some useful commentary next to his Catholic links. He does attempt to identify official Catholic documents and positions. But he also has some links to material not endorsed by the Church. This can be helpful for learning and dialoging with those who hold other positions and beliefs, as long as these links are clearly identified as non-Catholic so they will not be confused with Catholic material. The author of this directory has tried to do this.

This directory is bound to grow. You may already find new topics on the main page not found in this book. I was happy, however, when John notified me of his new addition to this index—the unofficial guide to the Vatican's Website. As I have said before, frame-dependent homepages can be difficult to view or may not be supported by your Internet browser. So John has taken the Vatican site that uses frames and broken down its pages into a listing instead. This way you can bypass the frames and go directly to what you want to see.

You can get to anything mentioned in the main index on this Webmaster's directory in two ways: Click on the topic or subtopic on his main page or click on the topic and page down to the subtopic.

If you have suggestions or comments, please e-mail John Mark Ockerbloom at: spok+catholic@cs.cmu.edu.

CATHOLIC LITURGY AND WORSHIP

http://www.cs.cmu.edu/Web/People/spok/catholic/worship.html

Liturgy

There are several liturgical rites of the Catholic Church. Most English-speaking Catholics follow the Latin Rite. There are also a number of Eastern Rites. In our town of Petersham, there is a monastery that follows the Maronite Rite. Many times a Rite will be tied to a particular culture. So, for instance, many Lebanese follow the Maronite Rite. Eastern liturgies may come from different traditions and involve different customs, but the Sacraments are the same. Baptism is still baptism. The Mass is still the Mass.

The Mass (of the Roman Rite)

http://www.uccla.org/uccla/UCC/Mass.html

The last major revision of the Order of Mass was made in the late 1960s, after the Second Vatican Council. Here is the English and Latin for it, as of 1975. Some minor revisions and additional options have been added since then.

Catholic Masses in the CMU Vicinity
http://www.cs.cmu.edu/Web/People/spok/mass.html

CMU stands for Carnegie-Mellon University, where this directory is based.

Mass Scripture Readings for Upcoming Sundays and Major Holy Days
http://www.cs.cmu.edu/Web/People/spok/catholic/readings.html

It's helpful to read the readings before Mass. Even if you can't attend Mass, this is a great way to read and meditate on the Bible.

Today's Mass Scripture Readings
http://www.avenue.com/cgi-bin/cgiwrap/avenue/netdaily

Maybe you could make time to read this today. Some people's lives have been deeply enriched by one verse of Scripture.

Reflections on Today's Readings
http://www.veritas.org.sg/presentation_ministries/reflections/index.html

We need aids to meditating on the Scripture readings of the Mass. You will find one here.

Notre Dame Center for Pastoral Liturgy
http://www.nd.edu/~ndcpl/

This site has a commentary on liturgy.

The Divine Office (of the Roman Rite)
http://www.strath.ac.uk/~crac44/office.html

As a monk, I find the Divine Office or Liturgy of the Hours very important. But you don't have to be a monk to pray it. I know many laypeople who do so, too. You will want to see this page in the United Kingdom about the Divine Office.

The Byzantine Rite

The Byzantine Catholic Church in America
http://www.epix.net/~byzantin/byzan.html

You will want to see this unofficial page for the Byzantine Catholic Church in America. It opens with a beautiful icon of Our Lord. Follow the icon links to view these beautiful images, along with learning how to paint your own. There are tons of links to parishes, monasteries, and institutions, as well as links to information about the Churchs' Ecumenical Councils. You can find out about their spirituality as well.

Mass: The Byzantine Rite
http://esoptron.umd.edu/UGC/Liturgy1.html

Uses the liturgy of St. John Chrysostom, which you can find here. You can also look at the Orthodox version.

Mass: The Byzantine Rite (Orthodox)
http://www.ocf.org/OrthodoxPage/liturgy/liturgy.html

It is common to find Orthodox counterparts to Eastern Catholic Churches. After the split of Eastern Churches from the Catholic Church in A.D. 1054, some of these Churches returned to unite with her.

*Divine Office
http://www.airmail.net/saint_nicholas/services/

This page has the service texts to parts of the Divine Office as celebrated in the Orthodox Church. The Byzantine Catholic version is very similar.

Here are some Web pages from parishes in various eastern rites:

Melkite Church: St. George's Church in Wisconsin
http://www.execpc.com/~pstamm/

This is a nicely laid out homepage. You can find out about the Melkite Church, as well as take a virtual tour of St. George's parish. I find icons so beautiful, and the two on this page are no exception!

Ukranian Catholic Church: St. Michael's Church in Maryland
http://www.the-hermes.net/~hrycak/Welcome.html

You will want to see the distinctive architecture of this church. Also, there are liturgical links here, including vestments, customs, and music. Besides finding out about the Ukranian Church, you will want to follow the link on "Rites and the Catholic Church" for an overview in general.

The Coptic Rite

*The Coptic Catholic Church of St. Basil
http://www.frugal.com/~stmary/Liturgy.html

This liturgy is very similar to the Coptic Orthodox version. If I am not mistaken, when I visited the Church of the Holy Sepulchre in the Holy Land, there was a Coptic monk situated right behind the tomb of Our Lord's resurrection.

Prayer

Catholic Prayer Page by Kenneth Morrill
http://www.webdesk.com/catholic/prayers/index.html

An excellent collection of prayers and related resources. Spontaneous prayer is great, but we can also draw from a long tradition of written prayers, too.

A Treasury of Latin Prayers
http://www.cs.cmu.edu/Web/People/spok/catholic/latin-prayers/index.html

With English translations and commentary by Michael Martin.

The Rosary in Latin
http://www.sky.net/~mntssyst/ltrose.html

Why not learn the prayers of the Rosary in the language of the Church?

Information on Centering Prayer
http://www.io.com/user/lefty/Centering_Prayer.html

By Fr. Thomas Keating, O.C.S.O. He says his method is designed to facilitate contemplative prayer.

*Prayers from the Shrine of St. Jude Thaddeus
http://www.ultranet.com/~bellvill/wpcs/stjude/stjude.html

You usually will find this saint pictured with a club. This is because tradition holds that he was clubbed to death.

Orientations
http://www.oise.on.ca/~rboys/veltri.html

A large portion of this book on prayer by Jesuit priest John Veltri is online.

Music, Hymns, and Chant

Gregorian Chant Homepage
http://www.music.princeton.edu/chant_html/

Located at Princeton, this homepage is the definitive directory of chant-related resources. One of the more interesting such resources is:

Cantus: Database of Divine Office Gregorian Chant
gopher://vmsgopher.cua.edu/11gopher_root_music%3a%5b_cantus%5d

You need to have good lungs for this!

A Collection of Canticles
gopher://ftp.std.com/11/obi/book/Canticles

These are edited by Sarah Keefer. A canticle is a sacred hymn whose words are taken directly from the Bible. "The Magnificat" is one example.

CATHOLIC TEACHING

http://www.cs.cmu.edu/Web/People/spok/catholic/teaching.html

Catholic teaching is based on sacred Scripture and tradition, the deposit of Faith entrusted to the whole Church. The significance and interpretation of this deposit of Faith has been discerned over time. The magisterium, that is, the bishops in union with the Pope, have the authority and grace to discern and penetrate into this Sacred Deposit to give authentic teaching and correct doctrine in the area of Faith and morals. We should thank God that He has left us a sure guide in His Church. Who knows what we, as individuals on our own, would believe after 2,000 years! Another site to visit:

Sacred Scripture
http://www.cs.cmu.edu/Web/People/spok/catholic/scripture.html

Catechisms and Summaries of Catholic Doctrine
The Catechism of the Catholic Church is an excellent reference on Catholic teaching. See the Top 20 picks in Chapter 5 for this link.

The Baltimore Catechism
http://www.catholic.net/RCC/Catechism/Catechism.html

This is a late-nineteenth-century question-and-answer Catechism written for Catholic schoolchildren, based on the Catechism of Trent. Catholic.net has several versions:

Number 1
http://www.catholic.net/RCC/Catechism/1/Welcome.html

The simplest version.

Numbers 2, 3, and 4
http://www.catholic.net/RCC/Catechism/2/Welcome.html

Number 4 presents an explanation of the Baltimore Catechism, written for teachers.

The Summa Theologica
http://www.knight.org/advent/summa/summa.htm

This is St. Thomas Aquinas' thirteenth-century exposition of the Catholic Faith, written in a scholastic point-counterpoint style. That means he states the theological question along with various authors' opinions. He will give his answer then refute the opposing ones. A lot of people who read the *Summa* take a shortcut and just read St. Thomas' "I answer that. . . ." But it's good to read both parts.

Official Church Documents

Scripture
http://www.cs.cmu.edu/Web/People/spok/catholic/scripture.html

You can skip down to the subtopic "Scripture" later in this section if you like.

Ecumenical Councils

Also known as "general councils," these are councils of Bishops from the worldwide Church. Their pronouncements can rule on matters of doctrine, set Church discipline, and give counsel. The Church has had 21 Ecumenical Councils. Many times these Councils were called to protect the Church from those teaching error.

Nicea I (a.d. 325)
http://www.fordham.edu/halsall/basis/nicea1.txt

Documents from the First Council of Nicea, edited by Paul Halsall.

Catholic Encyclopedia Article on Nicea I
http://www.knight.org/advent/cathen/11044a.htm

Nicea's main purpose was to affirm that Father and Son are consubstantial in the Trinity.

Constantinople I (a.d. 381)
http://www.fordham.edu/halsall/basis/const1.txt

Documents from the First Council of Constantinople, also edited by Paul Halsall. Of importance here is an affirmation of the full Divinity of the Holy Spirit.

Ephesus (a.d. 431)
http://www.fordham.edu/halsall/basis/ephesus.html

Held in Asia Minor, modern-day Turkey, this council affirmed Mary as the Mother of God.

Chalcedon (a.d. 451)
http://www.fordham.edu/halsall/basis/chalcedon.html

This council was held in Asia Minor also. Here was explained the doctrine of two natures (Divine and Human) united in the one Person of Christ.

Constantinople II (a.d. 553)
http://www.fordham.edu/halsall/basis/const2.html

Constantinople is now the city of Istanbul, Turkey. Condemned the Nestorian heresy (this Christological error led to denying Mary as Mother of God) and the Monophysite heresy (only one nature in Christ). Remember, a heresy is an error put forward by someone regarding Church doctrine.

Constantinople III (a.d. 680–681)
http://www.fordham.edu/halsall/basis/const3.html

Same place (the council fathers seemed to have liked Asia Minor!). Here they affirmed that Jesus possessed both a divine and human will.

Nicea II (a.d. 787)
http://www.fordham.edu/halsall/basis/nicea2.html

The Catholic Encyclopedia Article on Nicea II
http://www.knight.org/advent/cathen/11045a.htm

This one was convoked to deal with right and wrong understanding of the veneration of holy images and relics.

Constantinople IV (a.d. 869–870)
http://www.fordham.edu/halsall/basis/const4.html

Back to Constantinople again! This council condemned iconoclasm (the denial of the lawfulness of venerating images or icons).

Lateran IV (a.d. 1215)
http://www.fordham.edu/halsall/basis/lateran4.html

This one was held in Rome at St. John Lateran church. A lot was done here, with 70 canons being issued, many of which affect us to this day.

Trent (a.d. 1542–1563) Complete Canons and Decrees:
http://history.hanover.edu/early/trent.htm

*Selected Decrees
http://listserv.american.edu/catholic/church/trent/trent.html

Trent, or Trento as the Italians call it, is a city in northern Italy. The work of this council was both dogmatic (dealing with a truth of faith or morals) and disciplinary.

Vatican II (a.d. 1962–1965) Documents of the Second Vatican Council
http://www.christusrex.org/www1/CDHN/v1.html

The council of our age, Vatican II. I shouldn't need to say anything about this council because you know all about it—right?

Writings of the Pope

Papal letters can take various forms such as constitutions, encyclicals, rescripts, bulls, briefs, or apostolic letters. These are often used to express Catholic teachings.

Archive of Writings Listed by Pope
http://listserv.american.edu/catholic/church/papal/papal.html

You won't find any Popes listed here that lived before the thirteenth century.

The Latest Papal Addresses
http://www.vatican.va/

These addresses can be so interesting. They cover a wide variety of topics and people.

John Paul II's Writings in PDF Format
http://dominiks-www.howard.edu/Encyclicals/Encyclicals.html

These PDF files can be read, viewed, and printed with Adobe Acrobat Reader. You can download this program free off this page.

Church Documents in German
http://kirche.kath.de/sdbk/

How's your German? Sometimes when you read the same thing in two different languages, you can catch some nuances that can be found in one language but not in the other.

Catholic Official Documents by Subject

http://www.cs.cmu.edu/Web/People/spok/catholic/by-subject.html

Here is a partial listing.

Apologetics and Explanation

Here are some pointers to sites with sizable collections of apologetics (which argue the truth of various Catholic teachings) and explanations of these teachings.

Catholic Answers
http://www.catholic.com/

These are edited by Karl Keating. You will find more details about this one in the Top 20 in Chapter 5.

Catholic Apologetics on the Internet
http://www.cwo.com/~pentrack/catholic/apolo.html

This page discusses the basics of apologetics, the Bible, the Commandments, Protestants, cults, and Catholicism. There is tons of information here, listed with easy-to-understand titles or questions.

New Advent Catholic Supersite
http://www.csn.net/advent/

You can check this one out in my Top 20 picks found in Chapter 5.

Apologetics for Catholics and Christians
http://net2.netacc.net/~mafg/

This page really is something to see, with St. Michael the Archangel as the background! Interestingly, on this page you will find: "Click here to solve the problem of Christian Unity!" Can we solve it that easily? You will find more than apologetics here with links to other Catholic resources, addresses of Church officials, and Eucharistic adoration information.

Catholic Doctrinal Concordance
http://www.infpage.com/concorda.htm

This is a collection of basic Catholic doctrines and where to find the biblical support for them. There is also a nice icon of Our Lord on this page.

 # Bibles

http://www.cs.cmu.edu/Web/People/spok/catholic/online-bible.html

As of this writing, there was not a complete authorized Catholic English translation of the Bible online. The Douay-Rheims Bible was still being proofread online. Unfortunately, a Catholic Bible is supposed to include explanatory footnotes, which I didn't find with this online Bible. To learn more, check out this report for more information.

 ### The Bible Gateway
http://www.gospelcom.net/bible?version=RSV

This site has most of the current complete online Bibles, including the Revised Standard Version and Vulgate.

 ### The Vulgate Bible of St. Jerome
gopher://ftp.std.com/11/obi/book/Religion/Vulgate

This is the standard Latin Bible for the Church. It's based in part on the Greek Septuagint (Old Testament), used by the New Testament writers. Here's where you can find copies. Browse all the books from OBI Gopher or search the non-Deutero-canonical books at:

 ### ARTFL
http://humanities.uchicago.edu/forms_unrest/VULGATE.form.html

 ### The Douay-Rheims Bible
http://www.cybercomm.net/~dcon/

This is an English translation of the Vulgate made in the sixteenth and seventeenth century, then revised by Bishop Challoner (d. 1781) in the eighteenth century. It was the most commonly used Catholic English Bible through the mid-twentieth century. The online version of the Old Testament is still being worked on as of this writing.

*The King James Version
gopher://ccat.sas.upenn.edu:3333/11/Religious/Biblical/KJVBible

You will find the Deuterocanonical books under "Apocrypha." The Protestants do not consider these inspired by the Holy Spirit, but the Catholic Church does. It's the Protestants who call them "Apocrypha."

Readings

Readings for Upcoming Sundays and Holy Days
http://www.cs.cmu.edu/Web/People/spok/catholic/readings.html

The text for the readings is from the Revised Standard Version of the Bible, courtesy of Bible Gateway listed previously.

Today's Scripture Readings
http://www.avenue.com/cgi-bin/cgiwrap/avenue/netdaily

This page is a good example of why red is a poor choice for text color (you will see this on the opening page). But fortunately, when you follow the hyperlink for the readings, you'll find they didn't use red.

Reflections on Today's Readings
http://www.veritas.org.sg/

Besides the present-day reflection, you can look through past reflections in the archive or find out how to read the whole Bible in one year.

Writings by Subject

http://www.cs.cmu.edu/Web/People/spok/catholic/by-subject.html

This page is the start of an attempt to group various Church documents by their subject. There is something here of interest to everone.

When you go to this page, you can select Church documents by subject or just page down to see the list. When you click on one of the subjects listed at the top, it's just a shortcut to get to it on the list. Why not give it a try! The subjects are: Abortion and Human Life Issues, Africa, America, Asia, Bible and Scriptural Studies, Bishops, The Church, Communication, Eastern Churches, Education and Evangelization, Errors and Heresy, The Eucharist, Europe, Lay People, The Liturgy, Marriage and Family Issues, Mary, Moral Teachings, Other Religions and Traditions, Priests, Sexuality, Social Justice, Women, and Not Classified Yet.

 CATHOLIC CULTURE

http://www.cs.cmu.edu/Web/People/spok/catholic/culture.html

The Church embraces so many things, culture among them. One can even speak of a "Catholic Culture," which embraces what is good in all cultures. It also embraces all forms of human knowledge as gifts from God. Sometimes these gifts, such as art or music, are employed directly in the service of the Church. Artists have sculptured statues and designed churches. Musicians have written great pieces of music for use in the Mass and other liturgical services.

Catholic Writings

2,000 Years of Catholic and Catholic-Related Writings
http://www.cs.cmu.edu/Web/People/spok/catholic/writings.html

This chronological link on the culture page is coming up later in this section under "Writings" so hang on.

Historical Links

Early Church Writings
http://www.cs.cmu.edu/Web/People/spok/catholic/writings.html#earlychurch

Perhaps you'd like to start at the beginning! It's always good to go back to the roots. Still, the Church moves forward and continues to deepen her understanding and applying of the Sacred Deposit of Faith that has been entrusted to her by Our Lord Jesus Christ.

Ecole Initiative: Early Church History on the Web
http://www.evansville.edu/~ecoleweb/

There is tons of information, an alphabetical index, a glossary, and much more here. This is a cooperative effort on the part of scholars across the Internet to establish an encyclopedia of early Church history that goes all the way up to the Reformation.

Internet Medieval Sourcebook
http://www.fordham.edu/halsall/sbook.html

With around 150,000 visitors to this site, you might want to stop by yourself. There is much material here. You can look at selected sources (an index of selected and excerpted texts for teaching purposes), full text sources (full texts of medieval sources arranged according to type), and saints' biographies.

Jesuits and the Sciences, 1600–1800
http://www.luc.edu/libraries/science/jesuits/ind.html

This is an interesting page where you can click on the names of different Jesuits or periods of history to learn how they were connected to science. You will see a sketch of each, too.

*A Short Hypertext History of Catholicism in Great Britain
http://www.iris.brown.edu/iris/RIE/religions/Catholic.html

The history of Catholicism in Great Britain is a story of holy kings and queens, learned monks, pious nuns, and literary laypeople.

Places

*Tour New Norcia Monastic Settlement (in Australia)
http://stour.iinet.com.au/heritage/1_INTRO.html

Care to go "Down Under?"

Tour St. Luke's Church (in Stroudsburg, Pennsylvania)
http://www.microserve.net/~fabian/files/slvtour.html

The author of this page, Scott Fabian, claims this is "The World's First Parish Virtual Tour!" You will definitely know both the inside and outside of this church when you finish this pictorial tour.

Heart of Mary Priory (in Denmark)
http://inet.uni-c.dk/~grant/kloster1.htm

With almost 20,000 visitors, this page must have something very interesting on it. I like the two buttons at the bottom of the page that allow you to choose either "I love this site!" or "I really love this site!" They have some interesting links here, including one to the catacombs of Rome. This page is mainly about the Cistercians and includes a photo tour of this particular priory.

*The Road of Monasteries in France
http://www.imaginet.fr/apollonia/monasteries/mona00.html

Even though I don't speak French, I'd like to take a trip to this one.

Catholic Church in England and Wales
http://www.tasc.ac.uk/cc/

An inspiring visit because the Church in England and Wales is alive and dynamic.

Catholic Life in Flanders and Belgium
http://www.kuleuven.ac.be/kadoc/

Why stick to your own country when you can find out about the Catholics in other ones?

Catholic Life in the Netherlands
http://www.kdc.kun.nl/

You'll be surprised how many of the Dutch words you can make out. I guess that's because both Dutch and English are Germanic languages.

Jerusalem Mosaic
http://www1.huji.ac.il/jeru/jerusalem.html

This one is at the Hebrew University in Israel. It includes some material on Christianity.

Art

Illustrations from the Book of Kells (in Ireland)
http://www.tcd.ie/kells.html

Brother Craig saw this artistic masterpiece in Dublin during the year he spent studying at St. Kieran's Seminary in Kilkenny.

Shroud of Turin Page
http://www.cais.com/npacheco/shroud/turin.html

If it were up to me, I wouldn't place this one under art. If it is really the burial cloth of Jesus (and I believe it is), then it certainly has on it a miraculous image not made by human hands!

*The Virtual Museum of the Cross
http://www.dev-com.com/~infoquest/museum/

You will want to see this if you can get to it.

Music, Hymns, and Chant
http://www.cs.cmu.edu/Web/People/spok/catholic/worship.html#MUSIC

This will take you to Mr. Ockerbloom's linked list on these subjects.

Writings

This listing shows authors in roughly chronological order. It is truly amazing how much is on the Internet. I hope you have a big enough hard drive to handle all this stuff!

The Early Church (1–500)
Following is a list of indexes to this time period. This is followed by the chronological author list previously mentioned.

Writings of Church Fathers/Doctors/Saints
http://listserv.american.edu/catholic/church/fathers/fathers.html

Augustine of Hippo is all three: a Father of the Church, a Doctor of the Church, and a Saint!

Selected Writings of the Apostolic Fathers

gopher://ccat.sas.upenn.edu:3333/11/Religious/ChurchWriters/Apostolic
Fathers

Hey, if you don't want to read them all, let someone else select some for you.

Documents from Early Church History

ftp://iclnet93.iclnet.org/pub/resources/christian-history.html

These have brief descriptions.

Nicene Creed

gopher://gopher.ncsu.edu/11/ref_desk/sacred/creed

Includes various versions.

The Early Church Fathers

http://ccel.wheaton.edu/fathers/

Can you name any of the Fathers of the Church?

St. Pachomius Library

http://www.ocf.org/OrthodoxPage/reading/St.Pachomius/

This one is on the Orthodox Church's page.

Scripture (to c. 100)

http://www.cs.cmu.edu/Web/People/spok/catholic/scripture.html

In case you didn't know, the "c." stands for *circa,* which is Latin for "about," and the numbers following are the years.

The Dicache (1st or 2nd Century)

http://listserv.american.edu/catholic/church/fathers/others/didache.txt

Also, called the Teaching of the Twelve Apostles. This document wasn't discovered until the eleventh century.

By Clement: First Epistle to the Corinthians (c. 96)

http://listserv.american.edu/catholic/church/fathers/others/clem-ep1.txt

This is a great witness to the primacy of the Pope. Pope Clement of Rome (A.D. 92–101) was writing to the Church in Corinth concerning problems there with the priests. He would never have written such a letter to Corinth if it was outside his authority.

Second Epistle to the Corinthians

gopher://ccat.sas.upenn.edu:3333/00/Religious/ChurchWriters/Apostolic Fathers/1Clement

Also attributed to this Pope, it was found along with the first epistle in the Corinth archives.

St. Ignatius of Antioch (d.c. 107)

http://listserv.american.edu/catholic/church/fathers/ignatius/ignatius.html

Here you will find all seven letters written by this heroic martyr as he was traveling to Rome where he was to be executed, martyred for the Faith. Here you can learn about the importance of obeying the local bishop. Also, he alludes to the Eucharist when he says that he is God's wheat and that he is to be ground by the teeth of wild beasts so that he may become the pure bread of Christ.

*St. Barnabas: Epistle of Barnabas (Letter c. 130)

http://listserv.american.edu/1/catholic/church/fathers/others/barn.txt

This one is attributed to Barnabas, a friend of St. Paul who traveled with him on many of his missionary journeys. Too bad we do not have a letter we are sure was written by him.

St. Polycarp (c. 69–c. 155): Epistle of Polycarp (c. 130)

gopher://ccat.sas.upenn.edu:3333/00/Religious/ChurchWriters/Apostolic Fathers/Polycarp

About Polycarp: The Martyrdom of Polycarp (Second Century)

gopher://ccat.sas.upenn.edu:3333/00/Religious/ChurchWriters/Apostolic Fathers/Martyrdom_Polycarp

This is the earliest detailed and authentic account of a martyrdom. St. Polycarp, according to tradition, was a disciple of St. John the Apostle and Evangelist.

Hermas (Second Century) The Shepherd of Hermas
http://listserv.american.edu/catholic/church/fathers/others/hermas.txt

The author of this work, Hermas, was said to have been the brother of Pope St. Pius I (d.c. 154). In the work itself, it seems that Hermas was a slave and then freed. He owned a farm on the highway between Rome and Cumae, which he lost because of financial problems. During a Christian persecution, Hermas' own children apostatized and betrayed him.

St. Perpetua (d. 203) The Passion of Saints Perpetua and Felicity
http://www.fordham.edu/halsall/source/perpetua.html

The story of these great early women martyrs can be found here.

Tertullian (c. 155–c. 220) Biographical Page and Writings
http://listserv.american.edu/catholic/church/fathers/tertullian/tertullian.html

More Tertullian Writings
http://ccel.wheaton.edu/fathers/ANF-03/

He wrote a lot but has never been recognized as a saint by the Church.

St. Cyprian (c. 200–258)
http://listserv.american.edu/catholic/church/fathers/cyprian/cyprian.html

St. Cyprian is one of the saints mentioned in the First Eucharistic prayer. He was the first African Bishop to die a martyr's death.

St. Athanasius (c. 295–373) On the Incarnation (c. 318)
http://ccel.wheaton.edu/athanasius/incarnation/0content.html

This saint was very heroic throughout much persecution from the Arian heretics who denied that the Son was consubstantial with the Father.

St. Cyril of Jerusalem (c. 315–c. 386) The Procatechesis or Prologue to the Catechetical Lectures
http://www.ocf.org/OrthodoxPage/reading/St.Pachomius/Greek/Catech/lexr0.html

 First Catechetical Lecture
http://www.ocf.org/OrthodoxPage/reading/St.Pachomius/Greek/Catech/lexr1.html

 Second Catechetical Lecture
http://www.ocf.org/OrthodoxPage/reading/St.Pachomius/Greek/Catech/lexr2.html

St. Cyril was made a Doctor of the Church in 1883. You will want to read these early catechisms of the Church in Jerusalem.

 St. Gregory of Nyssa (c. 335–c. 394)
http://www.ucc.uconn.edu/~das93006/nyssa.html

This saint was the younger brother of St. Basil the Great (d. 379). Their sister was St. Marcrina (d.c. 303).

 St. John Chrysostom (c. 346–407) Homilies on the Gospel of St. Matthew
http://ccel.wheaton.edu/fathers/NPNF1-10/

 Homilies on Acts and Romans
http://ccel.wheaton.edu/fathers/NPNF1-11/

 Homilies on Galatians, Ephesians, Philippians, Colessians, Thessalonians, Timothy, Titus, and Philemon
http://ccel.wheaton.edu/fathers/NPNF1-13/

Homilies on the Gospel of St. John and Hebrews
http://ccel.wheaton.edu/fathers/NPNF1-14/

St. John Chrysostom was a Doctor of the Church and the Archbishop of Constantinople. As you can see, we have many of his homilies on the New Testament.

St. Jerome (c. 347–420) Vulgate Bible
gopher://ftp.std.com/11/obi/book/Religion/Vulgate

Letters and Selected Works
http://ccel.wheaton.edu/fathers/NPNF2-06/

This great translator of the Bible lived in a cave right near the cave of Our Lord's Nativity in Bethlehem.

*St. Augustine of Hippo (354–430) Against the Epistle of Manichaeus Called Fundamental
http://ccel.wheaton.edu/fathers/NPNF1-4/augustine/bk_fundamental/bk_fundamental.html

*Answer to the Letters of Petilian, the Donatist
http://ccel.wheaton.edu/fathers/NPNF1-4/augustine/bk_petilian/bk_petilian.html

*Concerning the Nature of Good, Against the Manichaean
http://ccel.wheaton.edu/fathers/NPNF1-4/augustine/bk_good/bk_good.html

Confessions
http://ccel.wheaton.edu/augustine/confessions/confessions.html

De Dialectica (HTML)
http://ccat.sas.upenn.edu/jod/texts/dialecticatrans.html

Enchiridion (Handbook on Faith, Hope, and Love)
http:// ccel.wheaton.edu/augustine/enchiridion/enchiridion.html

*Letters (HTML)
http://ccel.wheaton.edu/fathers/NPNF1-1/

*On Baptism, Against the Donatists
http://ccel.wheaton.edu/fathers/NPNF1-4/augustine/bk_baptism/bk_baptism.html

On Christian Doctrine
http://ccel.wheaton.edu/augustine/doctrine/doctrine.html

*Of the Morals of the Catholic Church
http://ccel.wheaton.edu/fathers/NPNF1-4/augustine/bk_mmc/bk_mmc.html

*On The Morals of the Manichaeans
http://ccel.wheaton.edu/fathers/NPNF1-4/augustine/bk_mm/bk_mm.html

*Reply to Faustus the Manichaean
http://ccel.wheaton.edu/fathers/NPNF1-4/augustine/bk_faustus/bk_faustus. html

*A Treatise Concerning the Correction of the Donatists
http://ccel.wheaton.edu/fathers/NPNF1-4/augustine/bk_correction/
correction.html

*Two Souls, Against the Manichaeans
http://ccel.wheaton.edu/fathers/NPNF14/augustine/bk_2souls/bk_2souls
1.html

Some consider St. Augustine to be the greatest Father of the Church.

St. Patrick (c. 389–461): Confession of St. Patrick
http://ccel.wheaton.edu/patrick/confession/confession.html

Not many people realized that we have writings of St. Patrick. Not many people also realized that St. Patrick wasn't Irish but was, it seems, a Roman Britain. He went to Ireland to evangelize the then pagan Irish.

Later Writings

Although these are called later writings, they seem pretty early to me. Many of these writings are from the following site:

Christian Classics Ethereal Library
http://ccel.wheaton.edu/

St. Benedict (480–547): Rule of St. Benedict
http://www.osb.org/osb/rb/text/toc.html

He is called the Father of Western Monasticism.

Cassiodorus (c. 490–c. 585): Excerpts from Institutes
http://www.fordham.edu/halsall/source/cassio1.html

Early monastic writings exploring the idea of Christian scriptural study.

St. Bernard of Clairvaux (1090–1153): On Loving God (HTML)
http://ccel.wheaton.edu/bernard/loving_God/loving_God.html

This Cistercian monk and Doctor of the Church is called the "Honey Sweet Doctor" for the tenderness of his writings about Jesus and Mary.

St. Thomas Aquinas (c. 1225–1274) Summa Theologica (HTML)
http://www.knight.org/advent/summa/summa.htm

St. Thomas' great genius was his ability to arrange and order the different truths of theology and put them into his brilliant *Summa*.

Pope Boniface VIII (c. 1235–1303)
http://listserv.american.edu/catholic/church/papal/boniface/boniface.viii.html

Did you know that Boniface meant "good face"?

*Julian of Norwich (1343–1443) Revelations of Divine Love
http://ccel.wheaton.edu/catherine/revelations/

This is a favorite book of Brother Craig. Julian, also called Dame Julian and Mother Julian, was an English anchoress and mystic who was granted several visions and wrote about them. Though Julian was a Roman Catholic, the Anglicans or Episcopalians are devoted to her and even have a religious order that follows her spirituality.

St. Catherine of Siena (1347–1380): The Dialogue of the Seraphic Virgin (HTML)
http://ccel.wheaton.edu/catherine/dialog/dialog.html

This Italian Dominican saint and mystic is one of the two women saints who is a Doctor of the Church, along with the Spanish Carmelite mystic St. Teresa of Avila.

Thomas à Kempis (c. 1380–1471): The Imitation of Christ
http://ccel.wheaton.edu/kempis/imitation/imitation.html

Originally written in Latin.

Pope Paul III (1468–1549)
http://listserv.american.edu/catholic/church/papal/boniface/paul.iii.html

Here you can learn more about this Pope and what he wrote on slavery.

St. Ignatius of Loyola (1491–1556) Spiritual Exercises (HTML)
http://ccel.wheaton.edu/ignatius/exercises/exercises.html

A classic read by many. You can use it for a personal retreat.

St. Teresa of Avila (1515–1582) by St. Teresa: The Interior Castle (HTML)
http://ccel.wheaton.edu/teresa/castle/castle.html

The Life of St. Teresa of Jesus (HTML)
http://ccel.wheaton.edu/teresa/life/main.html

The Way of Perfection (HTML)
http://ccel.wheaton.edu/teresa/way/way.html

About St. Teresa: Lectio Divinia and the Practice of Teresian Prayer
http://www.ocd.or.at/ics/others/more.html

This great writer of spirituality is the Church's Doctor of Prayer. She was also a warm and loving person who had a great sense of humor.

St. John of the Cross (1542–1591) Ascent of Mount Carmel (HTML)
http://ccel.wheaton.edu/john_of_the_cross/ascent/ascent.html

Dark Night of the Soul, Translated by E. Allison Peers (HTML)
http://ccel.wheaton.edu/john_of_the_cross/dark_night/dark_night.html

Translated by Kieran Kavanaugh, OCD, and Otilio Rodriguez, OCD (HTML)
http://www.ocd.or.at/ics/john/dn.html

The Living Flame of Love (HTML)
http://www.ocd.or.at/ics/john/fl.html

 Sayings of Light and Love (HTML)
http://www.ocd.or.at/ics/john/dichos.htm

 A Spiritual Canticle of the Soul and the Bridegroom Christ (HTML)
http://ccel.wheaton.edu/john_of_the_cross/canticle/canticle.html

This saint was truly my inspiration to prayer and the contemplative life.

 *St. Robert Bellarmine (1542–1621) De Laicis (The Treatise on Civil Government) (HTML)
http://158.36.89.11/op/doctors/delaicis.htm

 The Temporal Power of the Pontiff (HTML)
http://158.36.89.11/op/doctors/papal.htm

Interesting historical documents written by this Jesuit cardinal.

 Brother Lawrence of the Resurrection (1661–1691) The Practice of the Presence of God
http://ccel.wheaton.edu/bro_lawrence/practice/practice.html

The thoughts on prayer of a Carmelite brother who worked in his friary's kitchen.

 Pope Benedict XIV (1675–1758
http://listserv.american.edu/catholic/church/papal/benedict.xiv/benedict.xiv.html

You can find out about this Pope, along with reading three of the documents he issued.

 St. Alphonsus de Liguori (1696–1787) Uniformity with God's Will (HTML)
http://ccel.wheaton.edu/alphonsus/uniformity/uniformity.html

We all should want to do God's Holy Will. Certainly studying this work will be a great help.

Pope Gregory XVI (1765–1846)
http://listserv.american.edu/catholic/church/papal/gregory.xvi/gregory.xvi.html

You can find out about this Pope here, along with his writing condemning the slave trade.

Pope Pius IX (1792–1878)
http://listserv.american.edu/catholic/church/papal/pius.ix/pius.ix.html

A short biography can be found here, along with three of his works—including the one on the Immaculate Conception.

John Henry Cardinal Newman (1801–1890)
http://dolphin.upenn.edu/~newman/newman_writings.html

Cardinal Newman was a well-known convert who led others into the Church. He is also considered one of England's greatest prose writers.

Pope Leo XIII (1810–1903)
http://listserv.american.edu/catholic/church/papal/leo.xiii/leo.xiii.html

There are extensive writings of this Pope to look through. He is sometimes called the Rosary Pope because he wrote a considerable amount on it. You can find some biographical information about him on this page too.

St. Pius X (1835–1914)
http://listserv.american.edu/catholic/church/papal/pius.x/pius.x.html

This Pope initiated a codification of canon law, completed in 1917, and encouraged frequent reception of Holy Communion. Many of his writings and more information about him can be found here.

Pope Benedict XV (1854–1922)
http://listserv.american.edu/catholic/church/papal/benedict.xv/benedict.xv.html

A great man of peace. He suffered much over the evils of World War I. Read a little about him and two of the works he wrote.

Pope Pius XI (1857–1939)
http://listserv.american.edu/catholic/church/papal/pius.xi/pius.xi.html

This heroic Pope condemned the Third Reich's "aggressive neopaganism" in the encyclical *Mit Brennender Sorge.* The encyclical *Divini Redemptoris* condemned Communism. Read more about him as well as his many works.

G. K. Chesterton (1874–1936) Heretics
ftp://uiarchive.cso.uiuc.edu/pub/etext/gutenberg/etext96/heret10.txt

Orthodoxy
http://ccel.wheaton.edu/chesterton/orthodoxy/orthodoxy.html

Additional writings
http://www-cgi.cs.cmu.edu/cgi-bin/book/authorsearch?chesterton

Additional writings on various topics by this famous English convert, who was a philosopher, essayist, poet, mystery writer, humorist, political analyst, and artist. Chesterton was much loved by all the children who knew him. He had an enormous sense of humor. A delightful Englishman and a perfect gentleman, his friends attest that he was always cheerful.

Pope Pius XII (1876–1958)
http://listserv.american.edu/catholic/church/papal/pius.xii/pius.xii.html

A pope who was so loved that people around the world knew the name of his pet birds. In 1950 this Pope proclaimed the dogma of the Assumption of Mary. Find out more about him and read his many writings.

*Blessed Titus Brandsma (1881–1942)
http://www.azstarnet.com/~chas/titus1.html

He was a Carmelite priest killed by the Nazis.

Pope John XXIII (1881–1963)
http://listserv.american.edu/catholic/church/papal/john.xxiii/john.xxiii.html

Beloved "Good Pope John," as he was called. Read about this Pope who began the Second Vatican Council. You can read nine of his works, too.

Edith Stein (Blessed Teresa Benedicta, OCD, 1891–1942) The Hidden Life: Hagiographic Essays, Meditations, Spiritual Texts
http://www.ocd.or.at/ics/edith/stein.html

Edith Stein was an amazing woman who was born in 1891. She was raised in a German Jewish family, but as a young teenager became an atheist, totally interested in philosophy. She was a brilliant philosophy student, the assistant to the phenomenologist Edmund Husserl. Reading the autobiography of St. Teresa of Avila converted Edith to the Catholic Faith. After some years of teaching and lecturing, especially on the vocation of women, she became a Carmelite nun in Cologne. She had to escape to Holland because of Nazi persecution. In time she was arrested and executed at Auschwitz.

Pope Paul VI (1897–1978)
http://listserv.american.edu/catholic/church/papal/paul.vi/paul.vi.html

A great pope who suffered much and bravely. He continued the Second Vatican Council begun by his predecessor, Pope John XXIII, to completion. As the first "Pilgrim Pope," he visited 16 countries on six continents, urging peace, justice, ecumenism, and brotherhood. His trip to the Holy Land was especially historic. Read about him and his many writings.

The Catholic Encyclopedia (1913)
http://www.knight.org/advent/cathen/cathen.htm

The Catholic Encyclopedia Project is working on putting the entire 1913 edition online. There's much to read here!

Pope John Paul II (1920–Present)
http://listserv.american.edu/catholic/church/papal/jp.ii/jp.ii.html

Be sure to read this one. He has written a lot, some of which can be found here.

Augustine Ichiro Okumura, OCD (1923–Present) Awakening to Prayer
http://www.ocd.or.at/ics/others/j.html

The original of this work was published in Japanese. You can find the translation here.

Terrye Newkirk (1946–Present) The Mantle of Elijah: The Martyrs of Compiègne as Prophets of the Modern Age
http://www.ocd.or.at/ics/others/newkir.htm

Accounts of the martyrs can be very interesting and edifying reading.

CATHOLIC PEOPLE

http://www.cs.cmu.edu/Web/People/spok/catholic/people.html

This page has resources about particular Catholic people and some of the vocations available to Catholics. You might want to contribute your homepage to this section. Go to "Catholics on the Net" further down in this section to see examples of what others have done.

Saints

Catholic Writings
http://www.cs.cmu.edu/Web/People/spok/catholic/writings.html

Writings of saints can be found here.

Catholic Encyclopedia
http://www.knight.org/advent/cathen/cathen.htm

A number of saints biographies can be found in these encyclopedias. Good thing you don't have to put these on your bookshelves. You would have to dedicate a whole shelf to them!

Index of Saints Biographies
http://www.pitt.edu/~eflst4/saint_bios.html

You will find this one listed in the Top 20 in Chapter 5.

List of Patron Saints
http://listserv.american.edu/catholic/other/patron.saints

Can you find yours? I found mine for this book. St. Francis de Sales is the patron of writers.

Franciscan Calendar of Saint
http://listserv.american.edu/catholic/franciscan/francisc.calendar.html

You won't find any biographical material here, just when their feasts are celebrated.

Irish Calendar of Saint

http://listserv.american.edu/catholic/other/irish.calendar

Saints be praised! Here is a list of the holy men and women of the land of saints and scholars. No biographies are given.

Vocations

Here are some of the vocations in the Church and pointers to some resources concerning them. (They are not all mutually exclusive.) Now don't get into your mind that your vocation is to be a pope!

Clergy

http://www.cs.cmu.edu/Web/People/spok/catholic/religious.html

See special resources for clergy and religious. This one is put together by the Webmaster of this directory.

The Pope—List of Popes Through History

http://www.knight.org/advent/Popes/ppindx.htm

The odds of this becoming your vocation are not high. As a matter of fact, you are more likely to win the lottery!

Bishops—Dioceses and Archdioceses

http://www.cs.cmu.edu/Web/People/spok/catholic/organizations.html#dioceses

This is the Webmaster of this directory's page on dioceses.

Marriage—Worldwide Marriage Encounter

http://www.scri.fsu.edu/~sollohub/wwme/wwme.html

Answers to Questions About Divorce and Annulment

http://www.rc.net/lansing/st_fran/questions.html

Married couples will want to see these two homepages. I'm hoping not many will need to look at the latter!

Religious Life—Catholic Vocations Page
http://www.weblifepro.com/vocations/

Web Pages for Religious Orders
http://www.cs.cmu.edu/Web/People/spok/catholic/organizations.html#orders

I want you to read the former page here. So many times I have encountered people who do not understand the distinction between religious priests and brothers. You can find out about the sisters, too.

Secular Institutes
http://www.cs.cmu.edu/Web/People/spok/catholic/organizations.html#secular

Many people do not know about these. These are communities of consecrated life whose members live in the midst of the world. You will find a couple listed here.

Catholics on the Net

Hey, John Ockerbloom almost stole the title of my book here! Catholics can write to spok+catholic@cs.cmu.edu to list their Web pages here. I encourage you to do this. Of course, I think you will have to offer something of interest to Catholics besides a picture of your dog, as cute as he or she may be. I found these pages impressive. It shows you what you can do with a little spare time. Why not give a homepage a try?

Homepages of Individual Jesuits
http://maple.lemoyne.edu/~bucko/sj_pers.html

Besides these individual homepages, you will find a table of contents at the bottom with some important links.

*Jonathan Day
http://www.ionet.net/~dday/jonpage.html

Here is a homepage by a Catholic teen—so says the Webmaster of this directory.

Francis C. C. F. Kelly
http://www.igs.net/~fccfkelly/

This page features help for those doing research in philosophy, theology, and history. They will help you locate or translate Latin documents along with documents in many other languages. You may want to check out the "Sacred Images" link here also.

Philip Kingry
http://www.netdepot.com/~phil/

Author of the Monk's Cell. I haven't the slightest idea what the "Monk's Cell" is about because this homepage was still under construction when I visited it. Of course, I do know what it is like to live in a monk's cell!

Yuri Koszarycz
http://honey.acu.edu.au/~yuri/

This is a neat page. He includes a Church history and ecclesiology page. But I am especially interested in his "Laughter and Religion" link. Yuri looks like a fun guy, as his picture attests. Why not find out about his family and friends while you're here?

*Timothy Kuczinski
http://tjk127.rh.psu.edu/

Ice Man's Catholic Page. The "Ice Man" has grown cold, perhaps because of a deep freeze last Winter. Good luck finding him.

Will Potter
http://www.ghawk.com/~wspotter/

Here you can check out the beautiful religious screen savers. If you really like one, you can order it from him. You are going to want to click on the "Mother of All Screen Saver," then on the "Image Collection," and finally on "Images of the Blessed Mother" to see these wonderful images. You will find links to other religious art collections. You will also want to click on the "National Shrine Grotto of Lourdes," too. I visited this grotto located in Emmitsburg, Maryland.

Diana Seago, OSB
http://www.benedictine.edu/diana.html

She is a Benedictine from Mount St. Scholastica in Atchison, Kansas. Learn about this nun who, besides fishing for souls, managed to catch a 32-pound rainbow trout. There are a good number of links here, some of interest for women.

Fr. Michael Walsh
http://www.geocities.com/MotorCity/1197/index.html

You can learn about the Irish Augustinians in Rome, where Father was for many years. Father is now located in Nigeria and has some photos from there.

Mary Weaver
http://www.geocities.com/Athens/1104/

She is a Catholic freelance writer. You can read about her, along with sampling some of her writing. I sure wish Mary could have helped me with this book! Anyway, if you are looking for a writer for your Catholic newspaper or magazine, check this homepage.

Kurt Welton
http://www.terracom.net/~psalm40/

You can click on Kurt's license plate for Psalm 40. He calls this his "Fun Page" and indeed has tried to make it interesting. You might want to check out "Attitude Is Everything!" You will want to see how he copes in an insane world. Did you know that Kurt has designed some local parish homepages? Probably not. He's willing to do more for free if your parish is in the area. Look Kurt, with the Internet you could design one for a parish in the North Pole!

CATHOLIC ORGANIZATIONS

http://www.cs.cmu.edu/Web/People/spok/catholic/organizations.html

This page lists official Catholic organizations and independent noncommercial organizations related to Catholicism. If your organization fits into either of these categories, you will want to submit your homepage here.

If your parish, school, or other Catholic organization needs a Web page, see the following:

RCNet
http://www.rc.net/

This site offers free Web space to qualifying organizations. See also:

PJ Kenedy Official Catholic Directory
http://www.nd.edu/~theo/RCD/Directory5.html

The Vatican

Official Vatican Web Site
http://www.vatican.va/

Obviously, you will want to look at this one. You can find out more about it by looking at the Top 20 in Chapter 5. If you want to bypass the frames or go straight to the pages that interest you, see "The Vatican (non-frames, unofficial)" later in this chapter.

Tour the Vatican
http://www.christusrex.org/

Imagine that you can take a tour of the Vatican from the comfort of your home.

Vatican Library Exhibit
http://sunsite.unc.edu/expo/vatican.exhibit/Vatican.exhibit.html

You begin here by learning about the city itself. At the bottom, be sure to click on the "Main Hall" to enter the exhibit. This exhibit at the Library of Congress in Washington D.C. presents some 200 of the Vatican Library's most precious manuscripts, books, and maps. Many of these played a key role in the humanist rediscovery of the classical heritage of Greece and Rome.

List of Popes Through History
http://www.knight.org/advent/Popes/ppindx.htm

Some popes were saints; others seemed far from it. Still the Church continued on.

List of Cardinals
http://www.avenue.com/v/rccardn.html

Here you can find them listed by name, nationality, age, date of birth, the year they became cardinal, and their current and past ecclesiastical positions. This is really good material for a Catholic trivia game!

Radio Vaticana News
http://www.uni-passau.de/ktf/vatican.html

This one is in German. This is probably easier to do with a short-wave radio.

Catholic Dioceses and Archdioceses
http://www.cs.cmu.edu/Web/People/spok/catholic/dioceses.html

Is yours listed? You will find this listing of the Webmaster of this directory later in this chapter.

Catholic Parishes and Local Churches
http://www.wsnet.com/~alapadre/churches.html

Is yours listed here? Ditto on the above.

Religious Orders and Prelatures

Now it is understandable that homepages by religious orders are going to tell you about their order. They will give you links to their various houses around the world and sometimes an individual member's homepage. Many times you will find a lot more than this. I will introduce you to what the order is. If you want to know more, you will have to visit their pages!

Secular Institutes
http://www.cs.cmu.edu/Web/People/spok/catholic/organizations.html#SECULAR

See this page on secular institutes. They need to be better known.

Assumptionists
http://www.assumption.edu/HTML/Assumptionists/AssumptionNet.html

They follow the Rule of Saint Augustine. Their apostolates are: teaching, preaching, and counseling in universities, high schools, parishes, publishing houses, hospitals, or on the street. You can find everything you ever wanted to know about the order here, along with foundational documents and texts on Assumptionist education.

*Order of St. Augustine
http://www.geopages.com/Athens/1534/osa.html

Our community follows the Rule of St. Augustine, as do many others. St. Augustine gives some basic guidelines for communal living. Some families might benefit from his Rule also. Look it up on the Internet!

Irish Augustinians in Rome
http://www.geocities.com/MotorCity/1197/irishosa.html

Irishmen in Rome! I would sure like to hear Italian with an Irish brogue.

Order of St. Benedict
http://www.osb.org/osb/

Followers of what Rule do you think? That's right, St. Benedict's. Read the Rule in English, Latin, Hungarian, or Spanish. There is a lot of monastic information here. You can also find out about Benedictine Oblates, men and women living in the world according to the spirit of Saint Benedict. Use their geographical index to find a monastery nearest you.

Capuchin Friars (in Italy)
http://www.wnt.it/religione/frati.cappuccini/i_home.html

This one is mostly in English. They follow the Rule of—this one's a little harder to figure out—St. Francis. Find out their history, see their constitutions, read the "Saint Francis Testament," enter their poetry contest (if you can write in Italian), and find out about their missionary activity in the world.

Carmelite Order
http://middletown.ny.frontiercomm.net/~ocarmvoc/carmelites.html

Homepage of North American Province of St. Elias. Their primary mission is to follow Jesus Christ through prayer, fraternity, and prophetic service and presence in the spirit of Mary and Elijah. Find out about Carmelite history and spirituality, get a free Brown Scapular, go to other Carmelite links, and look into the Third Order (lay Carmelites).

Carmelite Friars in the UK
http://www.york.ac.uk/~intm72/carm/info.htm

Province of the Assumption in England, Scotland, and Wales (not whales!)

Order of Discalced Carmelites (in Austria)
http://www.ocd.or.at/

Practice your language ability by reading about them in English, Spanish, Italian, French, and Dutch. This is the reform order started by St. John of the Cross and St. Teresa of Avila. Their mission is to live the contemplative life in the Catholic Church and to show people the way of friendship with God. Here you can find out about the Mount Carmel restoration project, their history and spirituality including the Rule, some links concerning St. Thérèse of Lisieux, Carmelites around the world including Secular Carmelites, joining their mailing list, and Carmelite literature.

Claretian Missionaries (official)
http://www.claret.org/

The Eastern Province in the United States maintains this page. They seek to share the Good News throughout the world like their founder, St. Anthony Mary Claret. They aim to be present especially to the poor, to youth and families, and to the unchurched. Here you can see their "News Center," find other homepages of the order, learn about their volunteers and lay members, see photos of individual Claretians, and learn about their founder.

Claretian Missionaries (in the UK)
http://http1.brunel.ac.uk:8080/depts/chaplncy/cmfs.htm

Subscribe to the order's mailing list here.

Congregation of Holy Cross
http://www.nd.edu/~vocation/

Its roots go back to the early nineteenth century in France. Father Basil Anthony Moreau gathered a community of priests and brothers to assist the Church's ministries wherever needed—as educators, foreign missionaries, and in a variety of auxiliary services. He also established the Holy Cross Sisters, who today continue to minister in the spirit of their founder. Find out about their history and constitutions as well as their universities and high schools.

Congregation of Holy Cross
http://server.cs.stedwards.edu/holycross/home.htm

This one is maintained by the Southwest Province.

Congregation of the Marians of the Immaculate Conception
http://marian.org/

The Congregation has these three basic ends in view: to promote devotion to Mary, to bring relief to the suffering souls in Purgatory, and to conduct apostolic work through assistance to pastors, especially in educating and ministering to those most in need of mercy. They are the great promoters of the Divine Mercy Devotion, as revealed to Blessed Faustina. You can learn a lot about this devotion here. They also have a prayer line where you can give them prayer requests, and much more.

De La Salle Christian Brothers
http://www.catholic.org/delasalle/

Dedicated to the education of youth, especially those normally excluded from education. Learn about their founder St. John Baptist de la Salle, the Rule, educational institutions, and the community worldwide.

(U.S.) Dominican Central
http://www.op.org/DomCentral/

Maintained by the American Central Province. The Dominicans follow the Rule of St. Augustine and were founded by St. Dominic. Their mission involves preaching, theological education, and the promotion of peace and justice. Listen to "A Gospel Line," a new musical play along with the other sounds associated with their pages. There is plenty here so I suggest you give them a visit.

(European) Dominican Web
http://www.op.org/op/

Find out what's happening with this community in Europe.

Franciscan Web
http://listserv.american.edu/catholic/franciscan

The Franciscans were founded by Saint Francis of Assisi. The Franciscan Orders include the Friars Minor (Order of Friar Minor, OFM), Order of Friars Minor Capuchin (OFM Cap), and Order of Friars Minor Conventual (OFM Conv), the Poor Clares, and the Secular Franciscans. Go Franciscan crazy here with everything you want to know about them, including their mailing lists, publications, calendar of events, news, colleges, universities, and more. You can also take a tour of Assisi, see their clip art, find out about St. Anthony of Padua, and check out their calendar of saints.

Franciscan Missionaries of the Eternal Word
http://www.ewtn.com/motew.htm

This is a new group for men founded by Mother Angelica—you know, the Poor Clare Nun who started the Eternal Word Television Network.

Franciscan Cyberspot
http://www.serve.com/melita

This is a joint project by the Franciscans in Malta and in the Holy Land. There is a lot here to check out, including information about the Holy Land: sanctuaries, news, and documents; and links to Israel, Palestine, and Jordan. Make sure you don't miss the pictorial pilgrimage of the Way of the Cross accompanied by reflections. Music can be found here too. The Holy Land page information can be found in my Top 20 in Chapter 5.

Franciscan Friars of the Immaculate
http://www.connix.com/~ffi/

This community is very much motivated by the spirituality of St. Maximilian Mary Kolbe. You can find out more about him there. Also you will find documents about Mary, Franciscan saints, books on Catholic topics, the Franciscan Third Order, and a new organization for Marian apostles. Visit their download site to get music, computer wallpaper (background graphics for your computer screen), art, and much more. Give them your prayer requests and listen to the Vatican Radio.

Conventual Franciscan Friars
http://www.cris.com/~Mtstfran/msf.htm

These friars wear black habits and sometimes gray. Did I tell you that the habit I wear is gray? Anyway this page is about the friars in Southern Indiana. You can find links for more information about their multipurpose center called "Mount St. Francis."

Conventual Franciscan Homepage
http://www.franciscans.org/vocations/ofm_conv.html

Here is a little trivia. Why are they called Conventual Franciscans? I would give you the answer, but I'd rather you find it on their page. There is, of course, vocational information to be found there, too.

Jesuit Homepage
http://maple.lemoyne.edu/~bucko/jesuit.html

Begun by St. Ignatius of Loyola and his six companions, Jesuits are committed to any apostolic endeavor enjoined on them by the Pope. Here learn everything you wanted to know about the Jesuits. Learn about their founder and read his famous work, "The Spiritual Exercises." Also, you can find out about their retreat centers.

*Maryknoll Missioners
http://www.academic.marist.edu/maryknoll/

This United States–based Catholic mission movement includes three distinct organizations: The Maryknoll Society (priests and brothers), Maryknoll Congregation

(Sisters), and the Maryknoll Mission Association of the Faithful (laity, priests, and religious). Find out about each of these branches here.

Monks of Adoration
http://www.rc.net/org/monks/

Certainly the best homepage on the Internet with movies, graphics, theater sounds, 3-dimensional experiences . . . well, perhaps I've exaggerated a bit. Other than the chat area, you won't find anything fancy here. But you will find more than 150 articles on prayer, articles for children, our magazine, a monk speaker available, a prayer line, vocation page, gift shop, Eucharistic adoration information, and more.

Montfortian Religious
http://ourworld.compuserve.com/homepages/Montfort/

A group of three religious congregations that take their inspiration from St. Louis Marie Grignion de Montfort (d. 1716). Learn more about these branches, their founder and what he wrote.

Opus Dei (official)
http://www.opusdei.org/

Founded by Blessed Josemaria Escriva (d. 1975), their spirit follows his saying, "God is calling you to serve him in and from the ordinary, material and secular activities of human life." They are a personal prelature. Learn about the founder and their history. See their books and documents along with links to them around the world.

Opus Dei (in Spain)
http://web1.cti.unav.es/english/opus.dei/index.html

As expected, everything is in Spanish.

Passionist Homepage
http://www.pcn.net/passionisti/

(In English, Spanish, or Italian.) Following the example of their founder, St. Paul of the Cross (d. 1775), the Passionists make a special promise to promote the memory of the Passion of Jesus by word and deed. They do this especially in preaching and various ministries among the poor and the marginalised in whom they see the Crucified Jesus today. Learn about their founder and look at their links to other Passionist homepages, especially the retreat houses.

Piccola Opera Della Divina Providenza, di Don Orione
http://www.vol.it/donorione/

In Italian. I can't translate everything for you, but I can make out that this one is founded by Blessed Don Orione (d. 1940). Whatever their name is, they have Divine Providence in it—that's good enough for me!

*Poor Clares of Perpetual Adoration
http://www.ewtn.com/poorclar.htm

They have several houses of their community in Ohio. This is also the order to which Mother Angelica belongs.

Sisters of St. Joseph (U.S.)
http://www.nd.edu/~csjus/home.html

A voluntary union of all Sisters of Saint Joseph of the United States who claim a common origin in the foundation at LePuy, France.

Daughters of St. Paul (in Canada)
http://www.netrover.com/~pauline/

Visit the Pauline book and media centers all over the world. There is much more here, including information on their founders, history, lay associates, and children's electronic magazines.

Paulist Missionary Society
http://www.paulist.org/

They are priests who serve as missionaries in the United States and Canada. Their directory will take you to everything they are involved in. They have a photo gallery of their members.

Priestly Fraternity of St. Peter
http://www.ewtn.com/fssp/fsp_html.htm

A Society of Apostolic Life of Pontifical Right founded for the formation and sanctification of priests in the framework of the traditional Liturgy of the Roman Rite (Tridentine).

Redemptorists
http://www.redempt.org/

They were founded by St. Alphonsus Liguori to preach the Gospel of Christ to the poor. Here you will find their online publications and catalog along with information about the founder, their worldwide family, associates and lay missionaries, food for thought, and resources for prayer.

Salesians of Don Bosco
http://www.sdb.org/

(In English, Italian, or Spanish.) Learn about St. John Bosco and the spiritual family he founded to work with youth. You will find links to their homepages and documents. Learn about the Don Bosco volunteers. Find out about the saints, blessed and venerable members of the order.

Salesian Studies
http://www.allencol.edu/salesian/salesian.html

Maintained by the Oblates of St. Francis de Sales. Their mission is to spread the spirit and charism of their patron St. Francis de Sales on a global level.

Congregation of the Sisters, Servants of the Immaculate Heart of Mary
http://www.marywood.edu/www2/ihmpage/

A Belgian Redemptorist priest, Father Louis Florent Gillet, went to Michigan in the 1840s. There in 1845, with the cooperation of Mother Theresa Maxis Duchemin, he founded this congregation. Learn more about them and check out their "Resource Collection."

Order of Friar Servants of Mary (Servites)
http://www.weblifepro.com/vocations/osm_home.html

The charism of the Servants of Mary is lived through three elements: fraternity, Mary, and service, especially to the poor and the sick. Learn about the order: their mission, history, spirituality, charism, Marian character, vision, confraternity, and the Servite laity. Also, find information about the Servite Rosary, Saint Peregrine (the patron of cancer patients), their newsletter, and links to the vocation's homepage and events.

Society of the Sacred Heart
http://www.rscj.org/rscj/

Saint Madeleine Sophie Barat (d. 1865) founded the Society of the Sacred Heart in Paris in 1800. In 1818 Saint Philippine Duchesne (d. 1852) carried this vision across the ocean to America. They are involved in education apostolates. Learn more about them and what they do.

Salvatorians (Society of the Divine Savior)
http://www.sds.org/

(In English, German, Italian, and Portugese.) They were founded to proclaim to all people the salvation that has appeared in Jesus Christ, so that by the lives they live and in their apostolic activities, all may come to the only true God. Find out here about their history, location, other homepages, and apostolates.

Catholic Educational and Academic Organizations

Primary and Secondary Catholic Schools
http://www.microserve.net/~fabian/files/school.html

Looking for a Catholic school? You will want to see Scott Fabian's list in Chapter 11.

Universities and University-Level Departments
http://www.cs.cmu.edu/Web/People/spok/catholic/schools.html

The Webmaster of this directory has put together a page of links to Catholic schools, colleges, and academic departments.

Student Organizations and Ministries
http://www.cco.caltech.edu/~newman/OtherNC.html

You will want to see this extensive listing of Newman Centers found in Chapter 9. See also:

Catholic Education Page from Aquinas Software
http://www.avenue.com/v/cef/cef.html

Here you will find six discussion forums for teachers, parents, and students.

Publications, Radio, and TV

The Internet has really transformed our idea of media. It combines many mediums into one. You can read publications, listen to the radio, or watch a television program. But these do not have to be mutually exclusive. Now somebody can have a publication that you can read, hear, and watch! But don't get too excited yet—the Internet is still too slow with special effects. But, there are plans in the works to speed it up.

Catholic Commentary
http://www.top.net/cathcom/

Information (by MMR Publishing). The intent of Catholic Commentary (in electronic format here) is to provide reporting and commentary on events occurring within the Catholic Church and in the world, which impact in a most serious way on the faithful of the Church. MMR Publishing is a small, family apostolate dedicated to the publication and distribution of Catholic books, pamphlets, audiotapes and videos, and other religious articles.

Catholic Family Perspectives Weekly
http://www.vivanet.com/~jwagner/cfpw.htm

The editors, John F. Wagner, Jr., and Helen Ann Wagner, live in Rochester, New York. They are the parents of six children.

*The Catholic Post

http://www.itek.net/~diocese/post/

Peoria, Illinois, diocesan newspaper.

The Catholic Spirit

http://www.hgo.net/~spirit/

Wheeling-Charleston, West Virginia, diocesan newspaper. A colorful page that uses two frames. You can scroll through the articles that give you a little summary of what they are about. Some information here is not exclusively local.

Catholic Worker

http://www.cais.com/agf/cwindex.htm

This is an unofficial site. You can see a picture of Dorothy Day and learn about her. Further, you can find out about this movement and where their houses are located.

Catholic Worker Roundtable

http://catholicworker.org/roundtable/

The Catholic Worker is a great apostolate for helping the poor and promoting peace and justice. Here you can find out more about their mission, read their essays, search for their houses, and participate in their message board.

*Companions

http://www.gonzaga.edu/Companions/index.html

This is a Jesuit ministry magazine. Did you know that the Jesuits used to be called the Company or Companions of Jesus? Now they are called the Society of Jesus.

Company

http://www.luc.edu/or/sj/Company/index.html

This is an American Jesuit magazine. It offers news, features, books, and references from the Society of Jesus on its ministries, friends, history, and members.

Compass: A Jesuit Journal
http://www.io.org/~gvanv/compass/comphome.html

This one is from Canada. They claim that their journal is recognized as the best Catholic magazine in North America. Now that is quite a claim! Anyway, *Compass* is a forum for lively debate on contemporary, social, and religious questions. You can look over entire back issues and get excerpts from the current one.

*Information on In a Word
http://www.interpath.net/~mdoyle/wordhome.html

Kath Fernseharbeit beim ZDF
http://kirche.kath.de/kfa/

Perhaps you guessed—this one is all in German. They have a cute table of contents that will reside on the bottom of your screen. You can look at children and TV, spirituality, religion, and more that I can't translate for you. It might be fun to try to figure out some of these.

Little Storytellers of God
http://www.interaccess.com/users/lilstory/

There are children's religious stories! Don't think only children will enjoy these!

Living the Word
http://www.interpath.com/~toddwall/ltw/ltw.html

This is a weekly real audio radio program from the Raleigh diocese. You will want to tune in to this one!

Information on the Lumen Vitae Review
http://www.luc.edu/or/sj/lumen/index.html#lv

The *Review* contributes to theological and pastoral thinking on all important Christian issues. They have subscribers in nearly a hundred countries. It is also available in French and Spanish.

North Carolina Catholic Newspaper
http://www.interpath.com/~mdoyle/regnews/regnews.html

You will find this one under the "Southern Catholic Review." There is almost always information in Catholic newspapers of interest to everyone.

Patchquilt
http://www.interpath.com/~mdoyle/appalachia/ccahome.html

This is the newsletter for the Catholic Committee of Appalachia, an area in the United States known for economic hardship. This committee strives to keep its membership informed of issues relevant to their presence in the mountains.

Pax Christi
http://listserv.american.edu/catholic/other/paxchristi/paxchristi.html

This is an unofficial information site on this Catholic peace group. You can read about them and find out more about their spirituality of nonviolence and peacemaking.

Presentation Ministries
http://w3.one.net/~presmin/

Various publications associated with the Archdiocese of Cincinnati. This is a private lay association of small covenanted communities and of ministries of the Word of God. You will want to move around on their table of contents found at the bottom of their page.

Radio Vaticana Reports
http://www.uni-passau.de/ktf/vatican.archiv.html

You are just going to have to learn German. Listening to it is a great help.

Salt of the Earth
http://www.claret.org/~salt/

A Claretian social justice magazine. It is a bimonthly review of social justice issues and practical ways men and women across the United States are seeking social change.

Southern Catholic Review
http://www.interpath.com/~mdoyle/regnews/regnews.html

Stories from southern U.S. Catholic newspapers. This is a private project, not sponsored by any of the dioceses involved. You can connect to ten diocesan papers here.

The Wire
http://www.roehampton.ac.uk/link/wire/

Catholic communications quarterly in the United Kingdom. I couldn't quite fit their whole page on my screen. The screen resolution they recommend at the bottom is probably not the one I have! Isn't that the way it always is? Anyway, you can still read everything and move around with the table of contents located at the bottom of the page.

Other Organizations

Catholic Alumni Clubs International
http://www.clark.net/pub/cac/

Social organization for single Catholics. Most of the information pertains to the clubs, but they do have other Catholic links, too.

Catholic Biblical Association of America
http://www.cua.edu/www/org/cbib/

Their purpose is to promote, within a context of the Faith, scholarly study in Scripture and related fields.

Catholic Charismatic Center
http://www.garg.com/ccc/

Located in the diocese of San Jose. There is enough information and links here to keep you busy for awhile. You will want to check out "The Roman Catholic Web-Ring" located near the bottom of this page.

Courage
http://www.allencol.edu/pastoral/courage.html

Officially endorsed ministry for homosexual persons. Straightforward text on this page with a link to the Church's teaching on this issue.

Cursillo Movement
http://www.sound.net/~eering/

Short courses on Christian living. "De Colores!" is their favorite expression. Find out why! Find out everything about this life-transforming movement. Just select one of the pushbuttons they have provided on what you would like to know.

The FAITH Movement
http://www.compulink.co.uk/~faith/Welcome.html

In the United Kingdom. Their particular focus is the promotion of a new synthesis of Catholicism, a synthesis of science and religion that makes sense of the modern scientific world while remaining true to the Church's Magisterium.

Free the Fathers
http://www.voyageronline.net/~jdavies/index.htm

Helping priests imprisoned in China. They already have acquired freedom for several Catholic priests who were being held in captivity.

Friendship House
http://www.friendshiphouse.org/

Catholic interracial apostolate, affiliated with the Diocese of Chicago. Started by Catherine Doherty (d. 1985), who was also foundress of the Madonna House apostolate.

International Youth Network
http://www.dsdelft.nl/~mpr/

In the Netherlands. Discusses what World Youth Day is and the next one coming up.

Madonna House Lay Apostolate
http://www.geocities.com/Heartland/3905/

Dedicated to loving and serving Christ in each other and in all men and women. Not a bad idea for all of us!

North Dakota Catholic Conference
http://rrnet.com/~sedaqah/ndcc4.html

Represented here is the Diocese of Fargo and the Diocese of Bismarck in public policy matters. There are some good links here.

Saint Antoninus Institute for Catholic Education in Business
http://www.ewtn.com/antonin/ANTONIN.HTM

They are dedicated to saving souls in the workplace and marketplace through word, action, and prayer. This is a must-visit for those who want to learn more about the social teachings of the Church and how to implement them in their daily lives.

Schoenstatt Movement
http://www.schoenstatt.org/

(In English, German, or Spanish.) Characterized as a movement of comprehensive education in the Faith. They have many beautiful shrines to Our Lady, and you can find their addresses here plus links to their other Web sites.

Society of Our Lady of the Most Holy Trinity
http://www.solt.org/solt/solt.html

Their goal is that all people will experience the peace of living their lives in union with the Trinity through following Jesus and Mary. Consists of priests, religious brothers and sisters, deacons, and both married and single laypersons called apostles.

Sphaira
http://incolor.inetnebr.com/mdavis/

An ecumenical organization dedicated to the unification of all people into one Christian family by spreading Christ's message through rational discourse.

Spiritual Retreats in Assisi, Italy
http://linex.com/~assisi/

You are invited to join a spiritual retreat in Assisi, Italy, with committed people from the United States and several European countries. Learn more about it here.

Woodstock Theological Center
http://guweb.georgetown.edu/woodstock/

Run by the Jesuits, this center engages in theological and ethical reflection on many topics. There is a lot here.

Dioceses

This page lists Catholic dioceses, eparchies, and Bishop's organizations with Web pages. It is organized by country. All dioceses are Latin Rite unless otherwise noted. See also:

Tim DeRyan's Catholic Directory
http://www.catholic-church.org/cid/

What is a diocese? It is a territory under the jurisdiction of an ordinary (usually a Bishop) that has been canonically erected by the Holy See. It embraces all the parishes and people within its given area. An archdiocese is a large diocese run by an Archbishop. Finally, an eparchy is the name used for dioceses of the Eastern Catholic Church.

Given that the diocese embraces all the activities of Catholics under its area, you can expect a lot of information to be listed on a diocesan homepage. A typical page will tell you something about the ordinary in charge and perhaps have a message from him. The diocesan paper will normally be online. Also, there will be a ton of diocesan information concerning parishes, missions, parochial schools, colleges and universities, and other institutions (such as religious communities, hospitals, retreat centers, and lay associations). These may include links to homepages if they exist and possibly e-mail addresses for people involved in them.

Now I could have written an entire book just on what's available on diocesan pages. Instead I just try to point out those things that may make one diocesan page distinct from others. If you want to know about the Church anywhere in the world, you will want to start with the diocesan pages. As this present list has dioceses from all over the world, feel free to test your language ability!

Algeria:

Virtual Diocese of Partenia
http://www.partenia.org/

Written by the former bishop of Evreux. Has a version of the homepage in English. See a map of where the diocese is located. Unfortunately, the fancy stuff here wouldn't work so I was limited to a letter from the bishop and a list of Internet links.

Austria:

Diocese of Eisenstadt
http://www.kathpress.co.at/kathweb/pdat-at/pdi-ei.htm

All these are in German. (Good luck!) These Austrian pages are hosted by KathWeb. You can play around with the table of contents for fun to see where it will take you.

Diocese of Feldkirch
http://www.kathpress.co.at/kathweb/pdat-at/pdi-fk.htm

Did you know that most Austrians are Catholic? This page has little information on it.

Diocese of Graz-Seckau
http://www.kathpress.co.at/kathweb/pdat-at/pdi-gs.htm

The Alps have always been fascinating to me. On this page you will find another page with factual information.

Diocese of Gurk-Klagenfurt
http://www.kathpress.co.at/kathweb/pdat-at/pdi-gk.htm

Austria reminds me of "The Sound of Music." This page reminds me of bare bones information.

Diocese of Innsbruck
http://www.kathpress.co.at/kathweb/pdat-at/pdi-ib.htm

Brother Craig spent a day in Innsbruck once (he took a train from northern Italy). I remember this place because the Olympic Games were once held there.

Diocese of Linz
http://www.kathpress.co.at/kathweb/pdat-at/pdi-lz.htm

I just wish I knew Austria better so I'd know where some of these places are.

Diocese of St. Pölten
http://www.kathpress.co.at/kathweb/pdat-at/pdi-sp.htm

Archdiocese of Salzburg
http://www.kathpress.co.at/kathweb/pdat-at/pdi-sb.htm

This was the archdiocese of the von Trapp family singers.

Archdiocese of Vienna
http://www.kathpress.co.at/kathweb/pdat-at/pdi-wn.htm

Since there are so many coffee houses in Vienna, perhaps you should enjoy some coffee while looking at this homepage. Personally, I hate coffee!

Canada

Canadian Conference of Catholic Bishops (official, in English and French)
http://www.cam.org/~cccb/index.html

You will find an introduction to the conference, recent news, their public statements, press releases, publications, background information (some interesting links here), a map of Canada organized by zones (where you can get information on the Catholic Church by clicking on a zone), and more.

Archdiocese of Halifax, Nova Scotia
http://www3.ns.sympatico.ca/rc.halifax/mainpage.htm

What's on the Internet for Catholics?

This is their official homepage. You may want to look at their "RC Links." You can't get lost on this one, as the table of contents is right in the middle of the page.

Archdiocese of Ottawa, Ontario
http://www.igs.net/~cyberchurch/

Hear the Rector of the Basilica's audio clip and look at their multimedia archive with various Catholic documents such as papal encyclicals, information on Catholic religious rites, photographs, and sound clips.

Diocese of Sault Ste. Marie, Ontario (official, in English or French)
http://www.isys.ca/cathome.htm

You will know where they are located, as a colorful map jumps out at you on the opening page. (They really want you to know where they are!) The same map is on the "English" page.

Ukranian Catholic Archeparchy of Winnepeg, Manitoba (official)
http://www.freenet.mb.ca/iphome/u/ukrcath/index.html

Beautiful icon of Our Lady with her Son. Although still under construction, this page provides you with links to Ukrainian Catholic youth.

Croatia

Catholic Church in Croatia
http://www.hbk.hr/

I presume the language here is Croatian. An impressive picture of Our Risen Lord. There is some English. You will find links to the Church in Croatia, the Conference of Bishops, statistical data, news about Catholic churches damaged or destroyed in the latest war, and some Catholic links.

Germany

Information on German Dioceses
http://www.kirchen.de/_kat-inh.html

Although you might not understand the language, you can still look around for familiar sights as a tourist does! The background is an eye-opener. I learned a new word in

German here—"neu." Can you guess what that means? Anyway, all the following pages are in German.

Archdiocese of Berlin
http://www.kirchen.de/dioezesen/berlin/_berlin-inh.html

Here you will see "Kirche Online" in the background. Can you guess what that means?

Diocese of Eichstdtt
http://www.ku-eichstaett.de/BISTUM

Here you will find a line drawing of the cathedral. You may want to check out the forum there.

Diocese of Essen
http://www.kirchen.de/dioezesen/essen/_essen-inh.html

I do know a little German, such as "foto." You will want to select that here to see their group picture. I hope that's not the whole diocese!

*Diocese of Köln (Cologne)
http://www.kirchen.de/dioezesen/koeln/_koeln-inh.html

They tell me they moved here, but apparently they have not finished moving yet.

Diocese of Limburg
http://kirche.kath.de/bistum/limburg/

They do have some Catholic links here and use a little yellow to brighten up their page.

Diocese of Mainz
http://kirche.kath.de/bistum/mainz/

Hey, I am learning my German! I think I figured out what "Willkommen" means. This page has a purple background and a bunch of links.

*Diocese of Passau
http://www.vgp.de/red/iop/

This is a time when I really would appreciate a visit from Helga, our German hairdresser friend!

Diocese of Rottenburg-Stuttgart
http://www.kirchen.de/dioezesen/drs/_drs-inh.html

You can see pictures of a couple of churches here, as well as be awakened by the bright yellow background.

Diocese of Trier
http://www.dioezese-trier.de/

This page is a little easier to figure out because they have provided some graphical images. The diocesan newspaper articles reside in the middle of the page with other selections around the border. They have also provided a search engine to search their page.

Italy

*Diocese of Rome
http://www.glauco.it/Chiesa.Cattolica.it/Diocesi/Roma/

Although I couldn't quite locate this one on the Internet, I believe it is big enough to be an archdiocese—so how could I miss it?

Mexico

Archdiocese of Yucatan
http://www.yucatan.com.mx/especial/iglesia/iglesia.htm

(In Spanish.) Find out its history and most relevant activities. There are links to information about the Church through the centuries, when the Pope visited, his two messages, the cathedral, and its four centuries of history and the organization Catholic Action. Their link of Church documents include the 3rd Diocesan Synod, the Eucharistic Year, Sunday The Day of the Lord, and two pastoral letters from the archbishop. There are some Catholic links here, including devotions and traditions.

Diocese of Zacatecas
http://www.logicnet.com.mx/~eferriz/

(In Spanish.) Even if you don't speak the language, you can tour the virtual museum and look at the photos. These photos, along with the articles, express the Catholic culture here. Also, you will find a commentary on the Gospel for each Sunday, public documents of the Bishop, the diocesan newspaper, and an extensive history of the diocese from 1546 to the present.

Norway

Archdiocese of Oslo
http://www.katolsk.no/okb/

In Norwegian. The table of contents is across the top. The only word I understood was probably the one you will want to pick also, "Hjelp."

Diocese of Tromso
http://www.katolsk.no/nn/

In Norwegian. Apparently designed by the same person as the page above.

Diocese of Trondheim
http://www.katolsk.no/mn/

In Norwegian. On this one, you will want to click on the shield in the upper-left corner so you can see some pictures.

Singapore

Archdiocese of Singapore
http://www.veritas.org.sg/

Care to go to Singapore? This one has popped up before in this book. There are some useful things here. You will want to view their new "Web Links," their "Users Resource Page," and "What's Hot?" They even give you the local time so you can see how far ahead or behind you are.

United Kingdom

Catholic Church in England and Wales
http://www.tasc.ac.uk/cc/

See the latest Catholic news, link to the Bishops' Conference. Find educational resources, liturgical resources, the Catholic Church's social teaching, and Church information about these two countries.

Ukrainian Greek Catholic Church in Great Britain
http://christusrex.org/www1/CDHN/exarch.html

See their beautiful icon of Our Lady with Jesus. Make sure you follow the link to Peter Hrycak's homepage called "St. Michael the Archangel Ukrainian Catholic Church," where you can learn a lot about the Eastern Catholic Church.

Diocese of Dunkeld, Scotland
http://www.cali.co.uk/dunkeld/

Who knows? Perhaps you want to know the Mass times there. You can also find out about the Catholic Church in Scotland.

Diocese of East Anglia, England
http://ourworld.compuserve.com/homepages/doea/homepage.htm

Here you'll find official reports of the Bishops' Conference, an interesting link to the Church in Europe (put together by the Media Commission of the Council of European Bishops Conferences), and information about their priests helping in South America.

Archdiocese of Glasgow, Scotland
http://ourworld.compuserve.com/homepages/Glasgow_Archdiocese/

You can read Cardinal Winning's Pro-Life speech. Also there is a link to "Other Catholic Places on the Web" and "A Map of the Scottish Dioceses."

Diocese of Hexham and Newcastle (unofficial)
http://www.ugkc.lviv.ua/CDHN/index.html

Some interesting links here. You can explore Tynedale or the city of Newcastle and these homepages: Is There a Need for the New Catechism?, Our Lady's Page, A Catholic Prayer Book and Study Guide, Calligraphy in Our Diocese, Mental Prayer, Selected Papal Letters, A Meditation on Our Creator, Catholic Software Resources, and When Life Loses Value.

Diocese of Northampton, England
http://www.cableol.co.uk/diocese/

This one has very little information on it. Still, you can e-mail them.

Diocese of Portsmouth
http://www.portsmouth-dio.org.uk/index.html

Official homepage. This one is laid out in a straightforward way. They have a link to a "General Christian Resources" page.

Diocese of Westminster
http://www.rmplc.co.uk/eduweb/sites/wdes2/

(An education service.) Some useful links here, including an extensive list of Church documents listed in the RE and Catechesis Department page. Also a link to Church Net UK, a site where much information on all the Christian Churches in England and Wales, together with news on their educational and RE contributions, can be found.

United States

Diocese of Buffalo, New York (official)
http://www.buffalodiocese.org/

Check out the links to The 46th International Eucharistic Congress in the Archdiocese of Wroclaw Poland; "The Father Justin Rosary Hour" (predominantly in Polish); Holy Infant Jesus Shrine in North Tonawanda; the St. Columban retreat center in Derby, New York; and the youth and young adult pages.

Diocese of Charleston, South Carolina (official)
http://www.awod.com/gallery/probono/catholic/

The diocese currently operates three separate computer networks. They have useful information under "Technology" for others thinking of running or who are running networks. Read current articles from their newspaper *New Catholic Miscellany,* along with links to other Catholic publications. Also learn about the history of the diocese.

*Melkite Catholic Eparchy of Newton, Massachusetts
http://www.execpc.com/~pstamm/eparchy.html

Unofficial. I could actually get in the car and physically visit this one!

Diocese of Sacramento, California (official)
http://www.cwo.com/~diocsacr/index.html

Here you can find links to two Catholic chat areas, one at EFNet and the other at Undernet. I didn't know they existed until going here. Just out of curiosity, you might want to look at their summer camp page.

The Holy See
http://www.vatican.va/

Yes, it's official! You can check out the Top 20 Picks in Chapter 5.

MORE INFORMATION

http://www.cs.cmu.edu/Web/People/spok/catholic/moreinfo.html

More Catholic Sites

Listserv Catholic Newsgroup
news:bit.listserv.catholic

This is about the same thing as a bulletin board where people post messages or files that everyone can see and respond to.

KathWeb
http://www.kathpress.co.at/kathweb

Catholic information in German. You will find the Austrian diocesan home-pages listed in the previous section hosted by them also.

Catholic Theology and Resources in German
http://www.wifak.uni-wuerzburg.de/wilan/theo/infos/tzi-hp-d.htm

At Wuerzburg. These guys are pushing it by trying to fit four frames on my screen. You might want to follow the link to "Theolog. Fakultäten in Europa" in the lower-right frame window.

Catholic Answers
http://www.catholic.com/~answers/

Edited by Karl Keating. Now where in this book did you see this one before? If you don't know, I'm not going to tell you.

Catholic Christian Outreach
http://www.sasknet.com/~cco/

This is a university student movement dedicated to evangelization. Find out about them and how to set one up in your school.

Information on Catholic Information Net
http://www.cs.cmu.edu/Web/People/spok/catholic/cin.txt

Free BBS with Internet mail services. You can find out a lot more about them in my Top 20 in Chapter 5.

Et Cum Spiritu Tuo
http://www.cwo.com/~pentrack/catholic/index.html

By David Pentrack. Here you will find Catholic spiritual growth and reference material. This one is clearly laid out. Here you can find out more about what I mentioned before—how to get EWTN by satellite.

St. Michael's Depot
http://web.sau.edu/~cmiller/religion.html

Includes lots of historic texts. With more than 100,000 visitors, this one has got to be good. There are tons of good links here, besides helpful commentaries. Check it out!

Avenue of Catholicism
http://www.avenue.com/v/catholic.html

I like the picture of the tabernacle on this page. The table of contents on the left side has some good links under "Catholic Knowledge" and "Catholic Prayers." The "Catholic Net Daily" has some interesting links under it, including a "Catholic Education Discussion Group" and a search tool that uses more than 40 search engines.

Catholic Resource Center
http://www.serve.com/crc/

This is a free lending library of books, videos, and audiotapes. I think this is a great idea, and recommend you go here to find out more about it. Besides the library, they have a "My Catholic E-Pal Project," where you can make e-mail pals instead of pen pals.

Selected Sites on Related Topics

Here are a copule of selected sites on topics that may be of special interest to Catholics. I am sure this one will grow larger in time!

Abortion/Pro-Life Links:

*Pro-Life Newsletter
http://www.pitt.edu/~stfst/pln/AboutPLN.html

LifeLinks
http://www.wwns.com/~lara/lifelink.html

COMMERCIAL SITES

These are Web pages for commercial establishments that may be of interest to Catholics or that make a special effort to market to Catholics. If you want to be on this list, write to spok+catholic@cs.cmu.edu with your URL and a brief description of your business. There is no fee charged for listing here.

This sure makes shopping for Catholic goods a lot easier. At times you can even see what you purchase online. Credit card information is still something people feel a little hesitant about giving over the Internet. I don't blame them. But apparently there are relatively good programs now for scrambling this kind of information so that nobody can steal it. I think an interesting development here would be for someone to initiate a Catholic online mall. There are malls already on the Internet. Why not a Catholic one?

The Companies

100% Roman Catholic
http://www.qni.com/~catholic

Here you will find three pages of religious goods to buy. At the bottom of the first page, you will find the index to everything. There are pictures, too. One that interested me was the "Catholic Questions and Answers Game!"

*Aquinas Software
http://northshore.shore.net/~aquinas/

Featuring consulting and the Catholic PrayerWare.

Ave Maria
http://users.aol.com/kapelle888/heaven.htm

You will want to find out about their new recording, "Heaven's Hymns," that is made up of favorite Catholic songs. These songs were picked after conducting an Internet survey. (I remember because I was sent the survey!) You may want to read their hymn stories and look into their Catholic links.

Be Still and Know That I Am God
http://www.nashville.net/~troppo/bestill.htm

Here you will find sound recordings of nature and scripture along with some sound files. Living out in the woods, I don't think I will need this one!

Cal-Hellas
http://gpg.com/calhellas/

Icons in Eastern Church styles. This is one of those places that you want to go even if you are not interested in buying anything. They have three collections to look at.

Calling All Angels
http://poconos.net/angels4u/

Angel figurines can be purchased here. You cannot miss the "Product Information" link here.

*Carolina Catholic Music Publishing
http://www.infi.net/~ccmp/

Catholic Knights Insurance Society
http://www.execpc.com/~ckis

Everybody is into insurance these days. You even need insurance for your insurance policies!

Catholic Video Club

http://www.inetbiz.com/cvc/

Looking for a video? We have the catalog of this company for our bookshop. They have more videos than I have ever seen. If they don't have the video you want, it probably hasn't been made.

 CCC of America

http://www.connect.net/ccca/

Catholic animated children's videos. These are impressive cartoons. We have sold their video on Fatima. That one comes with a colorful book, too.

 Chimney Sweep Books

http://antiquarian.com/chimney/

Catholic and other religious out-of-print books. There are always classics that you would like to get your hands on but can't find in print. Well, don't give up; look here for them.

 Couple to Couple League International Inc.

http://www.missionnet.com/~mission/cathlc/ccl/home.html

Natural family planning information.

 *Church Data Helper Plus

http://www.oanet.com/mall/ga-tech/cdhp.htm

Church database management software. I suppose that if you are a pastor or work in a Church office this site will be of much interest to you.

 Ecclesia Web Service

http://www.catholic-church.com/

Low-cost sites for Catholic organizations. You can find out more about this one in Chapter 11.

Goliard Music Press

http://users.aol.com/GoliardMP/goliard.htm

Service music for choirs. Nudge your choir director to get with it and go see this one.

Guardian Angel Books

http://www.sesi.com/angel/index.html

Children's books. For some reason angels are the "in" thing right now. You have to be careful, as the New Age has infiltrated this area and produces what look like wonderful books, but inside they are full of errors.

Good News by Mail

http://www.uniserve.com/goodnews/

Catholic mail-order book service. I guess the name will have to be changed to e-mail-order book service.

Ignatius Press

http://www.ignatius.com/

Catholic books and periodicals. Father Joseph Fessio, S.J., is the publisher. They put out many good works.

*Journey Publishing

http://www.nsbol.com/nsbol/3busines/journey/welcome.htm

Features Rosary recordings. My mother to this day walks while listening to a chanted Rosary recording. Such a tape can be a great aid to praying.

Verlang Kath. Bibelwerk

http://kirche.kath.de/kbw/

German Catholic publishing house. Why not be different and order something in German?

*Mercy Foundation
http://www.xroads.com/~jbperry/Mercy.html

Catholic video documentaries. We have a great documentary by the Mercy Foundation in our shop—about a holy little girl in our diocese of Worcester named Audrey.

 Oregon Catholic Press
http://www.ocp.org/index.shtml

Liturgical music and missals. Imagine they hold more than 10,000 music copyrights that they represent! They have some music in Spanish as well.

 Parish Registry System
http://ourworld.compuserve.com/homepages/gdwilson/wilson3.htm

Shareware for parish records. If you know that your pastor doesn't enjoy record-keeping, you may suggest he look here.

 *Principal Solutions
http://www.brigadoon.com/school/vendor/psi/psi.html

Software and Net service for Catholic schools and parishes. If you have anything to do with a school, you will want to track this one down.

 Rowan and Associates
http://www.polaris.net/~chp/rowan/home.htm

Consultants in religious education and parish ministry. Obviously, this one is not for everyone.

 St. Andrew's Book, Gift and Church Supply
http://mastermall.com/andrews/

Here you will find an easy-to-use index along with a search engine for their site at the bottom.

St. Bede's Publications
http://www.stbedes.org/

Books on monastic spirituality and theology. They have links to other publishers as well. You might want to find out about what a "colophon" is. I certainly didn't know until I followed their link. They are the masters of Gregorian Chant so you will want to follow their link to information about it. Why don't you give their page a visit?

*St. Gabriel Gift and Book Nook
http://www.electriciti.com/gabriel/catalog.html

It may seem strange to some that we call the angel Gabriel "Saint." It has become a custom of respect for these great archangels who have played such important roles in mankind's history.

St. Joseph Communications
http://www.saintjoe.com

Catholic audiotapes and videos. With this one I learned something—I could change the size of the frame by dragging it to the right or left. I certainly needed to, as all three frames would not fit on my screen. Anyway, this one claims to be the largest international Catholic audiotape and video reproduction and distribution company in the country so you might want to look here.

St. Mary's Press
http://wwwsmp.smumn.edu/

The emphasis here is on the youth. Whether you are young, feel young, look young, or work with the young, you may want to look at what they offer.

*Serenity Place
http://www.serenity-place.com/index.html

Catholic gifts and books. Serenity is something we all would like, isn't it?

Sophia Institute Press
http://catholicity.com/market/sophia.html

Excellent Catholic publisher. One of the employees there, Richard Rotondi, is a good friend of our monastery. They have fine books that are both scholarly and literary. They are well done in every way. They also reprint Catholic classics.

Sutton Enterprises
http://ally.ios.com/~rsutto29/index.html

Of interest here is an auto Rosary. I hadn't the slightest idea what to expect here so I looked into it. An auto Rosary is a compact Rosary designed to mount easily and safely on your car's dashboard or anywhere you may find it useful.

Vision Software and Publishing
http://www.wsnet.com/~alapadre/vision.html

Software for church organizations. This one has a limited audience.

THE VATICAN (NON-FRAMES, UNOFFICIAL)

http://www.cs.cmu.edu/People/spok/catholic/vatican.html

The Vatican has unveiled its new official Web site with lots of information. Some Web browsers may have a problem with the site as it stands now, due to its dependence on frames and its bandwidth requirements. This present homepage is designed to give quick, frameless access. The main menu on the Vatican site as of this writing is: The Holy Father, The Roman Curia, News Services, The Vatican Museums, Jubilee 2000, and Archive. You can click on any of these heading to jump to them on this Webmaster's page.

As usual, the Church gives the title of documentsin Latin. Since most of you are probably not Latin scholars, the substance of the main theme of each document is spelled out. I am sure you wll find something here to interest you! This frameless guide was mostly put together by John Ockerbloom and is still under construction.

The Vatican does not officially sponsor this guide. For definitive information and the most up-to-date links, use their site directly.

Vatican English-Language
http://www.vatican.va/home_en.html

 OTHER REFERENCES FROM THE INDEX

http://www.cs.cmu.edu/Web/People/spok/catholic.html

Parishes and Local Churches
http://www.wsnet.com/~alapadre/churches.html

This one you will find in Chapter 7.

9

Catholic Resources on the Net–Tad Book

http://davinci.marc.gatech.edu/catholic/web/

Here is another example of a straightforward opening page. Since this is meant to be an index, there isn't anything out of the ordinary in this homepage design. You will see a list of topic headings (similar to the ones I list following) that you can click on for the Catholic homepages that fall in that category. The Webmaster has one topic called "Ecumenical" that I did not include since this book is really concerned with *Catholic* homepages and information. You will probably find new topics added since I looked at his site, which is not surprising as this type of directory is supposed to grow.

When you click on a topic, you will be taken to the page with Catholic homepage links that fall into it. There are no commentaries here—just lists of links. You can get back to the main page two ways: click on the "Return to the Index" found at the bottom of this page or press the "Back" button on your Internet browser program.

This index of Catholic sites was done by the Catholic Center at Georgia Tech. You can send comments, make suggestions, or report any bugs to Tad Book at: tad@ davinci.marc.gatech.edu.

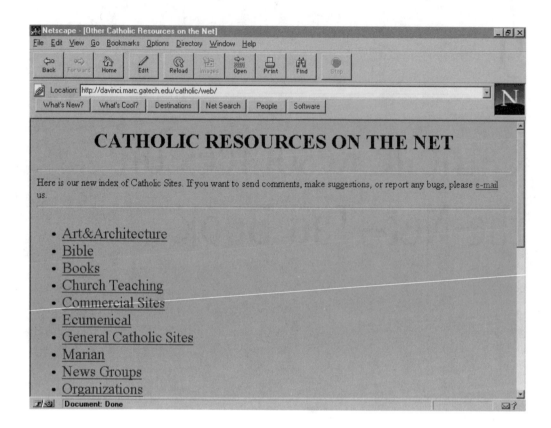

♫ ART & ARCHITECTURE

http://davinci.marc.gatech.edu/catholic/web/art.html

The Church has always been a supporter of art and has employed it for the glory of God. Art is used to raise our minds to heavenly realities or as a teaching aid to the Faith. It must be remembered that not long ago, many people could not read. The art found on church ceilings, walls, and stained glass were a means of catechesis.

Architecture is another fascinating subject. There have been so many different methods employed in the design of churches. Men have gone to great lengths to come up with unique buildings for the glory of God. To this day I marvel at how these tremendous buildings were constructed out of stone, without modern day cranes and other equipment to help lift things and put them in place. The famous Michelangelo (d.1564) did the design for St. Peter's Basilica that we see today. I have never been there, but I believe it is the largest church in the world!

St. Andrei Rublev Icons
http://maple.lemoyne.edu/~bucko/andre.html

You can learn about icons here. Also, you will find some prayer novenas (certain prayers said for nine days) and many beautiful pictures of icons to look at.

Vatican Tour
http://www.christusrex.org/

This one is found at Christus Rex. Definitely worth looking at, it has many images. Save yourself some traveling money and take this inexpensive tour.

*The Virtual Museum of the Cross
http://www.netline.net/novus/museum/index.html

This is worth pursuing. Use a search engine to locate it.

THE BIBLE

http://davinci.marc.gatech.edu/catholic/web/bible.html

The Church encourages us to know and read the Bible. If you follow the daily Mass readings, you will go through a lot of it. It may be helpful to take a chapter a day and read the Bible from cover to cover, as I once did. When you read the whole Bible, you get a better feel for how a particular part fits into the whole.

Catholic Bibles include all the books that the Church considers to be inspired by God. Other Christians have thrown out some books of the Bible for various reasons, but their scholars are currently coming to realize that perhaps this was a mistake. A Catholic Bible is supposed to have notes explaining various difficult texts in the light of Church tradition. In one of his letters, St. Peter says that the writings of St. Paul are hard to understand. Now if he thought so, imagine how difficult it is for us 2,000 years later, being from a different culture and having a different language!

When the Church approves an edition of the Bible, she says that you can be sure the translation substantially retains the meaning of the original text. Now when I say original text, I don't mean that we really have the original pages of the Bible, because we do not. We do have some early copies.

Bible Gateway
http://www.calvin.edu/cgi-bin/bible?

The Bible in six languages. Look under "Examples" to learn about how you can use the gateway to turn scripture references into a hyperlink in your own documents. You can search the Bible by passage or by word and see a cross reference and footnotes. Further, you can see what the Bible says about over 22,000 topics.

Clementine Vulgate
http://davinci.marc.gatech.edu/catholic/scriptures/vulgata-clementina.html

The Latin Vulgate Bible. Make sure you follow the link to St. Sophia's Library—The Digital Scriptures Collection of the Catholic Center at Georgia Tech.

English Douay-Rheims
http://www.cybercomm.net/~dcon/drbible.html

Translated from the Latin Vulgate. Diligently compared with the Hebrew, Greek, and other editions in different languages.

French Louis Segond Bible
http://humanities.uchicago.edu/forms_unrest/BIBLE.form.html

Can you read French? Reading the Bible in a foreign language is one good way to learn that language along with the spiritual benefits you receive.

German Elberfelder Bible
http://ourworld.compuserve.com/homepages/mawolter/elberfe.htm

The table of contents is in English on this page; it is worthwhile to see their Bible reading plan.

Italian Bible
http://www.crs4.it/~riccardo/Letteratura/Bibbia/Bibbia.html

Besides looking at each book, you can search by word also.

Latin Clementine Vulgate

http://ukanaix.cc.ukans.edu/carrie/vulgate_main.html

Here you can select any book of the Bible and get the Latin text.

Old English "Bible"

http://davinci.marc.gatech.edu/catholic/scriptures/saxon-bible.html

Electronic Old-English texts of Biblical literature. The term "Old English" describes a number of dialects in use on the isle of Britain from about A.D. 400 to 1100. It is also called Anglo-Saxon. For fun here, you will find a glossary of Old English that even includes some sound samples.

*Spanish Bible

http://www.lsl.com.mx/~turbo/rvr/

I can read Spanish because I studied theology while living in Puerto Rico and Columbia.

Easton's Bible Dictionary

http://ccel.wheaton.edu/easton/ebd/ebd.html

An alphabetical index of Biblical words. Clicking on them will bring up the relevant information.

Vulgate Bible of St. Jerome (Gopher)

gopher://ftp.std.com/11/obi/book/Religion/Vulgate

The table of contents is broken down by books of the Bible. You can see St. Jerome's Latin translation. St. Jerome spent 30 years translating the Bible. Now that's perseverance!

BOOKS

http://davinci.marc.gatech.edu/catholic/web/books.html

Here are a few books of possible interest. Credit for many of these goes to:

Harry Plantigna's Christian Classics Ethereal Library

http://ccel.wheaton.edu/

If you know of any other books of general Catholic interest on the Web, please e-mail Tad, the Webmaster of this homepage, at tad@davinci.marc.gatech.edu

With the advent of TV, book reading has somewhat fallen by the wayside. Many people prefer very short books or magazines, if they read anything at all. I do not consider myself a book reader either, but I do find them very helpful in spiritual life. There are just so many great works and great people in Church history to read about!

*Catechism of the Catholic Church
http://webzone1.co.uk/www/jcrawley/ccc.htm

A must! This is just about required reading as far as I'm concerned.

Documents of the Church
http://listserv.american.edu/catholic/church/church.html

These are not written to collect dust in the Vatican archives, but are written for our good. We need to read those that pertain to our vocation in the Church.

The Baltimore Catechism
http://www.catholic.net/RCC/Catechism/Catechism.html

During the nineteenth century, the American bishops held a series of provincial and national meetings in Baltimore, Maryland, to pave the way for Church expansion and mission work in this country. The Catechism was one of the fruits of these meetings.

Anonymous Theologia Germanica, Text
http://ccel.wheaton.edu/theo_ger/theologia_germanica.txt

This work was first discovered and published in 1516 by Martin Luther. It has since appealed to Christians of all persuasions. No, I don't know who wrote this.

St. Thomas Aquinas Summa Theologica
http://www.knight.org/advent/summa/summa.htm

(In Latin)
http://ccat.sas.upenn.edu/jod/Texts/aquinas.html

(In English)
http://ccat.sas.upenn.edu/jod/texts/thomas.html

St. Thomas answers the question: Should Christ have committed his doctrine to writing? I bet you never thought about this before.

St. Augustine
http://ccat.sas.upenn.edu/jod/augustine.html

"De Musica" in Latin
gopher://ccat.sas.upenn.edu:5070/11/tml

"The Rule of St. Augustine"
http://ccat.sas.upenn.edu/jod/augustine/ruleaug.html

You just have to read some works of this great Father of the Church.

Boethius—"The Consolation of Philosophy"
http://ccat.sas.upenn.edu/jod/boethius/boecons.html

(In Latin)
http://ccat.sas.upenn.edu/jod/boethius/boethius.html

(In English)
http://ccat.sas.upenn.edu/jod/boethius/boetrans

*"De musica"
gopher://ccat.upenn.edu:5070/11/bomus

"The Consolation of Philosophy" was written just before this author's execution.

Blessed Elizabeth of The Trinity—"Letters"
http://www.ocd.or.at/ics/trinity/lt.html

Very beautiful and inspiring letters written by this French Carmelite nun (d. 1906) whose spirituality was focused on the blessed Trinity dwelling within her soul.

*St. Ephraim of Syria—"The Pearl"
http://davinci.marc.gatech.edu/catholic/web/ephraim/pearl/pearl.html

In his lifetime this saint (d.c. 373) was known as a great writer, orator, poet, commentator, and defender of the Faith. He was made a Doctor of the Church in 1920.

*St. Eucherius of Lyons—"De Contemptu Mundi" (HTML)
http://davinci.marc.gatech.edu/catholic/web/eucherius/contempt/on_
contempt.html

Monk, hermit, then bishop, St. Eucherius lived around the year 450.

John Gower (c. 1327–1408)—"Confesio Amantis" (HTML)
http://etext.lib.virginia.edu/cgibin/browse-mixed?id=GowConf&tag=public&
images=images/modeng&data=/lv1/Archive/mideng-parsed

Who the heck is this person? He was an English poet who was a prolific writer. This work is a discussion of the seven deadly sins.

St. Gregory the Great—"Moralia or Commentary on the Book of Blessed Job"
Book 1
http://ccat.sas.upenn.edu/jod/texts/moralia1.html

Book 2
http://ccat.sas.upenn.edu/jod/texts/moralia2

Book 3
http://ccat.sas.upenn.edu/jod/texts/moralia3

Book 4
http://ccat.sas.upenn.edu/jod/texts/moralia4

Book 5
http://ccat.sas.upenn.edu/jod/texts/moralia5

Have you ever felt like everything was going wrong? If so, you will certainly want to read about Job.

Walter Hilton (d. 1396)—"The Scale (or Ladder) of Perfection," RTF
http://ccel.wheaton.edu/hilton/ladder/ladder1.0.RTF

One of the classics of the school of spirituality known as the English Mystics. Walter was an Augustinian.

W. R. Inge — "Light, Life and Love." [U.S. only], RTF
http://ccel.wheaton.edu/inge/US_ONLY/light_life_love/light_life_love1.0.RTF

Selections from German Mystics, also called the Rhineland Mystics.

St. John of the Cross
http://www.ocd.or.at/ics/john/gen.html

"Counsels to a Religious"
http://www.ocd.or.at/ics/john/couns.html

"Precautions"
http://www.ocd.or.at/ics/john/prec.html

Poems
http://www.ocd.or.at/ics/john/p.html

Letters
http://www.ocd.or.at/ics/john/lett.html

He is considered one of the greatest poets in Spain to this day.

Junillus (Sixth Century)
http://ccat.sas.upenn.edu/jod/junillus.html

"Instituta Regularia Divinae Legis"
http://ccat.sas.upenn.edu/jod/texts/junillus.intro.html

(In Latin)
http://ccat.sas.upenn.edu/jod/texts/junillus.text.html

(In English)
http://ccat.sas.upenn.edu/jod/texts/junillus.trans.html

Learn about some of the thinking of early Mesopotamian Christianity.

 *Pope John Paul II—Encyclicals and Other Writings by Pope John Paul II
http://cfa-www.harvard.edu/~dhoffman/Encyclicals/Encyclicals.html

The Pope is even recognized by nonbelievers for his wisdom.

 Sam Anthony Morello, OCD—"Lectio Divina and the Practice of Teresian Prayer"
http://www.ocd.or.at/ics/others/more.html

Lectio divina is Latin for "divine reading" or the more familiar usage, spiritual reading. You may want to see how this author works this in with methods of prayer taught by St. Teresa of Avila.

 John of Ruysbroeck—"The Adornment of the Spiritual Marriage" and Other Works, [U.S. only], RTF
http://ccel.wheaton.edu/ruysbroeck/US_ONLY/adornment/adornment1.0.RTF

 Text
http://ccel.wheaton.edu/ruysbroeck/US_ONLY/adornment/adornment1.0.txt

This one certainly has an interesting title.

 Therese of Lisieux—"Mit Leeren Handen"
http://www.ocd.or.at/ci/on-line/lh.html

She was a French saint (d. 1897), but this work is in German.

Non-Theological Books

 G. K. Chesterton—"The Innocence of Father Brown"
http://ccel.wheaton.edu/chesterton/innocence/title.html

"The Man Who Was Thursday"
http://ccel.wheaton.edu/chesterton/thursday/thursday.html

 "The Wisdom of Father Brown"
http://ccel.wheaton.edu/chesterton/wisdom/title.html

These are Chesterton's works of fiction. Father Brown was his priest-detective character.

 *Gary McDonogh—"Black and Catholic in Savannah, Georgia"
http://www.lib.utk.edu:70/UTKgophers/UT-PRESS/Sampler/front-McDonogh.html

This sounds like an interesting one, doesn't it?

CHURCH TEACHING

http://davinci.marc.gatech.edu/catholic/web/teaching.html

As Catholics, we are so lucky that Jesus established His Church as our guide for what we are to believe. Even in the time of the Apostles, people were already teaching and believing erroneous doctrine. If the Church had not constantly pointed out the truth, I don't know what we would believe by now!

 *Encyclicals and Other Writings by Pope John Paul II
http://dominiks-www.physics.wisc.edu/Encyclicals/Encyclicals.html

(In Adobe Acrobat format) *Encyclical* means "circular letter." These usually deal with affairs that pertain to the general welfare of the Church.

 Faith and Science
http://www.cco.caltech.edu/~newman/sci-faith.html

The Catholic perspective on this from Pope John Paul II and other Catholic and Christian sources.

Women in the Church
http://www.cco.caltech.edu/~newman/women.html

Catholic perspective on women in society and in the Church.

INFO COMMERCIAL SITES

http://davinci.marc.gatech.edu/catholic/web/commercial.html

I would guess that it is very rewarding to work at or own a Catholic business. Besides the reward of your work, you get the bonus of feeling that you are helping people love each other and God more!

St. Bede's Publications
http://www.stbedes.org/

They sound so familiar. Now where did I come across them before?

Be Still . . . and Know That I Am God (music)
http://www.nashville.net/~troppo/bestill.htm

A nature walk through the great Smoky Mountains with God. There are some sound files here to listen to also.

Catholic Answers
http://www.catholic.com

Books, audiotapes, and other resources about the Faith. This site was mentioned in the Top 20 of Chapter 5.

*Catholic Books
http://www.businessview.com/cb

This sounds like a good one. I wonder what they sell?

The Catholic Shop
http://transporter.com/cathshop/index.htm

Here you will find Bibles, books, music, videos, statues, pictures, Rosaries, vestments, crucifixes, medals, candles, cards, and much more.

 Heart of Mary Ministry
http://www.neosoft.com/~mary/

Founded by Sister Mary Lucy Astuto, R.S.M., this nonprofit ministry has for its purpose evangelizing, reaching others with the love of God, and helping to spread the messages Our Blessed Mother has given us in our modern day. Sister also has recorded tapes of her excellent singing.

 Liturgical Publications, Inc.
http://www.execpc.com/~lpi/

They will work with you to create inspirational church publications that enhance your message and effectively reach your audience. Find professional ministry resources here. Also, follow the link to the Catholic Catalog Company where you can take an "elevator ride" through their departments.

GENERAL CATHOLIC SITES

http://davinci.marc.gatech.edu/catholic/web/general.html

This looks like one of those catchall categories. Some homepages are hard to classify as they just have such diverse information and links on them. Some sites have grown from towns into virtual cities!

 Catholic Answers
http://www.catholic.com

This one is for Catholic apologetics and evangelization. They have a lot here that you can find out about by looking at the Top 20 in Chapter 5.

 *Catholic Chat Site
http://tjk127.rh.psu.edu/

This one sounds like a great idea. (I have a chat area on our homepage, too!)

Montessori Catholic Council
http://transporter.com/mcc/index.htm

See various essays about Maria Montessori and her excellent child development methods, discussions about Maria Montessori and Catholicism, FAQs, and job listings throughout the United States.

New Advent Supersite Page
http://www.knight.org/advent

Here you will find general Catholic information. For more about them, see my Top 20 picks in Chapter 5.

SOLT Ministries
http://www.solt.org/solt/index.html

This homepage is by the Society of Our Lady of the Trinity, some of whom were in my classes at the seminary.

The Rock
http://www.nervline.com/therock

Here you will find another Catholic resource index of links. You might want to see their colorful banner as well.

NEWS GROUPS

http://davinci.marc.gatech.edu/catholic/web/newsgroups.html

News is a very interesting thing. I learned when I was in the Philippines how it can be distorted or taken out of context. I was there when an actual event took place, a protest at a university. My parents in the United States saw it on the news and were led to believe that something like a war had broken out. One thing about Internet news groups is that you can talk to people who perhaps were eyewitnesses to an event taking place. But beware, you could start with a story about the fisherman that caught a minnow and end up with a story about the whale he caught!

 ORGANIZATIONS

http://davinci.marc.gatech.edu/catholic/web/organizations.html

Because the Church is universal, it embraces a multitude of vocations and apostolates. As you can see from nature, God certainly likes variety! So it is with the graces He bestows. People feel called to different works and ways of life. Like trees in a forest, organizations spring up and sometimes disappear as well. The Holy Spirit is constantly at work in the Church, bringing out new growth to meet the needs of the times.

Religious Orders

St. Benedict's Abbey
http://www.benedictine.edu/Abbey.html

This abbey in Kansas is home for 75 monks of the Order of St. Benedict.

The Benedictine Monastery of Christ in the Desert
http://www.christdesert.org/pax.html

This monastery has been featured in various articles for their Internet work. Here you will find information about seeking God, their monastery, monastic studies, and monastery news.

Mount Saviour Monastery
http://www.servtech.com/public/msaviour/

A New York monastery. Here you will find news about them with pictures, their history, a 12-picture tour of the monastery, information about their sheep farm, an article about monastic life, and more.

Divine Word Missionaries
http://www.vais.net/~svd/

Missionaries whose work heavily depends upon the needs of the local Church and the particular expertise of its members. Find out where missionaries are around the world, learn more about Blessed Arnold Janssen and the many communities he founded, follow links to their other homepages, download a multimedia presentation about them, and look at the liturgical calendar in English or Vietnamese.

Fraternity of Mary
http://members.aol.com/FOMQC

A private Clerical association composed of diocesan (secular) clergy living in community, loyal to the Magisterium and committed to serving their brother priests.

*Teresian Carmel (OCD)
http://info.risc.uni-linz.ac.at/misc-info/ocd/ocd.htm

The Order of Carmelites Discalced trace their spirituality to Elijah in the Old Testament.

Dominican Web Page
http://www.op.org/op/

There is a tradition that St. Dominic met St. Francis of Assisi.

*The Sisters of Saint Joseph
http://www.nd.edu/~csjus/home.html

The saint that this community takes as its patron has a growing popularity in our time. The silent one in the Gospels, now has many devotees.

The Sisters of Saint Joseph of Florida, USA
http://ballingerr.xray.ufl.edu/sisters.html

Service for them means a consistent effort to promote union among their neighbors and with God.

Franciscans International
http://listserv.american.edu/catholic/franciscan/fi/fi.html

The Franciscans are present as a nongovernmental organization (NGO) at the United Nations. Read articles from their *Cord* magazine, then find out about the World Food Summit and Habitat II.

What's on the Internet for Catholics?

Franciscan Province of Our Lady of Consolation
http://www.weblifepro.com/vocations/olc_prov.html

Find out about the province as well as follow a link to the Conventual Franciscan homepage.

Pallottines
http://www.dare.uni-essen.de/sac/

Their main activities include: lay apostolate, ecumenical initiatives, missions, charity, social apostolate (social justice), and mass-media. Learn about their founder Saint Vincent Pallotti (d. 1850), view some of the homepages they maintain, and look at their directory.

Jesuit
gopher://gopher.luc.edu:7000/1

If you want to know everything about this order founded by St. Ignatius of Loyola and his six companions, this is the place to go.

DIOCESES

There are many more dioceses listed on the homepage, but I have covered them already or will cover them in Chapter 12.

Diocese of Phoenix, Arizona
http://www.catholicsun.org/

See their newspaper appropriately named *The Catholic Sun*, read what the Bishop writes, look into the "News and Events" (where you will find a lot of local information, including some on retreats). There is a nice summary of their activities listed by month for last year, called "The Year in Review." Besides finding out about each parish, you can get driving directions to them as well.

*Archdiocese of Seattle, Washington
http://www.psrnet.com/index.html

This diocese was established in 1850 under a different name. In 1907 the name was changed to Seattle; then in 1951, it was made an archdiocese.

Other Religious Organizations

*Knanaya Community
http://biophysics.coe.drexel.edu/knanaya.html

All the way from India!

Legion of Mary
http://transporter.com/lom/

This group held their meetings at our monastery some time back. They do great work. I especially like their door-to-door efforts of evangelization.

Most Holy Mother of God Catholic Church
http://www.pond.net/~jeffclang/mostholy/index.html

In Vladivostok, Russia. See a picture of the church and read about its history. You may want to help them with their needs. There are essays you can read here, along with area news, links to other churches, and Catholic sites.

*Opus Dei
http://web1.cti.unav.es/english/opus.dei/index.html

From the Universidad de Navarra. All in Spanish.

Institutes

Apostolate Alliance of the Two Hearts
http://www.ici.net/mantle

A cooperative effort of religious institutes via their affiliated apostolates, which are dedicated to spreading devotion to the Sacred Heart of Jesus and the Immaculate Heart of Mary. Find out about the promoters of these devotions, the devotions themselves, and the story of this apostolate.

Office for Social Justice—Archdiocese of St. Paul and Minneapolis
http://www.mtn.org/justice

These pages contain information about resources available from their office, social justice issues in the Twin Cities area, and the teaching of the Catholic Church on social justice.

International Institute Lumen Vitae of Pastoral and Catechetical Studies
http://members.aol.com/icmwebsite/index.html

They offer a two-year formation program in healing ministry as well as provide prayer-ministry referrals to healing teams of Western Washington and Northern Oregon. Find out about this ministry here.

*Pontificia Universita San Tommaso d'Aquino "Angelicum"—Rome
http://www.informedia.it/dipiu96/st/st_index.htm

Here is a title in Italian that you can practice translating. You will find it in English elsewhere in this book.

Pope John Center for the Study of Ethics in Health Care
http://www.pjcenter.org/pjc/

Is it morally permissible to refuse medical treatment? Look here to find out the answer to this and to other important questions in the medical world.

Rosary Center
http://www.teleport.com/~rosary/

This is the Dominican Fathers' headquarters for The Rosary Confraternity. Listen to their nice music while learning about their worldwide movement for peace. You can find out about the Rosary here, read their newsletter, and follow their links to more information.

Other Organizations

*The Catholic Evidence Guild—Ann Arbor, Michigan
http://www.us.itd.umich.edu/~ximenez/cegintro.html

This group began some years ago in England and was greatly aided by the Catholic apologists and publishers Frank Sheed (d. 1981) and Maisie Ward (d. 1975). They were known for teaching about the Faith on street corners and at Speakers Corner in London's Hyde Park.

http://davinci.marc.gatech.edu/catholic/web/pastoral.html

Passing on the Faith to the next generation is always an important consideration and apostolate. Any school that calls itself "Catholic" has to have some program of religious education. To this day I don't know how I learned all the basic prayers and doctrine that I know. I am sure they were taught to me in the Catholic elementary school I attended, but I can't remember.

Being members of the Church, our experience of the Faith is not limited to doctrine. As a community, we share it with each other. Now people often feel most comfortable sharing in peer groups. This is true with the youth as well. Seeing others their age living the Christian life is great incentive to them. It also forms a support group to deal with those pressures in society that work against such a life.

Catholic Christian Outreach
http://www.sasknet.com/~cco/

A Canadian university student movement dedicated to evangelization. Find out about CCO, how they can benefit your diocese, and how to start a chapter. Read their online *Grapevine* newsletter. If you are into music you might want to look at their music chart.

Catholic Educational Resources
http://www.microserve.net/~fabian/re.html

This one is put together by Scott Fabian, the Webmaster of the "Ecclesia" site mentioned in Chapter 11.

Catholic School Times
http://ballingerr.xray.ufl.edu/cst/index.html

This newsletter is connected to the education department of the Archdiocese of Miami. Learn about the accomplishments and challenges of Catholic education at the elementary and secondary level.

*Joyful Noise
http://www.geopages.com/TheTropics/1552/

Catholic liturgical music. Sometimes I wish choirs would choose simple melodies so the congregation can sing along.

Retrouvaille—A Lifeline for Married Couples
http://www.vicnet.net.au/~retro

Family life is the basic fabric of any society. Once you lose the family, you lose the society as well.

PERIODICALS

http://davinci.marc.gatech.edu/catholic/web/periodicals.html

At the monastery we are fortunate to get donated subscriptions to some Catholic periodicals. Unlike a book, a periodical gives you the story in brief. And if you are a busy person, you don't have time for much else!

Catholic Issues and Facts
http://www.catholic.net/RCC/Periodicals/Issues/Welcome.html

Addresses topics, such as the Galileo affair, that frequently trouble Catholics and non-Catholics. There are also some apologetic issues addressed here. To be versed in some common questions and their answers, you will want to stop here.

Catholic World News
http://www.catholic.net/RCC/Periodicals/CWN/index.html

Keep on top of what is going on in the Catholic world. The news article links are listed by month.

News from the Holy See in English
http://www.christusrex.org/www1/news/news.html

In Italian
http://www.christusrex.org/www1/news/notizie.html

En Español
http://www.christusrex.org/www1/news/noticias.html

Why not try reading the news in all three languages?

This Rock
http://www.electriciti.com/~answers/thisrock.html

The emphasis of this magazine is on the scriptural, historical, and rational grounds for Catholic teachings. You can select full-text articles from recent issues here.

*The Saint Augustine Catholic
http://128.227.164.224/diocese/sac/sac.html

The patron saint of this publication was not baptized until he was 33 years old. In spite of this late start, he went on to become a priest, Bishop, and possibly the greatest Father of the Church!

TIME—John Paul II as Man of the Year
http://www.pathfinder.com/@@STBgQgAAAAAAABPa/time/magazine/domestic/1994/941226/941226.cover.html

This article appeared in *Time* magazine. Find out why they named the Pope "Man of the Year."

*TIME—John XXIII as Man of the Year
http://www.pathfinder.com/@@STBgQgAAAAAAABPa/time/special/moy/1962.html

Another article from *Time* magazine. Imagine that—two Popes made it as "Man of the Year!"

Vatican Information Service
http://www.vatican.va/vis/englinde.html

Don't miss this one! There is obviously plenty of good information here.

Notizie dal Mondo
http://www.christusrex.org/www1/news/mondo.html

In Italian. This is a hyperlink index of world news by the month.

http://davinci.marc.gatech.edu/catholic/web/prolife.html

Defending life from conception to natural death has become an issue that nobody can avoid getting involved in these days. Those opposed to life keep spreading their poisonous views from country to country around the world. In Third World countries these views are pushed upon the people, whether they like it or not, by those with power and money. Some governments now decide how many children a family will have. With all this going on, it is good to keep in mind that the only binding laws of a government are those for the common good that do not go against God's laws. Just because something is made legal does not automatically make it moral! We have to work at getting the human laws to correspond to the divine ones.

The Alliance for Children
http://www.adoption.com/alliance

Based in the Commonwealth of Massachusetts and the state of Rhode Island, this nonprofit adoption agency will help you find a child to adopt if you live in those areas. Even if you don't, this page has links to adoption agencies all over the world, FAQs for adoptive parents, and a story of an adoption.

The American Family Network
http://www.customcpu.com/personal/mneligh/cop/

The American Family Network and the Coalition of Parents have combined. Their mission is to assist those who have been falsely accused of rape, child abuse, child neglect, spousal abuse, and sexual harassment in defending themselves, restoring their good names, and gaining compensation and justice for the harm done to them and their families. The Coalition of Parents has further established for itself the purpose of restoring fair, honest, and decent methods of law enforcement.

America's Crisis Pregnancy Hotline
http://www.easy.com/crisis/

Designed to provide facts about the many services and resources available across the United States for women experiencing unplanned pregnancies. You will be put in touch with available resources, FAQs, and related links.

Fray Antonio
http://www.best.com/~mlacabe/puigjane.html

A well-known nonviolent activist, defender of human rights, and voice for the "disappeared" in Argentina, as well as a vocal opponent of the government. He is currently in prison for a crime he did not commit. Find out how to help get him released as well as read his case, biography, letters, and more.

Natural Family Planning
http://www.usc.edu/hsc/info/newman/resources/nfp.html

References to several contemporary methods for spacing, postponing, avoiding, or enhancing the possibilities of conception, without any chemical or physiological alterations of the reproductive system (female or male).

Our Lady's Crusaders for Life
http://www.tiac.com/users/wooly/olcl.htm

A group of Catholics from the Boston area who believe that the murder of pre-born babies must be publicly opposed. Their newsletter and Web site offer a commentary on our "Age of Impurity." They expose the evils of certain sex education programs and provide "Holy Lessons" from the Faith. Links regarding these issues can be found here.

The Precious in His Sight—Internet Adoption Photolisting
http://www.adoption.com/

Their primary goals are to provide quality adoption information so each individual can make an educated decision about adoption options, help find families for as many children as quickly as possible, simplify and shorten the process of prospective adoptive parents searching for a child to adopt, and provide resources to adoption professionals to assist them in serving their clients.

I just know you want to see all the photos of these beautiful children. Of course, to see them is to love them, and to love them is to want to adopt or at least pray for them. Here you can see a photolisting of international children awaiting adoption, adoption daily news, the adoption resource mall (adoption-related vendors), the library, chat room, and much more.

 REFERENCE

http://davinci.marc.gatech.edu/catholic/web/reference.html

Many times a question comes up regarding the Faith and we don't know where to begin searching for the answer. This is where reference books come in handy. Now you can find what you are looking for on the Internet as well. Some major works that could be found only in large Catholic libraries are now available to you. Even if you can't find the answer you need, you will probably come across someone who can at these sites.

 Apologetics
http://transporter.com/apologia/

The index here is clearly explained to easily guide you to information about the Catholic Church and other denominations. You will definitely want to learn about "12 Painless Ways to Evangelize" by clicking on the book with this title.

 *Apologetics
http://users.aol.com/jamesakin/apologetics.html

Did you know that St. Justin Martyr (d.c. 165) is regarded as the most important of the second-century apologists?

 The Apologetics Page
http://www.htp.com/raistlin/apology/apology.htm

The author of this page presents a rational defense of Christianity. He tells you what he intends to do and not to do. Besides this, he gives you links to related sites and has a mailing list.

 A Large Collection of Church Documents
http://listserv.american.edu/catholic/church

This link will take you to a page that looks similar to what you see when looking at the directories on your hard drive. For easiest viewing, click on "church.html" to see a linked list of references for Church documents.

Documents from Early Church History
ftp://iclnet93.iclnet.org/pub/resources/christian-history.html

This one is clearly laid out with a table of contents and a hyperlinked listing of texts along with brief descriptions.

The Ecole Initiative
http://cedar.evansville.edu/~ecoleweb/index.html

An encyclopedia of Church history. You can see an alphabetical listing here if you like. Besides getting tons of historical information here, you will want to pursue the "Images" link for sure.

*Jesuits and Sciences
http://www.luc.edu/~scilib/jessci.html

Jesuits have been involved in the sciences. Find out exactly who and what was involved here.

Liturgical Calendar
http://www.easterbrooks.com/personal/calendar/index.html

Did you know that some days commemorate more than one saint? For instance, four saints are remembered on May 25.

The Popes
http://listserv.american.edu/catholic/other/listof.popes

This is a list of Popes, along with the dates each reigned.

*The Theology 100 Online Glossary
http://www.nd.edu/~jvanderw/theo100/glossary.htm

If you can't find this one, go to Notre Dame University and sign up for Theology 100!

Shroud of Turin Homepage
http://www.cais.com/npacheco/shroud/turin.html

Although the Carbon-14 dating tests said the material of the shroud was from around the fourteenth century, this finding could be off. The reason is that scientific tests did not take into account the fact that the shroud was involved in a fire centuries ago, which could have changed the results of the carbon dating.

SAINTS

http://davinci.marc.gatech.edu/catholic/web/saints.html

This section brings to mind the Gospel reading I heard at Mass today. Certain Jewish leaders were trying to prove that there was no resurrection from the dead. Jesus answered that the Old Testament recorded God saying to Moses, "I am the God of Abraham, the God of Isaac and the God of Jacob." Jesus concludes from this that God is the God of the living, not of the dead. So the saints, although dead, are alive. Just as they interceded for others with God during life so they continue to do so now from Heaven. They can be a great aid to us, who still are on a pilgrimage of Faith. Let's get to know them better!

L.P.H. Book of Saints
http://www.netaxs.com/~rmk/saints.html

Put together by Our Lady of Perpetual Help homeschoolers, this site includes a paragraph on each of 50 different saints. You must read these cute accounts of the saints written by these children. Follow the "L.P.H. Resource Center" link to find out how your children can be part of this homeschooling effort.

Index of Saints
http://www.pitt.edu/~eflst4/saint_bios.html

This page is listed in the Top 20 in Chapter 5. It was put together by Ed LoPresti, a recent electrical and computer engineering graduate from Carnegie-Mellon University. Ed is now a graduate student in bioengineering at the University of Pittsburgh. We definitely need some good Catholics in this field. Good luck, Ed!

Spiritual Resources
http://davinci.marc.gatech.edu/catholic/web/spiritual.html

Many of us take care of our bodies, which is good. But not all of us give a thought to the care of our souls. Just as we need to feed our bodies to stay healthy so should we do likewise for our souls. Take in a little spiritual nourishment every day so you will have life now and in the life to come.

*The Taizé Community's Johannine Hours
http://saturn.colorado.edu:8080/Christian/JHours/hours.html

Johannine normally refers to St. John the Evangelist. What Johannine Hours means by this, I haven't the slightest clue. But I can tell you that Taizé is an ecumenical community located in France. There are some Catholics in this community.

Information on Centering Prayer
http://www.io.com/user/lefty/Centering_Prayer.html

By Fr. Thomas Keating, O.C.S.O. I'm sure you have seen this one earlier in this book.

Treasury of Novenas
http://www.nd.edu/~mary/Novena.html

Here you will find 11 novenas, some with a history given. Do you know when the first novena took place?

A Longer Compilation of Rosaries
gopher://wiretap.spies.com/00/Library/Religion/Catholic/Rituals/rosary.txt

Now don't get confused. Normally when we refer to the Rosary, it is the one with 15 meditation Mysteries. But there are other prayers said with beads, usually called "chaplets." Here you will find a long list of chaplets with information on how to pray them.

Ignatian Spiritual Exercises
http://www.cs.pitt.edu/~planting/books/ignatius/exercises/exercises.html

This is an 8- or 30-day program.

Mass Readings for Today
http://www.veritas.org.sg/

If you haven't read them yet today, read them right now!

Secular Institutes

http://www.coffey.com/~bryan/main.html

Mainly about the Society of Our Lady of the Way, yet this page also provides information for those who want to know more about secular institutes.

*Stations of the Cross

http://www.nd.edu/~jvanderw/stations/stations.htm

Did you know that you can gain a plenary indulgence by making the Stations of the Cross? If you don't know what a plenary indulgence is, look up the prayer article on indulgences on our monastery's homepage.

IN LATIN

Cantus: Database of Divine Office Gregorian Chant

gopher://vmsgopher.cua.edu/11gopher_root_music%3a%5b_cantus%5d

I know nothing about music and can't read a note, yet I can chant. You can too.

Gregorian Chant Homepage

http://www.music.princeton.edu/chant_html/

St. Pope Pius X said that this type of chant contains in the highest degree the qualities characteristic of sacred music—true art and holiness.

*Regula Benedicti

http://www.osb.hu/l_regula/

The Rule of St. Benedict with English translations and commentary. Did you know that someone trying to kill this saint put poison in his wineglass? Fortunately, he made the Sign of the Cross over the glass and it broke. It pays to say grace before meals!

A Treasury of Latin Prayers

http://www.cs.cmu.edu/Web/People/spok/catholic/latin-prayers/index.html

With English translations and commentary.

The Tridentine Mass
http://www.cs.cmu.edu/Web/People/spok/mass-parallel.txt

Latin in one column and the English translation in another. In some places the Bishop has given permission for certain priests to still celebrate the Tridentine Mass. If you don't remember it, this page will show you what it was like.

Charismatic

Catholic Charismatic Center
http://www.garg.com/ccc/

A lot of information here about the Charismatic movement. You can also see a calendar of events and a directory of Charismatic organizations. There are FTP site links for Christian ClipArt and documents of the Church. Further, you will find links to the Bible, Catholic sites, and some notable articles.

STUDENT ORGANIZATIONS

http://www.cco.caltech.edu/~newman/OtherNC.html

The student organizations are organized by geographical location. Now for those who don't want to bother paging down, you can click on the geographical location link of the place you are interested in. This will take you directly to that section in the list. So, for example, if I were interested in student organizations in Michigan, I would click on "MidWest." In each section, you will find these organizations arranged in alphabetical order for your convenience.

This listing is a great way for Catholic students around the world to get connected to each other. Also, you may be attending one of these schools and be unaware that there is a Catholic student community!

These students are doing a lot of fun stuff! I especially like looking at the pictures of their activities.

There will be some common information on many of these pages. For each organization, you most likely will see a listing that includes their Catholic chaplain, their Mass schedule, announcements, and perhaps even a newsletter.

Many if not all these student organizations are located at non-Catholic colleges. So don't be surprised if you find the Catholic community information listed on a page with information or links to other religions and their ministry at the college or university.

 ## OTHER REFERENCES FROM THE INDEX

http://davinci.marc.gatech.edu/catholic/web/

Marian
http://davinci.marc.gatech.edu/catholic/web/marian.html

Although this is one of his main categories, I didn't give its listing because almost all these sites are found in other parts of this book. You still may want to check out his list as he may have added new ones.

10

▼▼▼

Catholic Kiosk:
From Cincinnati

http://www.erinet.com/aquinas/arch/dio.html

This page was put together by the Aquinas MultiMedia Design Studio. Although this page seems to be dedicated to information in Cincinnati, I chose it because it is also a resource directory of Catholic sites on the Internet. I believe it is a good example of a service that can be provided to the Church. What do I mean? Aquinas Studio has provided a public service directory to online Catholic groups, parishes, and organizations in southwestern Ohio. They have also hosted some of them, too. (The Archdiocese of Cincinnati maintains its own homepage that provides official information and news.) Although a diocese may have a homepage on the Internet, that doesn't mean they can either construct or pay for homepages for all the institutions located within it. So it is up to the laity to assist their local Church in getting a presence on the Internet. I think Aquinas Studio will give you ideas of how you can set up your site for the local Church in your area.

Here you will find the table of contents along the left-hand side or bottom of the page. As you go from page to page, the table of contents will stay with you. There are other links in the middle of the page that I put under "Other References from the Index" in my book.

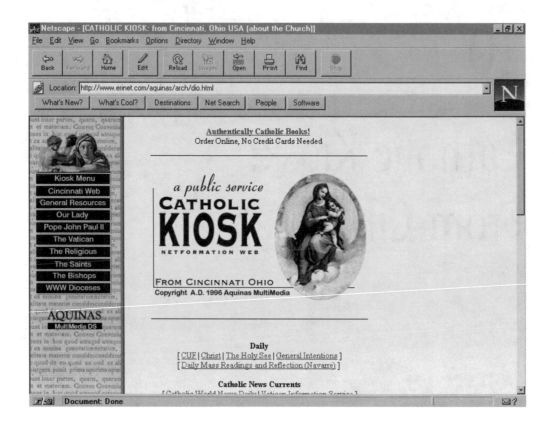

Netscape - [CATHOLIC KIOSK: from Cincinnati, Ohio USA [about the Church]]

File Edit View Go Bookmarks Options Directory Window Help

Location: http://www.erinet.com/aquinas/arch/dio.html

What's New? What's Cool? Destinations Net Search People Software

Kiosk Menu
Cincinnati Web
General Resources
Our Lady
Pope John Paul II
The Vatican
The Religious
The Saints
The Bishops
WWW Dioceses

AQUINAS
MultiMedia DS

Authentically Catholic Books!
Order Online, No Credit Cards Needed

a public service
CATHOLIC
KIOSK
NETFORMATION WEB

FROM CINCINNATI OHIO
Copyright A.D. 1996 Aquinas MultiMedia

Daily
[CUF | Christ | The Holy See | General Intentions]
[Daily Mass Readings and Reflection (Navarre)]

Catholic News Currents

Document: Done

TOP TEN RECOMMENDED CATHOLIC WEB SITES!

INFO

http://www.erinet.com/aquinas/arch/recs.html

Now I think you can count as well as I can. So why aren't 10 sites listed? Because I axed some of them! (No, not because he didn't agree with my Top 20 picks!) This list, I am sure, will change constantly so you may not find all of the following links.

The Catechism of St. Pius X

http://abbey.apana.org.au/official/catechisms/piusx.htm

Pope St. Pius X's partial realization of a simple, plain, brief, popular Catechism for uniform use throughout the whole world. It was directed to laypeople. It was used in the ecclesiastical province of Rome and for some years in other parts of Italy.

Adoremus

http://www.erinet.com/aquinas/arch/adoremus.html

A distinguished group of lay and religious Catholics (including Mother Angelica, Father Joseph Fessio, S.J. of Ignatius Press, and writer/historian James Hitchcock) has formed Adoremus: the Society for Renewal of the Sacred Liturgy.

This Rock from Catholic Answers
http://www.catholic.com/~answers/thisrock.html

This Rock is a magazine of apologetics and evangelization. Catholic writers explain the faith and defend it against misrepresentations and misunderstandings. Particular emphasis is put on the scriptural, historical, and rational grounds for Catholic teachings. All articles reflect Catholic orthodoxy. It is published by "Catholic Answers," the largest lay Catholic apologetics and evangelization organization in North America. You can learn more about them in the Top 20 in Chapter 5.

*Suggestions on Eucharistic Adoratio
http://web.frontier.net/Apparitions/lucia.html

The contents of this file address frequently asked questions about Perpetual Eucharistic Adoration. Fr. Martin Lucia, director of this apostolate, wrote this article about Perpetual Eucharistic Adoration in response to our Holy Father's call to evangelization and especially to evangelize about the Real Presence of Jesus in the Eucharist.

The Angelicum
http://www.informedia.it/dipiu/st/st_index.htm

The Pontifical University of St. Thomas Aquinas traces its origins to the medieval studium of the Dominican Order in Rome. The College of St. Thomas was founded in the sixteenth century, and in the seventeenth century the Pope authorized it to confer academic degrees in theology.

CINCINNATI WEB/CATHOLIC CINCINNATI

http://www.erinet.com/aquinas/arch/cinti.html

The Catholic Cincinnati site may be of particular interest to Catholics in southwestern Ohio and northern Kentucky since these listings pertain to their area. Others who are curious or want to get ideas for constructing pages or directories for their local Church might want to look through these, too.

Schedules of Exposition of the Blessed Sacrament
http://www.erinet.com/aquinas/arch/expo.html

It would be great if all churches had exposition of the Blessed Sacrament with many people in adoration of Jesus.

Of Historical Interest

A History of the Cathedral of St. Peter in Chains
http://www.erinet.com/aquinas/arch/history1.html

At St. Peter in Chains in Rome, visitors can see the chains that are believed to have held St. Peter the Apostle. On this homepage you will find pictures along with an adaptation of a speech delivered by Fr. Donald Tenoever, architecture historian, at the celebration of the 150th anniversary of the Cathedral.

The Treasured Churches of Cincinnati
http://www.aquinas-multimedia.com/church

This project was in progress when I visited this page. In due course, more than 20 Catholic churches in Cincinnati will be included in this electronic book. Most churches will include an architectural tour, history, photos of the art and architecture; some will also include information on the artists and architects along with their sketches, drawings, and blueprints.

Parishes

St. Catharine of Siena Church (Westwood, Cincinnati)
http://www.aquinas-multimedia.com/church/catharin.html

This church has a great patronness in this saint who influenced many during her life and had a group of followers who traveled about with her. She even stopped wars between Italian towns—now that is a miracle!

Holy Family Church (East Price Hill, Cincinnati)
http://www.aquinas-multimedia.com/church/holy-fam.html

May the Holy Family be an inspiration and an example to all families everywhere.

St. Maximilian Kolbe Church (West Chester)
http://www.iac.net/~condittm/stmax.html

I don't know how he did it, but the patron (d. 1941) of this parish was superior of a large number of Franciscans that actually formed a town in Poland called Marytown. They published a daily newspaper that they delivered by plane!

University of Dayton Chapel
http://www.udayton.edu/~campmin/mass-gr.htm

This Catholic University is run by the Marianist Fathers and Brothers.

Catholic Schools and Universities

Chaminade-Julienne High School
http://www.udayton.edu/~cj/

There is an interesting blue background to this page. Marianists and Sisters of Notre Dame DeNamur staff this school. You can find out more about them along with other information here.

Archbishop Moeller High School
http://www.moeller.org

This is such a big school that their page wouldn't all fit on my screen! Anyway you can see an impressive drawing of the school along with a look at their homepages and "Hot Links" that really looks like it is on fire.

*Purcell Marian High School
http://www.rcch.com/purcell/pmhs.html

Archbishop Elder High School
http://miavx1.acs.muohio.edu/~knepflcr/

Of special interest here is their "Top Ten Web sites" and "Listen on the Web." The latter is Elder's football games broadcast "live" over the Internet.

International Marian Research Institute
http://www.udayton.edu/imri/

This is one of my Top 20 picks found in Chapter 5.

Cincinnati Catholic Organizations

One Bread One Body: Daily Readings
http://w3.one.net/~presmin/OBOB/daily/daily.phtml

Besides telling you where to find the Mass readings of the day, this page gives a short reflection on them. At the bottom of the page is the table of contents with other things to explore.

World Wide Marriage Encounters
http://www.rc.net/org/wwme_cin/

Enrich your marriage through this ministry. Links to other marriage encounter homepages can be found here, also.

Couple to Couple League
http://www.itek.net/~mission/cathlc/ccl/

Former Archbishops

Archbishop Joseph L. Bernadin 1972–82
http://www.archdiocese-chgo.org/bio.html

You can find out a lot more about him by following this link.

Archbishop Daniel E. Pilarczyk 1982–Present
http://www.archdiocese-cinti.org/archbishop/curvitae.htm

Ditto here.

http://www.erinet.com/aquinas/arch/educate.html

Here you will find a listing of Catholic resources. At the top of this page you will find helpful shortcuts to topics that interest you. By clicking on them, you can jump down the list to that topic. Otherwise, just page down until you see what you like. The only drawback I experienced here was that when I pursued a link then returned to this page, I ended up at the top again. I would then have to select the topic I left off at to jump back down.

Now don't expect to find the following listing exactly as you see it on the Internet. This Webmaster updates his page frequently and has already added and taken away from what is listed.

Catholic History and Tradition

The Catechism of the Catholic Church
http://christusrex.org/www1/CDHN/ccc.html

The great guide for our age. If you want to find out more, see my Top 20 in Chapter 5.

The (1917) Catholic Encyclopedia Project
http://www.knight.org/advent/cathen/cathen.htm

This is a great encyclopedia. We have the old-fashioned set—the actual books—in our library. Imagine that!

The Baltimore Catechism
http://www.catholic.net/RCC/Catechism/Doit.html

A lot of people still like this one. You can compare it to the new one.

A Guide to the Church Councils
http://abbey.apana.org.au/councils/~index.htm

Find out what an ecumenical council is and read the texts of all the councils except Trent and Vatican II.

The Douay-Rheims Bible Project
http://www.cybercomm.net/~dcon/drbible.html

Find out about this project, mentioned before.

The Ecole Initiative: Early Church History
http://www.evansville.edu/~ecoleweb/

Another great resource to look up. It is great to know the roots of the Church.

Catholic Recommended Readings Bookshelf
http://ccel.wheaton.edu/shortlist.html

A selection of 11 books with both an abstract and the text.

The Labyrinth: A Server for Medieval Studies
http://www.georgetown.edu/labyrinth/labyrinth-home.html

This is a dedicated site for those interested in Medieval history in general and the Church in those times in particular.

Guide to Early Church Documents
ftp://iclnet93.iclnet.org/pub/resources/christian-history.html

The study of the Early Church is fascinating and can teach us many lessons even today.

Writings of the Apostolic Fathers
gopher://ccat.sas.upenn.edu:3333/11/Religious/ChurchWriters/Apostolic Fathers

I hope you remember who they are.

Divine Mercy Homepage
http://www.cais.com/npacheco/mercy/faustina.html

This is a very special homepage. Twice I have attended Divine Mercy Sunday at the Marian Fathers' shrine in Stockbridge, Massachusetts.

Shroud of Turin Homepage
http://www.cais.com/npacheco/shroud/turin.html

Fortunately this most important relic was saved from destruction by fire for the second time. A fireman carried it out before it suffered any damage in this recent fire.

*Dead Sea Scrolls
http://sunsite.unc.edu/expo/deadsea.scrolls.exhibit/intro.html

Can you believe that these important scrolls were found by a boy tending sheep?

What is Catholicism?

The Catechism of the Catholic Church
http:// christusrex.org/www1/CDHN/ccc.html

It was Cardinal Law of Boston who suggested a universal catechism.

The Catechism of St. Pius X
http://abbey.apana.org.au/official/catechisms/piusx.htm

St. Pius X was the Archbishop and Patriarch of Venice before becoming Pope.

The Gallagher's Catholic Apologetics
http://net2.netacc.net/~mafg/

Catholic Answers:
http://www.catholic.com/cgi-shl/index.pl

Catholic Apologetics. If you haven't looked at this one that I put in my Top 20 picks of Chapter 5, please go look at it now!

This Rock
http://www.catholic.com/Rock/ThisRock.htm

Monthly magazine. Put together by the group above.

Defending the Faith Conference Tapes
http://listserv.american.edu/catholic/other/defend.faith

You can obtain the teachings, exhortations, and workshops from the 1993 "Defending the Faith IV Conference" at Franciscan University.

*Catholic Apologetics Articles
http://www.sky.net/~mntssyst/catholic.html

Another resource for you on Catholicism.

*The Immaculata Homepage
http://nyx10.cs.du.edu:8001/~dprabowo/Immaculata.html

This one is about Our Lady.

Catholic Art and Architecture

Vatican City Pictorial Tour
http://www.christusrex.org/www1/citta/0-Citta.html

Be sure to take this tour, even if you have actually been there.

The Raphael Stanze and Loggia
http://www.christusrex.org/www1/stanzas/0-Raphael.html

The Italian Renaissance painter and architect Raphael Sanzio was born in 1483 and died in 1520.

A Worldwide Tour of Churches
http://www.christusrex.org/www1/splendors/splendors.html

Take a whirlwind tour of churches throughout the world.

The Image of Divine Mercy
http://www.cais.com/npacheco/mercy/dmpaint.html

The white and red rays coming out from this image represent the Blood and Water that flowed from the wounded side of Jesus after he was struck by the soldier's lance.

Catholic Theology

*The Theology 100 Online Glossary
http://www.nd.edu/~jvanderw/theo100/glossary.htm

St. Thomas Aquinas: Summa Theologica
http://www.knight.org/advent/summa/summa.htm

His great work, in which he tried to bring all of theology together into one work.

Catholic Prayers and Missals

Apostleship of Prayer
http://www.ewtn.com/ap/ap.htm

A worldwide association of Catholics and other Christians who strive to make their ordinary, everyday lives apostolically effective. They do this by offering themselves and everything they do each day in union with Christ's sacrifice in the Mass. They thereby cooperate with Jesus in His mission of bringing salvation to everyone. Find out everything about them. Also, read about the 12 Promises of Jesus to Saint Margaret Mary Alacoque and the homily from Saint Claude la Colombière's canonization Mass by Pope John Paul II.

Prayers of the Monks of Adoration
http://www.rc.net/org/monks/ourprays.htm

These are the specific prayers we monks pray every day. Please join us in praying them.

*A Prayer to Our Lady of Guadalupe
http://www.nd.edu/~taranda/lupe.html

I wish more people from the United States and Canada would visit this Mexican shrine.

Kenneth Morrill's List of Prayers
http://webdesk.com/catholic/prayers/index.html

This is a very large list of prayers. Why not pray your way through them?

*St. Dominic's Nine Ways of Praying
http://www.ultranet.com/~bellvill/wpcs/stjude/nineway.html

This is a great aid to prayer given to us by a great saint. Even though I write a column on prayer, I had never heard of this before.

Information on Centering Prayer
http://www.io.com/user/lefty/Centering_Prayer.html

Ignatian Spiritual Exercises
http://ccel.wheaton.edu/ignatius/exercises/exercises.html

Latin Resources

A Treasury of Latin Prayers
http://www.cs.cmu.edu/Web/People/spok/catholic/latin-prayers/index.html

Ora pro nobis. Do you know what that means?

A Collection of Canticles (in Latin)
gopher://ftp.std.com/11/obi/book/Canticles

The Rosary

The Marian Hour Rosary (with audio)
http://netpage.bc.ca/marianhr/

L' Heure Mariale Radio Rosaire
http://netpage.bc.ca/marianhr/francais.html

Same as the previous but in French.

The Rosary Center: The Rosary Confraternity of the Catholic Church
http://www.teleport.com/~rosary/

A wonderful group to join. A great way to share in the prayers of this worldwide prayer group. To be a member of this confraternity is a great blessing.

*The Rosary for the Web
http://www.nd.edu/~jvanderw/rosary/rosary.htm

It's great the Rosary is on the Web. Do you remember when the Pope John Paul II opened the last Marian Year by leading a worldwide Rosary via satellite? Perhaps the next one will be via the Internet!

*A "Catholic Answers" Article on the Rosary
http://www.csn.net/advent/tracts/rosary.htm

The Rosary is attacked by those who do not understand it. Learn how to defend it.

*Laetitiae Sanctae: Commending Devotion to the Rosary
http://listserv.american.edu:70/catholic/church/papal/leo.xiii/l13ro3.txt

Encyclical of Pope Leo XIII on Devotion to the Rosary.

Divine Mercy Chaplet

The Chaplet of Divine Mercy
http://www.cais.com/npacheco/mercy/faustina.html

How to pray it. I recommend this devotion for everyone. Be sure to pray it for the dying.

Devotion to the Divine Mercy
http://web.frontier.net/Apparitions/Faustina.homepage.html

A really wonderful devotion. Never despair of God's mercy. He will forgive and forget if you will be sorry and repent!

Way of the Cross

The Stations of The Cross with Meditations
http://convex.cc.uky.edu/~jatuck00/Religion/Stations.html

If you can't go to the Holy Land, why not make a spiritual trip there to honor the final path that Jesus walked before His death?

Gregorian Chant

Cantus: Database of Divine Office Gregorian Chant
gopher://vmsgopher.cua.edu/11gopher_root_music:[20_cantus]

Gregorian Chant has become very popular. The Benedictine monks in Spain have had great success with their Gregorian Chant CD.

*Gregorian Chant Homepage
http://www.music.princeton.edu/chant_html/

There is probably nothing more soothing than to listen to this chant.

Liturgy and the Liturgical Year

Adoremeus: Society for Renewal of the Sacred Liturgy
http://www.erinet.com/aquinas/arch/adoremus.html

See this directory's Top 10 sites for more information on this one.

*Joyful Noise
http://www.geopages.com/TheTropics/1552/

Catholic Liturgical Music. You don't have to have a super great voice to partici-pate in your parish choir. Why not give it a try?

Calculation of the Ecclesiastical Calendar
http://cssa.stanford.edu/~marcos/ec-cal.html

If you ever become trapped in the jungle with only your notebook computer and cellular phone, you now have the means to figure out the Church's calendar yourself.

*Mass Readings and Liturgical Calendar (Roman)
http://www.erinet.com/aquinas/arch/rcnov.html

Meditating on the Mass readings can be a great spiritual aid.

Catholic Education

*Christendom College
http://www.erinet.com/aquinas/arch/christdm/christdm.htm

This one is a small Catholic college in Virginia. You may want to look for it in the Catholic college list in Chapter 7.

Franciscan University of Steubenville
http://www.franuniv.edu/

A Catholic college known for its orthodox theology, dedication to the Church, and inspiring prayer life. This university is run by the Third Order Regular Francis-cans and its president is the well-known Father Michael Scanlon, T.O.R.

*Regina Coeli Academy
http://www.ictheweb.com/rca

Regina Coeli is Latin for Queen of Heaven, one of the titles given to Mary, the Mother of Jesus.

*St. Antoninus Institute
http://www.erinet.com/aquinas/arch/antonin/antonin.htm

You will find this one earlier in this book. It is dedicated to showing you how to bring Christ into the workplace.

Catholic Hierarchy and Organization

A Directory of Bishops' Conferences
http://www.erinet.com/aquinas/arch/bishops.html

Bishops' conferences are comprised of the Bishops of a country who meet periodically to discuss matters pertaining to the Church in that country.

*U.S. Ecclesiastical Provinces
http://www.erinet.com/aquinas/arch/province.html

A Church province consists of the territory of a metropolitan. So what's that? An archdiocese plus the surrounding dioceses.

Pro-Life and Resources

Human Life International (HLI)
http://www.catholic.org/hli/

(English, Spanish, Polish, or French.) Here you can locate an office nearest you by looking at a map of the world and clicking on a flashing dot for more information. Find out about the following issues: abortion, assisted suicide, chastity/sex education, contraception, euthanasia, feminism, fetal tissue research, homosexuality, natural family planning, AIDS, planned parenthood, population control, pornography, sterilization, and the United Nations. If that's not enough, look into their 10 different programs and services.

Priests for Life
http://www.priestsforlife.org/

Father Frank Pavone is the director of this officially approved association of Catholic clergy who give special emphasis to the pro-life teachings of the Church. They offer ongoing assistance to the clergy in addressing the topics of abortion and euthanasia, and training and resources to the entire pro-life movement.

 Ultimate Pro-Life Resource List
http://www.prolife.org/ultimate

Claimed to be the most comprehensive listing of right-to-life resources on the Internet. From looking at the page, they may just be right. There are discussion forums and a live chat area here. You can select from the following: Pro-life Infonet, Organizations, Adoption Resources, Pro-life News, Politics, Opinions, Educational Factsheets, Miscellaneous Info, Health Info, Abortion Alternatives, and What's New at Ultimate. You will also find post-abortion help, a twice-a-month newsletter, pregnancy assistance, and—believe it or not—even more. See them in my Top 20 picks in Chapter 5.

 *American Life League
http://www.ahoynet.com/~all/index.html

An excellent pro-life apostolate headed by the hard-working and dedicated Judy Brown.

 Couple to Couple League Int'l
http://www.missionnet.com/~mission/cathlc/ccl/

 Catholics United for Life
http://www.mich.com/~buffalo/

A nationwide organization with branches in a number of cities. They come together to pray and give witness for the protection of all pre-born babies. See pictures of different tombs or cemeteries dedicated to the many babies who have died. You will find documents about abortion, book links, and a lot of other pro-life links.

 Children of the Rosary
http://www.paloverde.com/~cor/corindex.html

Their purpose is to peacefully pray outside places where abortions are done legally. Also, they work to educate people about the truth of abortion, about pre-born babies, and the disclosure of the lies of the "pro-choice" agenda through the distribution of CoR Newsletters, Newsgrams, and flyers.

*The Pro-Life Shopping Guide
http://crnet.org/antonin/listab.htm

This one has an interesting title that you might want to look up.

*The St. Antoninus Institute Pro-Life Home Business
http://crnet.org/antonin/plhb.htm

Here is another interesting one on which you might want to find more information.

*St. Thomas Aquinas Pro-Life Organization
http://www.airmail.net/~stthomas/staplo.html

It certainly couldn't hurt to name a pro-life group after a saint who so earnestly pursued the truth.

Catholic Organizations' Resources

Adoremus: Society for the Renewal of Sacred Liturgy
http://www.erinet.com/aquinas/arch/adoremus.html

Find out more about them at the beginning of this directory under the Top 10.

*The Blue Army of Our Lady of Fatima
http://www.erinet.com/aquinas/arch/bluearmy/index.htm

This wonderful international apostolate was made as successful as it is today by the work of John Haffert. They are dedicated to Our Lady and her messages given at Fatima. The American center and shrine is in Washington, New Jersey.

*Catholic Relief Services
http://www.charity.com/crs.html

Aiding the hungry, the needy, and those suffering from disasters throughout the world. Look into this one to see all the good works in which the Church is involved.

*The Catholic Family Magnificat
http://www.erinet.com/aquinas/arch/magnificat/index.htm

This sounds great. Look them up.

Couple to Couple League
http://www.itek.net/~mission/cathlc/ccl/

Creative Communication Center
http://www.connect.net/ccca/

You can find out more about this group earlier in this book.

*Knights of Columbus Information
http://www.nd.edu/~knights/supreme/info.html

This is a Catholic men's group. They are in many countries. My father has been a member for years.

*Latin Liturgy Association
http://www.erinet.com/aquinas/arch/latinlit/lla.htm

Perhaps this site is for you—if you like Latin.

Legion of Mary
http://transporter.com/lom/

Would you like to join the Legion? They are major evangelizers in Korea as I learned when visiting there.

*National Association of Catholic Families
http://www.interaccess.com/users/dfroula/nacf.html

Families need to stick together to support each other in the Faith.

National Association of Hispanic Priests of the USA
http://www.christusrex.org/www1/NAHP/NAHP-index.html

An association of priestly fraternity and support for Hispanic priests in the United States. Some photos, some English and, of course, a lot of Spanish.

Newman Centers & Catholic Chaplaincies: Listed and Wanted
http://www.cco.caltech.edu/~newman/OtherNC.html

If your Catholic campus center is not on this list, now is the time to get on it.

Opus Dei
http://www.opusdei.org/

They have centers all over the world. The priest who founded them was recently declared Blessed.

Priests for Life
http://www.priestsforlife.org/

All priests should be priests for life. It is good to see an organized effort by priests to fight for life.

United States Catholic Historical Society
http://www.catholic.org/uschs

Founded for "the appreciation and preservation of American Catholic Heritage." The Society accomplishes its mission by publishing scholarly texts, conducting seminars and lecture series, and funding research projects.

Catholic Media Resources

Note: The following listing has been chopped down considerably by the Webmaster of this directory so you won't find some of those I list.

Catholic Answers
http://www.catholic.com/

Do you have questions about the Faith? Look them up here.

*Catholic Commentary (MMR Publishing)
http://www.top.net/cathcom/

Already mentioned earlier, you will find at least one questionable Catholic link recommended here.

Catholic Commentary
http://www.veritas.org.sg/

You will find this one on the Archdiocese of Singapore homepage.

*Corragio!
http://www.erinet.com/aquinas/arch/corragio/coraggio.htm

For Catholic youth. Is this in Italian? "Corragio" is Italian for courage.

Daughters of St. Paul (Canada)
http://www.netrover.com/~pauline/

They are very active in the media apostolate. After all, look who they took for their patron saint!

Daughters of St. Paul
http://pauline.inter.net/pauline/

These sisters publish books, magazines, videos, and audiotapes. I have visited their U.S. mother house located in Boston. It is a vast building with almost every type of media ministry.

EWTN: Eternal World Television Network
http://www.ewtn.com/

There center is in Irondale, Alabama, an unlikely place for a Catholic network as there are few Catholics residing there.

Franciscan University Press
http://Gabriel.franuniv.edu/press.html

This is the publishing house of the Franciscan University of Steubenville.

Ignatius Press
http://www.ignatius.com/

A great selection of books, including the theological writings of Adrienne von Spyer, the Swiss physican, mystic, stigmatist, and foundress.

*Immaculata Magazine
http://www.crnet.org/marytown/zine.htm

For some years this magazine wasn't being published. I'm pleased that it is being published again by the Conventual Franciscans at Marytown in Libertyville, Illinois. The magazine promotes the Marian spirtuality of St. Maximillian Kolbe.

KathWeb (Austria)
http://www.austria.eu.net/kathweb

In German. They host the Austrian diocesan homepages.

*Marytown Press
http://www.erinet.com/aquinas/arch/mtnpress/catalog.htm

This is the same Marytown I mentioned previously. I have visited this wonderful place to help maintain their Perpetual Eucharistic Adoration when the friars were occupied with a Marian congress.

*New Advent: Catholic Periodicals
http://www.knight.org/advent/linkperi.htm

New Advent was one of my Top 20 in Chapter 5 so I imagine their periodicals must be pretty good.

Notizie dal Mondo
http://www.christusrex.org/www1/news/mondo.html

News of the world, in Italian.

*The St. Augustine Catholic Magazine
http://128.227.164.224/sac.htm

Did you know that St. Augustine's sister also founded a religious community?

*Our Sunday Visitor
http://www.catholic.net/osv/

A publication for families that is the largest weekly national U.S. Catholic publication.

Radio Vaticana
http://www.uni-passau.de/ktf/vatican.html

In German. Did you know that in German you can link words together to form one long word?

*Radio Vaticana
http://www.milano.ccr.it/Radio/sc0408.html

In Italian. The people in Italy are very encouraging to foreigners trying to learn their language, or so I'm told.

Rowan & Associates, Catholic Publishers
http://www.polaris.net/~chp/rowan/home.htm

They bring in-service training, program evaluation, administrative support, and professional advice for catechists and other parish ministries.

Spirituality for Today
http://www.spirituality.org/

Don't visit this homepage tomorrow; do it "today."

St. Bede's Publications
http://www.stbedes.org/

Ordering books from St. Bede's is a way to help the publishers, the Benedictine Nuns of St. Scholastica's Priory.

*St. Elias Press

http://fellini.syr.vcomm.net/~pizzut19/

Normally we don't think of Old Testament figures as saints but some of them definitely were holy people, as Sacred Scripture attests.

St. Mary's Press

http://www.smp.smumn.edu/

A contemporary expression of the Catholic Church's mission to proclaim the Good News of Jesus Christ and the mission of the De La Salle Christian Brothers, to provide a human and Christian education to young people.

The Tabernacle (The Monks of Adoration)

http://www.rc.net/org/monks/

Newsletter with articles on Our Lady, on prayer, for children, about the monastery, the Eucharist and more.

*The Wire

http://www.roehampton.ac.uk/link/wire/The Wire/

Get wired by visiting this one.

Book and Video Distributors

*Marian Communications Online Catalog

http://mariancomm.org/CATALOG.html

This is an extraordinary apostolate that produces the finest religious documentary videos. I know the filmmaker Drew Mariani very well.

*Catholic Answers' Video/Audio Tapes

http://www.catholic.com/~edit/tapes.html

For those interested in knowing more about their Faith and sharing it with others.

*A List of Catholic Bookstores Throughout the Country
http://web.sau.edu/~cmiller/cbook.html

This can be a great help if you are looking for a book or are promoting a book.

The Catholic Shop
http://transporter.com/cathshop/

Need to do some shopping? You can find just about anything here. This is a family business owned and operated by Bill and Mary Peffley. They have actual shops in Pennsylvania and Virginia. See their online catalog of merchandise.

Sacred Heart Book Store
http://www.connix.com/~ffi/

This is a great page to look at even if you are not shopping. The opening page has a beautiful image of the Immaculate Heart of Mary. You can learn about the Franciscans who maintain this page and of their spirituality. Also, you will want to pay a visit to the "Marian Info-Center." Maybe you will have more luck finding the bookstore than I did.

*Serenity Place—A Catholic Gift Store
http://www.serenity-place.com/index.html

Try this one, too. We could all use a bit of serenity.

Catholic Focus Productions
http://members.aol.com/cathfocus/focus.htm

Their mission is to serve Catholics worldwide as a significant resource for audio and video programs that cover all aspects of the faith. They also maintain a complete audio and video production facility to serve priests, conferences, and organizations requiring this capability within the Catholic Church. They have produced some videos of talks that Brother Craig and I have given.

Any suggestions for additions to this list e-mail: aquinas@erinet.com

 OUR LADY

http://www.erinet.com/aquinas/arch/marian.html

It goes without saying that there is usually a listing for Mary in a Catholic directory. She has played and continues to play an essential role in our salvation. And there's more—all of us need a mother's love. Anybody who has implored Mary, in any way, has experienced her maternal care. She is not only a great intercessor before the throne of God; she is a great person to get to know.

Yes, Mary is right beside us, guiding us safely to where she already is. With all the apparitions of the Mother of God that have taken place throughout history, who could doubt that God wishes her to play an important role in our lives? She doesn't come by her own power but by God's power. So if God thinks she is important for our spiritual life, who are we to question it?

This Marian index changes regularly, so you may not find links to all of the following sites.

 The Marian Hour Rosary

http://netpage.bc.ca/marianhr/

With audio.

 Frequently Asked Questions About the Virgin Mary

http://www.udayton.edu/mary/questions.html

This page is maintained by The Marian Library/International Marian Research Institute. You will find 15 questions along with the answers concerning Our Lady. I wonder if they chose 15 in honor of the 15 mysteries of the Rosary?

 The Mary Page

http://www.udayton.edu/mary/

Maintained by the Marian Library/International Marian Research, an international center of research and study on the role of Mary in Christian life. The Marian Library holds the largest collection of printed information on Mary, and has developed into a center with many activities. You will certainly want to visit the "Gallery" for pictures with commentary of contemporary Marian art from around the world. This is a page you simply must visit!

Catholic Marian Centers USA
http://www.missionnet.com/~mission/cathlc/marian.html

Here you will find the addresses of centers by state. There is probably one near you.

Fatima Resources
http://www.cais.com/npacheco/fatima/fatres.html

Here you can find addresses for Fatima centers and how to acquire Fatima literature.

*Medjugorje at Huizen
http://huizen.dds.nl/~jgamleus/mary.html

If you can't get enough on the one above, try looking for this one.

Messages from Medjugorje at Stanford University
http://www-ksl.stanford.edu/people/decapite/docs/medj94.html

One of the visionaries who sees Mary receives monthly messages from her for the world. You can find these messages here.

Our Lady of Medjugorje at Stanford University
http://www-cs-students.stanford.edu/~marco/docs/medjugorje.html

There are some FAQs here about Mary and apparitions. You will find pictures here as well as previous and past messages. Toward the bottom is a sizable table of related links that you won't want to miss. One in particular called "Photographs of Mary" caught my eye.

Medjugorje Online
http://www.eclipse.it/medjugorje/

(English, Italian, German, or French.) Here you will find the publication entitled "Echo of Mary Queen of Peace" (formerly Echo of Medjugorje) in 16 languages, messages in many languages, related links, a nice photo of St. James Church in Medjugorje and one of Vicka, one of the visionaries.

Apparitions of Jesus and Mary
http://web.frontier.net/Apparitions/apparitions.html

A good spot to see major apparitions of the nineteenth and twentieth centuries arranged in chart form according to year, location, visionaries, and Church-approval status. You can find further information on some apparitions. Find out what Heaven is trying to tell us and what Church approval of an apparition means.

*Apparitions!
http://www.frontier.net/~mbd/apparitions.html

Reading about apparitions can truly enrich your spirituality. God loves us so much that He frequently sends Our Lady and saints from Heaven to direct us on our pilgrimage of Faith here on earth.

*Image of Our Lady of Guadalupe
http://www.nd.edu/~jvanderw/guadalup.gif

There is a lot of meaning in this image of Our Lady. Did you know that an atheist eye doctor was converted after seeing this image? He changed because he saw in the eyes of the image the same inverted image that you would see in any human eye.

Dickeyville Grotto
http://www.lafayette.edu/niless/awsthome.htm

Get a picture tour of this grotto with commentary.

POPE JOHN PAUL II

http://www.erinet.com/aquinas/arch/pope.html

The Pope, who is the bishop of Rome and successor of St. Peter, the first Pope, "is the perpetual and visible source and foundation of the unity both of the bishops and of the whole company of the faithful." (Vatican II, LG 23.) By reason of his office as

Vicar of Christ, the Pope has full, supreme, and universal power over the whole Church.

Now, obviously, the Bishops have authority in their own diocese; the Pope doesn't intervene unless there is very good reason. Also, he has many cardinals in various congregations at the Vatican who help him govern the Church. Far from dictators, the Pope and Bishops are pastors who serve the People of God.

There is no doubt that without the Vicar of Christ, the Church would have been splintered into a million pieces by the many assaults made on it throughout history. We should be ever thankful to God for giving us the great grace of having a pope.

*Papal Visit '95 (from Newark, New Jersey)
http://www.pope.pfmc.net/welcome.html

The pope always gives speeches appropriate to the country he is visiting. The media usually gives you about 10 seconds of them so you might want to read the entire text.

Speeches and Writings of Pope John Paul II
http://www.knight.org/advent/Popes/ppjp02.htm

They are ordered by date. You will find the Latin title, an English translation of it, and the date it was made.

The Unofficial Homepage of Pope John Paul II
http://www.erols.com/klnorman/Pope/Pope.html

Here you can find out about books and compact discs available by Pope John Paul II, a more or less complete bibliography of his writings, and links to other resources for Pope John Paul II.

Countries Pope John Paul II Has Visited
http://www.nj.com/popepage/map.html

Each country ordered according to the year of his visit. It gives the exact date also. John Paul II is the most traveled Pope in the 2,000-year history of the Church. I was exhausted just looking at the map of his journeys found here!

VATICAN

http://www.erinet.com/aquinas/arch/vatican.html

You probably already know this, but the Vatican is considered a country, separate from Italy. (It is surely one of the smallest countries in the world with only around 100 acres!) That is why the Church has diplomatic ambassadors to various countries. It is interesting how God arranged it so the Church could easily communicate with the modern world through channels it understands.

General Vatican Information

The Official Vatican Web Site
http://www.vatican.va/GB/

You wouldn't want to miss this one, though it does have frames. If you want to avoid the frames, see John Mark Ockerbloom's Vatican index in Chapter 8.

Tour of the Sistine Chapel
http://www.christusrex.org/www1/sistine/0-Tour.html

Built by Pope Sixtus IV, so it is called Sistine.

Vatican City Tourist Information
http://www.city.net/countries/vatican_city/

If you are going to Vatican City, you definitely want to see this page. Not a bad place for the just plain curious to visit either.

Vatican Art Exhibit
http://lcweb.loc.gov/exhibits/vatican/toc.html

First in a series of exhibitions that the Library of Congress plans to present about great libraries of the world.

Vatican News Sources

Vatican Radio Files in RealAudio
http://www.wrn.org/vatican-radio/

(English/French/German.) If you can't get it over the radio, why not through the computer?

Radio Vaticano (German)
http://www.uni-passau.de/ktf/vatican.html

How good is your German?

Sources for Vatican Documents

Recent Documents of the Church
http://www.cco.caltech.edu/~trwhite/Recent_Catholic_Documents.html

More important reading. We always like to read the latest.

Vatican Statements

These are statements issued by various Sacred Congregations and other ruling bodies in the Roman Catholic Church.

Letter to the Bishop of Boston
http://listserv.american.edu/catholic/church/vatican/holoff.txt

Concerning the issue of salvation outside the Church. The St. Benedict Center, which has a homepage, is one of the groups founded by a Jesuit priest in Boston who said the Church taught that only Catholics could be saved. This letter to the Archbishop of Boston explained that it is possible for those outside the Church to still be saved, *through* the Church. Unfortunately, some of this priest's followers continue to teach his error.

General Catechetical Directory (1971)

http://listserv.american.edu/catholic/church/vatican/gencatdi.txt

A guide for catechetics. Anybody involved in this work should read this.

On General Absolution (1972)

http://listserv.american.edu/catholic/church/vatican/p6absol.txt

Discusses this particular form for administering the Sacrament of Reconciliation. This is always an extraordinary way for receiving this sacrament.

Declaration on Procured Abortion (1974)

http://listserv.american.edu/catholic/church/vatican/cdfabort.txt

An urgently needed document. Any Catholic who has an abortion or assists in one is automatically excommunicated.

Declaration on Euthanasia (1980)

http://listserv.american.edu/catholic/church/vatican/cdfeuth.txt

Euthanasia refers to killing those who are ill, and to various forms of assisted suicide. Many are pushing to legalize this.

Declaration on Masonic Associations (1983)

http://listserv.american.edu/catholic/church/vatican/masons83.html

Catholics are not allowed to join the Masons, an anti-Catholic secretive society.

On Liberation Theology (1984)

http://listserv.american.edu/catholic/church/vatican/libtheo.asc

This is an important document, giving guidelines and pointing out errors.

On the Pastoral Care of Homosexual Persons (1986)

http://listserv.american.edu/catholic/church/vatican/gay.pastoral

Priests and others who do work in this area will want to read this document.

Shelter for the Homeless (Iustitia et Pax)
http://listserv.american.edu/catholic/church/vatican/housing.asc

(1988) A document encouraging compassion and caring. Like her founder, Jesus Christ, the Church always has a special concern for the poor.

Joseph Cardinal Ratzinger on AIDS
http://listserv.american.edu/catholic/church/vatican/ratzaids.html

(1988) Find out what the Cardinal has to say about this disease that is claiming the lives of so many.

Profession of Faith and Oath of Fidelity
http://listserv.american.edu/catholic/church/vatican/cathoath.txt

(1989) As Catholics we profess a common Creed of beliefs. On Sunday at Mass we pray the Creed that is a summary of what we assent to by belief.

Regarding Legislation on Gay People
http://listserv.american.edu/catholic/church/vatican/bishops.gay

(1990) The Church's teaching clearly stated on this issue.

Joseph Cardinal Ratzinger on Veritatis Splendor
http://listserv.american.edu/catholic/church/vatican/rat-onvs.txt

(1993) The Cardinal on the Pope's Encyclical on morality.

Agreement of Holy See and Israel
http://listserv.american.edu/catholic/church/vatican/vatisr.txt

(1993) This had great historic significance.

Responsum ad Dubium: Concerning the Teaching Contained in Ordinatio Sacerdotalis
http://www.electriciti.com/cin/cdfrad.html

(1995) A doubt was raised regarding how the teaching on women's ordination was to be taken.

 THE RELIGIOUS

http://www.erinet.com/aquinas/arch/religi.html

"The state of life which is constituted by the profession of the evangelical counsels, while not entering into the hierarchical structure of the Church, belongs undeniably to her life and holiness." (Vatican II, LG 44, paragraph 4.) The perfection of charity, to which everyone is called, is lived out in a special way in consecrated life. A person obliges himself or herself to poverty, chastity, and obedience within a permanent state of life recognized by the Church. Obviously God calls certain people to this vocation as can be seen throughout the history of the Church. Various communities have sprung up under the inspiration of the Holy Spirit to live out these counsels in a particular way. Each community has a special charism. This charism meets certain needs in the Church or the world at a particular time in history.

Franciscan Friars of Marytown
http://www.ewtn.com/marytown/mtown.htm

I have visited this friary. They have a beautiful chapel where the laity help the friars maintain perpetual Eucharistic adoration. Their chapel is featured often on Mother Angelica's television network.

 THE SAINTS

http://www.erinet.com/aquinas/arch/saints.html

Is it possible for a person to be canonized while living? Mother Teresa of Calcutta was called a "living saint." One reason no living people are canonized is that a saint has to have persevered and completed his pilgrimage on this earth and already be in Heaven. This doesn't mean that some people living today aren't saintly. There are good candidates for sainthood on earth, but we have to wait to see whether they become canonized! I hope your name is added to this listing one day!

 Catholic Online Saint's Page
http://www.catholic.org/saints/saints.html

There is a lot here. See their angel pages and saints index, and use their saints search. Learn all about saints, their feast days, Doctors of the Church, holy facts, Irish saints, patron saints, and each month's special saints.

By Individual Saint

Anthony of Padua
http://www.contrib.andrew.cmu.edu/usr/el28/Anthony.html

Meet this Doctor of the Church, great preacher, and helper who finds lost things (d. 1231).

*Antoninus of Florence
ftp://ftp.crnet.org/library/antonin/antoninu.asc

Learn about this Dominican Archbishop of Florence (d. 1459).

Aquinas, Thomas (Catholic Encyclopedia)
http://www.knight.org/advent/cathen/14663b.htm

Study the homepage of this scholarly saint.

Christina of Liege
http://www.contrib.andrew.cmu.edu/usr/el28/christina.html

Learn about this saint who seems to have come back from the dead!

Clare of Assisi
http://listserv.american.edu/catholic/franciscan/clare.info.html

Visit with this friend of St. Francis and foundress of the Poor Clares.

Edmund the Martyr
http://www.contrib.andrew.cmu.edu/usr/el28/stedmund.html

Read about this king of Norfolk who would rather die than betray his Faith.

Elizabeth Ann Seton
http://www.contrib.andrew.cmu.edu/usr/el28/seton.html

This wife, mother, widow, and foundress of a community of sisters is the first American-born person to be canonized.

Faustina Kowalska (Blessed)
http://www.marian.org/apostle.htm

Learn about this recently beatified Polish sister.

Francis of Assisi
http://www.contrib.andrew.cmu.edu/usr/el28/Francis.html

The beloved St. Francis, lover of holy poverty and friend of animals.

Francis Antony of Lucera
http://www.contrib.andrew.cmu.edu/usr/el28/lucera.html

Learn about this Italian saint (d. 1742) who had a special devotion to the Immaculate Conception.

Francis Xavier
http://www.stfx.ca/stfx/introducing/saint-fx.html

Check out this homepage about the great Spanish Jesuit (d. 1552) who was an apostle to India and is the patron of the Missions.

Isidore the Farmer
http://www.contrib.andrew.cmu.edu/usr/el28/isidore.html

Learn about this saint who would go to Mass while angels did the plowing for him.

*John Baptist de la Salle
http://www.dlsu.edu.ph/offices/sps/lasalliana/lasalle.txt

Visit with this French founder of the Christian Brothers.

John of the Cross
http://www.ocd.or.at/eng/juan.htm

Learn about this great Spanish Carmelite mystic, poet, and Doctor of the Church.

*John Duns Scotus (Blessed)
http://www.ici.net/cust_pages/ffi/scotus.html

Visit the homepage of this Franciscan Blessed (d. 1308) who was devoted to Our Lady and brilliantly explained the doctrine of her Immaculate Conception.

*John Henry Newman (Venerable)
http://dolphin.upenn.edu/~newman/bio.html

Learn about this English convert and Cardinal.

*Josemaria Escriva de Balaguer (Blessed)
http://web1.cti.unav.es/paginas/BJEB.html

The founder of Opus Dei.

Joseph
http://www.contrib.andrew.cmu.edu/usr/el28/joseph.html

Be sure to visit this homepage of the Patron of the Church, the dying, and workers.

Kateri Tekakwitha (Blessed)
http://www.contrib.andrew.cmu.edu/usr/el28/Kateri.html

Learn about this Native American woman (d. 1680) who lived a life of prayer and penance.

Martin de Porres
http://www.cais.com/agf/martindp.htm

Dominican brother, porter at his friary, friend of St. Rose of Lima, and thoughtful provider for hungry animals.

Margaret of Cortona
http://www.contrib.andrew.cmu.edu/usr/el28/Cortona.html

Find out about this great Italian penitent (d. 1297).

Margaret of Scotland
http://www.contrib.andrew.cmu.edu/usr/el28/MofScotland.html

Learn about this generous and charitable Queen of Scotland (d. 1093).

Maria de la Cabeza
http://www.contrib.andrew.cmu.edu/usr/el28/cabeza.html

The wife (d.c. 1175) of St. Isidore, the farmer listed earlier. I bet you didn't think any married couples were both canonized. Haven't you heard the expression, "He (or she) must be a saint to live with her (or him)?"

Blessed Virgin Mary
http://www.erinet.com/aquinas/arch/marian.html

Be sure to visit this homepage dedicated to the Queen of the Saints.

*Maximilian Kolbe
http://www.ici.net/cust_pages/ffi/whostmax.html

Polish Franciscan and heroic martyr of the twentieth century.

Patrick
http://www.mcs.net/~jorn/html/jj/patrick.html

Even if today is not March 17, don't be neglecting to stop in for a cup a tea with this patron of Ireland.

Philip Neri
http://www.contrib.andrew.cmu.edu/usr/el28/Neri.html

This cheerful saint is known for his great love of God—so great that his heart actually expanded and pushed out his ribs.

Pier Giorgio Frassati (Blessed)
http://www.cs.cmu.edu/~arivera/Frassati.html

Student and athlete (d. 1925), he is a great inspiration for the young.

Roch
http://www.contrib.andrew.cmu.edu/usr/el28/roch.html

Read about this saint who was put in prison by his own relatives (d. 1378). I sure hope that never happens to me!

Teresa of Avila
http://www.ocd.or.at/eng/teresa.htm

Have a chat with this strong Spanish Carmelite nun, foundress, talented writer, and loveable friend.

*Valentine
http://travel.it/relig/story.htm

Yes, this saint and martyr (d.c. 269) has his feast day on February 14!

THE BISHOPS

http://www.erinet.com/aquinas/arch/bishops.html

Besides the Pope, "the bishops too have been appointed by the Holy Spirit, and are successors of the Apostles as pastors of souls." (Vatican II, CD, paragraph 2.) They have the office of teaching, sanctifying, and governing the portion of God's people entrusted to them. We need to have a great love and reverence for these men that God has placed over us. You cannot just "follow the Pope." We are more specifically under obedience to the Bishop appointed over the diocese in which we reside. We follow our local Bishop, providing he is obeying the Pope.

Catholic Conference of Illinois (US)
http://www.archdiocese-chgo/conference.htm

People in Illinois will especially want to see this one. There is also more information here of benefit to everyone.

*Canadian Conference of Catholic Bishops (English)
http://www.cam.org/~cccb/english.cgi

Want to learn something about the Church in Canada? The conference page is a good place to start.

 The Canadian Conference of Catholic Bishops (French)
http://www.cam.org/~cccb/french.cgi

Want to improve your French and learn about the Church in Canada at the same time?

 Chilean Catholic Conference of Bishops
http://www.puc.cl/vic/texto/

(Español) If you read Spanish, you can learn about the Church in Chile. Of course, anybody can look at the map of the country they have there.

 Bishops' Conference of England & Wales (UK)
http://www.roehampton.ac.uk/link/AandB/bish_cnf

This page is designed to give a general picture of the Catholic Church in England and Wales, and to provide a "jump-off point" to their various dioceses and Catholic organizations on the Internet.

 Bishops' Conference of New Zealand
http://www.catholic.org/newzealand

Look at their news from New Zealand, of the Pope and the Catholic world. Read bishops' biographies and pastoral statements. Find out about the Jubilee year.

WWW DIOCESES

http://www.erinet.com/aquinas/arch/oth-dios.html

Now there are obviously a lot more dioceses listed in this directory on the Internet. I have pared it down to those not already in other diocesan listings in this book. You can still follow the other links to dioceses not listed here.

Foreign Dioceses

Diocese of the World
http://www.katolsk.no/utenriks/

This list of ecclesial jurisdictions is organized alphabetically by country. You will find a link to the diocese as well.

*Diocese of Edmonton Canada
http://www.supernet.ab.ca/Mall/Religion/Western/Parish/edmcity.html

The Historical Diocese of Zagreb, Croatia
http://bjesomar.srce.hr:1099/

Museum exhibit. You don't want to miss this virtual three-floor museum, with English commentary.

Foreign Parishes: Canadian Parishes
http://www.supernet.ab.ca/Mall/Religion/Western/parishdir.html

This page covers Alberta and the Northwest of Canada. You will find links to the dioceses of this area along with one to "Three Other Rites" found in Canada.

INFO OTHER REFERENCES FROM THE INDEX

http://www.erinet.com/aquinas/arch/dio.html

Following are some of the links found in the middle of the opening page. I did not put the obvious ones, such as the Vatican link. Others, like the "Treasured Churches of Cincinnati," take you to a certain section in a listing in the table of contents on the left or bottom of this page.

Christ
http://www.erinet.com/aquinas/arch/#christ

Clicking on this one will jump you further down the same homepage to some things to consider about Our Lord.

Daily Mass Readings and Reflection (Navarre Bible)
http://infoweb.magi.com/~menardd/gospel.htm

Gives you a reading for each day of the week.

Catholic World News Daily
http://www.cwnews.com

Their most visible service is the Daily News Briefs, but their services also include full global news coverage including feature stories, Vatican updates, interviews, news analysis, and opinion columns. You can see recent news or explore the archives.

Vatican Information Service
http://www.vatican.va/vis/daysv_en.htm#start

This is a Holy See information system instituted within the framework of the Holy See Press Office, which furnishes information on the pastoral and magisterial activity of the Holy Father and the Holy See.

Catholic Online Press Releases
http://www.catholic.org/cpi/

Remember Catholic Online? If you don't, you must have skipped an awfully big part of this book!

11

Ecclesia Web Service for Catholics

http://www.catholic-church.org/

Unlike the Internet directories listed in previous chapters, Ecclesia, which means "Church" in Latin, is a little different. You will not find Catholic homepages here organized alphabetically or under subject headings. You will only see a hyperlinked list of Web Sites that Ecclesia sponsors. So why did I pick this one to show you? Mainly because Scott Fabian, the President/CEO of The Fabian Corporation organized Ecclesia Web Service in early 1995 as a free resource and conferencing area for parish youth ministers around the world. Not only did I find youth ministry information here, but also an extensive directory of Catholic Schools on the Internet.

There is another reason for showing you this service. It began with a youth minister from St. Luke's parish in Stroudsburg, Pennsylvania, who used his computer talents to fill a need he saw in the Church. He started Ecclesia, which is now devoted to providing quality Web sites to Catholic organizations and promoting Catholic research and networking on the Internet. He even offers free Internet space to Catholic organizations. He can do this because Ecclesia Online Service owns a computer with a direct connection to the Internet. They do not go through someone else.

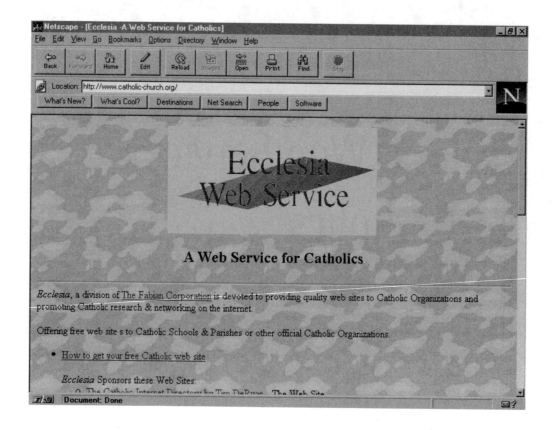

You, too, can use the talents God has given you to help the Church in her mission of bringing Christ to the world. The Internet opens up a vast array of possibilities for you. Pray about ways that you can contribute in this area.

The opening page you will see when you go to the Ecclesia Web page does not contain exactly the same categories as my headings to come. This is because I gave detailed listings only for information pertaining to youth or Catholic education. Scott, the administrator of these pages, has other links listed on his page that are under my section entitled "Other References from the Index."

Scott, now the director of religious formation at St Luke's church in Strouds-burg, received a Bachelor's degree in music from West Chester University and a Master's Degree in Religious Education from Marywood College. He has been married to his wife Joan for four years and they have a little boy, Thomas Matthew. If you have any suggestions, comments, or additions for this Web site, Scott Fabian can be e-mailed at: sfabian@poconos.net.

What's on the Internet for Catholics?

CATHOLIC YOUTH MINISTRY ON THE WWW

http://www.microserve.net/~fabian/ym.html

You will notice two sections on this page: youth ministry and Catholic pointers. I did not list the latter, as you can find them either in this chapter or in other chapters of this book. For the curious, you will find a link for Scott's biographical information at the bottom of the page. Scott did not provide a way of returning to his main page from this opening page. This is not a problem since you can just hit the "Back" button on your browser until you get there or bookmark his opening page so you can return. If you don't know how to use bookmarks, refer to Chapter 7.

Youth Ministry

 Youth Ministers Directory

http://www.microserve.net/~fabian/files/ymdir.html

Information is arranged by country and state. You will find the e-mail address of a contact person for each Youth Ministry, a description of what the ministry is doing, and more information. To be placed on this list free of charge, fill out the directory form on the page.

Franciscan Youth of Switzerland

http://communio.hcbc.hu/jfg.html

In English, German, Italian, or French. Addresses young people between the ages of 16 and 30 years old. Too bad I don't qualify! Read about the lives of St. Francis and St. Clare. Except for a few paragraphs in English concerning the Franciscan Youth group, all the rest of the linked information is in German. But if you follow the link to the lives of St. Francis or St. Clare, you will find photos and information on Assisi, including its monuments and basilicas, history, the city itself, outlying areas, festivals, and traditions. Also, on the youth page are other links, including churches in Switzerland and general information about this country.

Life Teen Ministry
http://www.lifeteen.org/

Great for teens and those who work with them. The purpose of the Life Teen Program is to create an atmosphere that leads high-school teenagers into a relationship with God through the teachings of Jesus Christ and His Church. I have talked about this page before in this book. You will want to see this bright page with the table of contents along the left-hand side. You can't miss the "Take Note" and the "Listen Up" in the middle of the page. I find the yellow shadow makes the words really stand out on the page.

Cross Fire
http://pages.map.com/~david/crossfire.html

Newsletter of the Holy Cross Youth Group, Holy Cross Church, Springfield, Massachusetts. You will not be disappointed when you "Click Here to Enter." The background is stunning in its own way. Since I commented on this page before, I will mention here that they used colored lettering well; it is not hard to read at all. And the table of contents is clear, also.

International Youth Network
http://www.dsdelft.nl/~mpr/

Youth can learn so much by interaction with other young people throughout the world. Here you will find out everything you wanted to know about "World Youth Day," past, present, and future. You can also find reference links.

Employment

Job Postings
http://www.microserve.net/~fabian/files/ymjob.html

This is not a general place to look for work! It is a directory of jobs in youth ministry, a vocation that is both fun and rewarding. The youth ministers I have met are truly committed people. While talking to one, I presumed he went on snow-skiing outings and other recreational trips with the teenagers. He surprised me by saying they had made pilgrimages to Lourdes and other holy places. The teenagers even suggested praying a Rosary at their meetings.

 Resume Bank
http://www.microserve.net/~fabian/files/ymres.html

If you would like to be a youth minister, submit your resume here. If you are looking for youth ministers, this is the place for you, too.

CATHOLIC RELIGIOUS EDUCATION ON THE WWW

http://www.microserve.net/~fabian/re.html

Just like the last page, you will find the same "Catholic Pointers" list on Scott's page. Basically everything I said about the last site applies here.

Catholic religious education is very important. Many people live the rest of their lives based on the religious education they received in their earlier years. Because this may be the last Catholic schooling people will receive this side of Heaven, Catholic educators need to build good foundations in the students they teach. If you are a Catholic educator, you can connect to other teachers on the Internet and get help in learning how to give your people a good Catholic foundation in the Faith.

 Religious Educators Directory
http://www.microserve.net/~fabian/files/redir.html

A listing of Catholic school catechists by country and state, along with other relevant information about them. There is an e-mail contact address for each of them.

 Religious Educators Sign In Form
http://www.microserve.net/~fabian/files/redirfrm.html

If you are involved in Catholic religious education and want your name added to the above list, fill out the form here.

Religious Education FAQ

http://www.microserve.net/~fabian/files/refaq.html

Paul D. Mazzurana is putting together a Catholic FAQ that will contain questions on the Catholic Church. This sounds like a great project and aid to Catholic educators. Please forward any questions that come up to him at pdmazz@austin.ibm.com.

CATHOLIC SCHOOLS ON THE INTERNET

http://www.microserve.net/~fabian/files/school.html

This page is maintained by Marty Kirwan and housed on the Ecclesia service provided by Scott Fabian. It is an Internet directory of primary and secondary Catholic schools. Some schools in this directory only have e-mail addresses. The schools are listed alphabetically by country, then by state/province if necessary, and then by name. City names have been provided to distinguish similarly named schools. I have kept his system here. As usual you may find things added or subtracted from Marty's directory since I looked at it. Don't panic!

As do other directories I've seen, Marty's page includes a list of the countries at the top. By clicking on any one of them, you can jump down his list to the country that interests you. He also has done this with the individual states of the United States of America. Another convenience he has provided is "Back to Top," which will do exactly what it says when you click on it. This way you can go to the country you want, look at the schools, jump back to the top, then click on another country to jump back down the list. This works the same way under the United States except now you can jump back and forth by state. If you prefer, you can use the "Find" tool on Internet browsers to accomplish the same thing.

Your school or parish can get a free site by going to http://www.catholic-church.org. You can add your school to their list! To do so, go to this page on the Internet, click on the words "Registration Form," and fill it out. If you need to update a link or have questions regarding this page, e-mail Marty at mkirwan@capaccess.org.

As you may imagine, the students from these schools have made some truly creative homepages. I think kids are more creative than adults! They also pick up how to use computers rather quickly, as they do languages. Soon they are showing their parents how to do things. They have additional incentive to design homepages, as they can show them off, literally, to the world!

I hope this directory will help link Catholic students. Many students give their e-mail address. (I guess instead of pen pals, they will be cyber pals!) This directory may also benefit parents who either have their children in these schools or are looking for a school. I was fortunate to have gone to a Catholic elementary school. When I switched to a public school in ninth grade, I was a year ahead of other students in learning. I was such a good student in elementary school that I went to school on many a Saturday. Actually, I went on Saturday because I got into trouble so much! (It was meant to be punishment!) I still recall fondly having to write, "I will not throw snowballs" 5,000 times. I am thankful because now I can spell "snowball." Seriously, a Catholic school is a great place to get an education.

Now it is obvious that school pages will give information on the schools they represent. Some information is of interest only to those attending that school. On the other hand, teachers like having students do interesting activities that result in all kinds of cute things you'll find on these pages. I really enjoyed looking through them to see what the kids are doing. One girl said something that really made me laugh. (You will find it following.) As usual, my comments are either on the homepage or off the wall.

Other Web Pages That List Catholic Schools

 1996 Catholic Internet Directory
http://www.catholic-church.com/cid

Remember this one? It was listed in Chapter 6 under Internet Directories. You can find out more about it there.

 *Augustinian Schools Worldwide
http://www.geocities.com/Athens/1534/augshoo.html

Hosted by Father John Pejza, this one would be of interest to those who are crazy about the Augustinians.

 Catholic Education Network
http://www.catholic.org/cen/school.html

About the same as what is listed following.

*Catholic K–12 Education Online
http://www.interaccess.com/catholic/schools.html

This is probably a good place to look for more information. You will have to search for it though.

Listing by Country

Here are the countries Ecclesia has registered so far: Australia, Austria, Canada, Estonia, Greece, Hong Kong, Hungary, Japan, Rep. South Africa, Russia, United Kingdom, and the United States. That's an impressive list!

Australia

Northern Territory

Stuartholme School, Brisbane
http://www.ozemail.com.au:80/~stuascho/

There is some interesting information here. Learn the background of the school and see the Southern Hemisphere's largest pictorial glass window, located in the Stuartholme chapel. Find out everything you ever want to know about Brisbane. After seeing the ninth-grade page project, I don't want to hear you say you can't design a homepage. Even if kids pick things up quickly, I'm still impressed that ninth graders who had never been on the Internet before put a homepage together. So if they can, why can't you? There are further links here to the association of Sacred Heart schools, interest groups within the school, an index of WWW sites organized into curriculum areas, another school's index, and other interesting Australian sites.

St. John Fisher College, Brisbane
sjfc@world.net

This English saint (d. 1535) was chancellor of Cambridge University and the Bishop of Rochester. Yes, originally both Cambridge University and Oxford University were Catholic.

St. Mary's College Woree, Cairns
stmarys@internetnorth.com.au

Just to confuse you, different countries do not have the same names for different levels of schooling. College in the United States for example, is where you go after grade 12, but the word college in some countries is used for grades equivalent to high school in the United States (grades 9 or 10 through 12).

South Australia

Blackfriars Priory School, Adelaide
http://203.23.125.33/index.html

A Dominican school with plenty of information on the homepage. Check out the news from their international water polo tour! See photographs of this team that only lost twice in the 1990s. Look at their "News & Views" along with their current newsletter, and check out student homepages. Need to find somebody in Australia? Here you will find links to both the white and yellow pages along with a link to international directories.

Christian Brothers' College, Adelaide
http://www.ozemail.com.au/~cbc/

Listen to their school song! You will, of course, want to see their special bulletins and events, and you should definitely follow the "World Links" from the Christian Brothers' College link library. You will find plenty on computing, audio, education, graphics, software, and search engines. You have to see and hear the "Wall-climbing Page" put together by the physical education athletes! You might also want to follow the link to the Christian Brothers' homepage.

Mount Carmel College, Adelaide
http://www.ozemail.com.au/~reed/mcc/mcchome.html

Named for Our Lady of Mount Carmel, the patroness of the Carmelite order. The feast of Our Lady of Mount Carmel was instituted among the Carmelites around the year 380 as a feast of thanksgiving in commemoration of favors received through the intercession of the Blessed Virgin. It was assigned to July 16, the traditional date on which the Blessed Mother appeared to St. Simon Stock and gave him the brown scapular.

St Kevin's, Toorak
http://www.stkevins.vic.edu.au

To find just about anything you want to know about or in Australia, you'll want to follow their "W3 Gateway." You can look at some photos from the school, also.

St. Joseph's College, Ferntree Gully
http://www.ozemail.com.au/~jbfox/school/

Run by the Salesians of Don Bosco. You might want to look at John Cull's Page. He is the Information Technical Coordinator at St. Joseph's. On this homepage, you will find samples of each student's work, see images from St. Joseph's, and can follow the link to the Salesian page. Other links off the main school page include Bosconet (homepage of the Australian Salesian Province of Mary Help of Christians) and "From the Newsletter" (updated regularly from the college information bulletin, college magazine, or weekly staff bulletin).

Austria

Aufbaugymnasium der Erzdioezese Wien, Hollabrunn
http://ourworld.compuserve.com/homepages/ag_hollabrunn/

This is a secondary school for students 14 to 18 years of age. The school is run by the Archdiocese of Vienna in Austria. Hollabrunn is located 50 km north of Vienna. Their pages are mainly written in German, but they also plan English pages.

Gymnasium Meinhardinum Stams, Tirol
http://www.stams.ac.at./meinhardinum/

This page is written in German also.

Canada

Alberta

St. Anthony/St. Matthew Schools, Drayton Valley
http://www.st-anthonys.drayton-valley.ab.ca/

See St. Anthony's "Yak Me" (live chat area), student Web pages, and everything you ever wanted to know about their school wrestling.

Grande Prairie and District Catholic Schools
gp28@terranet.ab.ca

You can e-mail them here.

Dufferin-Peel R.C.S.S.B. Schools
http://cs.dprcssb.edu.on.ca/more_html/schools.html

Here you will find a listing (some with links) to their elementary and secondary schools.

*Metropolitan Separate School Board
http://www.mssb.edu.on.ca/mssb.htm

They serve the K–12 needs of 104,000 Roman Catholic students in metropolitan Toronto. Good luck!

Ontario

Halton Roman Catholic School Board
http://www.haltonrc.edu.on.ca

Download songs from the special compact disc "Music for the Christ Child," performed by the students of St. Joseph's School, Acton, Ontario. You can also listen to "Touch the Stars" and "St. Francis Pride." They even have a "Photo Gallery" on this page! See the Web page created by the students.

Mary Ward School, Scarborough
http://www.io.org/~erwin

You will want to see the "Picture Gallery of Ward at Work!" found under "Overview." You can also find a link to Canada's "SchoolNet," learn about Toronto, and discover the many clubs at this school and what they are about.

St. Marguerite d'Youville Catholic Elementary School, Ottawa
http://www.ww3.sympatico.ca/marg.youville1/index.html

(Bilingual: English-French.) Read *Explore!* magazine that is published by the grade 5 French immersion students. As you can imagine, the magazine is all in French. But why not look at the impressive pictures anyway? You will also want to look at the children's page, look at a photo of the school, and read their newsletter. A must-visit is the link to "What's Up" with photographs.

St. Peter Catholic High School
marg.youville2@sympatico.ca

Great patron for a Catholic high school. This one is for e-mailing only.

Estonia

Tartu Katoliku Kool, an Elementary school in Tartu
http://www.rc.net/org/tartu

Find out everything you ever wanted to know about Estonia by following their link. Kids in grades 3 through 6 (and curious adults) have got to see the "A Why 'n' Not Education" homepage.

Greece

Ecole Jeanne D'Arc
ejdarc1@leon.nrcps.ariadne-t.gr

Send your e-mail to the attention of Theofilos Georgoussis. If I'm not mistaken, I believe St. Paul mentions a Theofilos in one of his letters. This is a private preparatory high school in Pireas operated by the Oblates of St. Joseph.

Hong Kong

Wah Yan College
http://www.wahyan.edu.hk/

Join their "Wah Yan Message Board!" This is an online threaded message bulletin board, which allows you to enter messages for everyone else to read. Then there is "Breaking the Barrier." This will take you to their bulletin board system (BBS) and mailing lists. You can follow their link to homepages of other secondary schools in Hong Kong also. There are some great photos here besides.

Hungary

Kalazantinum Piarist
http://www.piar.hu/index.html

This is a College of Theology and Teacher Training located in Budapest, Hungary's capital. The reason this page is listed here is because it has a link to the schools in Hungary, which the Piarist Fathers maintain. Their page has some interesting links on it, too.

Japan

Aichi

Hikarigaoka Girls' High School, Okazaki
http://power1.hikarigaoka.okazaki.aichi.jp

This school is run by Dominican sisters. You will find clear photos here, along with links to sister schools and information on the convent.

St. Joseph International School in Yokohama
sjislib@gol.com

Travel to Japan—well, sort of, because this is only for e-mail.

An Alumni Group for the St. Joseph International School, Yokohama
mendosan@erols.com

Why not strike up a conversation by e-mail with someone in Japan?

Republic of South Africa

Archdiocese of Cape Town Catholic Schools
afmsdbmo@iafrica.com

Here is another e-mail address for you.

Russia

A Letter from Siberia
http://dcn.davis.ca.us/~feefhs/lfs/frg-lfs.html

A newsletter (in English) from the Catholic bishop of Siberia (actually he is more properly titled the Apostolic Administrator for the Latin-Rite Catholics in Asian Russia). His "diocese" covers 10.3 percent of all the land on earth and is without question the largest ecclesiastical territory in the Latin Rite. You may find some information on schools in his newsletter.

United Kingdom

Ampleforth College and Abbey
http://www.ampleforth.org.uk/~college/

This school is a half-hour's drive north of York. Here you will certainly want to see their news and message board. The school is associated with Ampleforth Abbey so you'll want to read "Visions of Peace—the Way of the Monk" and about the fundraising bicycle ride of Abbot Timothy, too!

United States

Alabama

McGill-Toolen High School, Mobile
http://www.mcgill.pvt.k12.al.us

A tremendously big homepage of over 3,100 Catholic links can be found here by clicking on "The Catholic Mobile." This site is aimed at the more serious student of the Catholic Faith. Links are filed under the following headings: Church, Revelation, Liturgy, Justice and Peace, Morality, Spirituality, Evangelization, Theology, Religion, and Other. Oh yes, I forgot that we are looking at schools here. Under "Student Activities and Clubs," you can find some photo galleries. Under "Clio's Place" you will find history links. Look at "User Web Pages" for more interesting things. On top of all this, you will find the Ring of K–12 School Homepages.

Sacred Heart School, Anniston
http://www.buyersusa.com/nqc/al/shschool.htm

This is a K–8 school. I am fortunate to be working on this one on the Feast of the Sacred Heart, the Friday after Corpus Christi. Our Lord asked for Holy Communions of reparation to be made on this day to repair for the indifference He receives from the greater part of mankind, especially in the Holy Eucharist. On this homepage you can see a photo of some of the students.

Alaska

Archdiocese of Anchorage
71162.711@compuserve.com

You can send your e-mail to the attention of Brother Charles McBride, D.C. Perhaps you can ask him for information on the schools there.

California

Archbishop Riordan High School, San Francisco
http://www.crl.com/~riordan

This is an urban school for young men, run by the Roman Catholic Archdiocese of San Francisco and conducted by the Society of Mary, the Marianist. This page has an appealing look to it but not much on it yet. They are looking for ideas, especially on their "Up for Grabs" page, so give them some.

Bishop O'Dowd, Oakland
http://www.odowd.pvt.k12.ca.us/home.html

You will find a nicely organized set of links that was meant for the staff and students, but I'm sure they won't mind if you use them. They organized links under these categories: New, Reference, Books, Publishers, Cities, Countries, Languages, History, Images, Fun, Periodicals, Math, Museums, K–12 Schools, Science, Social Science, Sports, Theology, TV-Radio, Universities, Comments, and Alumni. Oh yes, back to the school again. The Congregation of St. Basil runs it. You can find out more about this order by following the link entitled "Basilian Fathers." The rector of the seminary I attended belonged to this community.

Marin Catholic, Kentfield
http://www.marin.k12.ca.us/~marcath

There is a very short audio welcome here, a video you can download from their library, student, and faculty homepages to look at, and more.

Moreau Catholic High School, Hayward
http://www.sfgate.com/~geigers/

Is your school connected to the Internet? Do you have a high-speed connection? If not, use someone's computer that's connected to find out about "NetDay" on this page. It is a grass-roots volunteer effort to wire schools so they can network their computers and connect them to the Internet. Labor and materials are provided by volunteers and support from companies, unions, parents, teachers, students, and school employees. On this page you can meet people involved with the school, including the students, view their photo and other things while you visit their page.

San Carlos School, Monterey
http://www.mbay.net/~scarlos

You can follow a few links about the Monterey location and community. There are also Catholic and educational tool links to be found here.

St. Francis High School, Mountain View
http://www.sfhs.com

This school is run by the Brothers of the Holy Cross, about whom you can find out more information here. Also, see some photos under "Athletics."

St. Francis Solano School, Sonoma
http://www.claytonwallis.com/Stfrncis.htm

A lot of interesting links to look at on this unofficial page for the school; although, there isn't anything here about the school!

St. Lawrence Elementary and Middle School, Santa Clara
http://members.aol.com/stlawren/stlaw2.htm

An example of more and more elementary schools that are getting on the Internet. This homepage has some links of interest, including the "Diocese of San Jose," "Family Education Network," and "Interesting Places for Kids" (like me!).

St. Therese School, Alhambra
http://www.sttherese.pvt.k12.ca.us

Look at the "St. Therese Resources" links for finding Internet-related educational Web sites. This has some of the best sites on the Internet for kids, parents, and teachers. You may have problems here with Java Scripts as they are trying to use the latest and best homepage technology that your browser may not support. They completely locked up Netscape Navigator that I was using.

Trinity Grammar and Prep, Napa
http://www.visioninteractive.com/trinity/

This is a grades 1–12 school offering parent-centered classical education in the Catholic tradition. I had some problems loading this homepage. You will find a list of "Keys to Educational Accomplishment" that they use.

St. Rose Catholic School
srscas@thegrid.net

If this school's patron is St. Rose of Lima (d. 1617), they picked a good one. She is the Patroness of South America.

Connecticut

Kolbe Cathedral High School, Bridgeport
kolbe@smartnet.org

When you e-mail them, make sure you send it to the attention of Father Marcel Sokalski.

Georgia

*St. Mary on the Hill School, Augusta
http://www.augusta.net/stmary/

Georgia reminds me of peaches and pecans.

St. Pius X Catholic High School, Atlanta
http://www.mindspring.com/~lion

This humble and gentle Pope is a great patron for a Catholic high school. This Pope recommended daily Holy Communion and the reception of Holy Communion by all children who have reached the age of discretion. This page opens with a picture of the school and the table of contents down the left side. To find out more about their patron saint, select "General" and then "Our Patron." Other students might want to make some e-mail pals by looking under "Students" into the "Student E-mail Directory."

Hawaii

*Catholic Schools Department, Kaneohe
http://www.pixi.com/~dever/index.html

Can you believe that I couldn't leave the airport of these beautiful islands. I was coming back from the Philippines, and because U.S. customs was to be done on the mainland, we were stuck in the Hawaiian airport.

Damien High School, Kalihi, Honolulu
http://www.damien.edu

You will find QuickTime Video on the physics pages here. Besides this, there is much to see here, including the "Joke of the Day."

*St. Joseph's High School, Hilo, Honolulu
http://www.pixi.com/~sjrelay/index.html

This island, I believe, is famous for having great waves for surfing. I tried surfing once but had no success.

Illinois

Marist Catholic High School, Chicago
http://www.marist.chi.il.us

This school is run by the Marist Brothers. You can find links to their schools around the world. With 25,000 people stopping by this page, I'd imagine you might want to see it yourself.

Mount Carmel High School, Chicago
http://www.concentric.net/~Caravan/

Hey, this one has my favorites—images and pictures. You will have to see it to believe it.

Notre Dame High School for Boys, Niles
http://nsls1.nslsilus.org/NotreDame/index.html

There aren't many all-boys schools anymore, but here's one. This page opens with a picture of the school, which is run by the Congregation of the Holy Cross. You can find links here to the other high schools, colleges, and universities that they run.

St. Alexander Elementary School, Villa Park
http://www.rc.net/joliet/st_alexander/

One link on this page caught my attention: "St. Alexander's is a Market Day school." What is this? You can find out about this way to raise funds for education, perhaps for your school, too. I'm not going to tell you more. Go find out for yourself! You will also find links to diocesean resources and other schools here.

*St. Stanislaus Bishop and Martyr School, Chicago
http://www.interaccess.com/catholic/ststans.html

I wonder about the name of this one. Are they training kids to be Bishops and martyrs? This saint (d. 1568) is from Poland, which I suppose you could tell by the name.

St. Benedict High School
sbhsinfo@TheRamp.com

You don't see many high schools named after St. Benedict. I bet this saint never imagined that centuries later a school would honor him by making him their patron.

Indiana

Bishop Dwegner High School, Fort Wayne
http://www.clearlake.com/bishop/dwenger.htm

You will find links to other Catholic schools, both in this state and across the country here. A link to "His Holiness, Pope JP II" is an interesting page to stop by.

St. Charles Borromeo, Bloomington
http://www.intersource.com/~stchucks/

If you are a student, you probably want to check out "Homework Hotlinks" under "About St. Charles School" on this one.

St. Joseph's High School, South Bend
http://sjcpl.lib.in.us/sjhhomepage/sjh.html

Owned and operated by the diocese of Fort Wayne-South Bend. You'll want to see their newspaper and the random collage of their graduates. Other links here are being worked on.

The Washington Catholic School
wchsb@dmrtc.net

This one is e-mail only. Perhaps if you are in the area, you can help them get up on the Internet.

Iowa

St. Malachy, Creston
http://aea14.k12.ia.us/schools/st_malachy.html

This saint was an Irish bishop who was a friend of St. Bernard. St. Malachy died in 1148. This is one of those straight text homepages.

Kansas

Hayden High School, Topeka
http://www.tyrell.net/~hayden/

You will find links to Topeka Catholic grade schools here besides information on the high school. Students will want to look into the "E-Mail Addresses" to get connected to their peers in Kansas.

Kentucky

St. Anthony Church and School, Covington
http://www.nkymall.com/anthony

I like this page. You can visit the church and school homepages, as well as meet some of the students—virtually that is.

Villa Madonna Academy Villa Hills
http://www.iglou.com/vma/

See pictures of the fourth, fifth, and sixth graders' travels to France and find out how the French students fared in Kentucky. Also, the high school students took a "Sound of Music Tour" to Heidelberg, Rothenburg, Eichstatt, Regensburg, Vienna, Salzburg, and Munich. You can see 16 photos of their journey. Their next adventure will be to Greece. Now why didn't I go to a school like this? Under "What's New at VMA," follow their "Sports Program" link to see pictures. Of course, there is much more here also.

St. Mary School System
smhs@vci.net

This is for e-mail only. I remember Kentucky for its rolling hills and well-known Kentucky blue grass. Others probably know it for the Kentucky Derby horse races. If you are a student, e-mail them and find out more about Kentucky.

Archbishop Blenk High School, Gretna
http://www.gnofn.org/~blenk

Some photos of students can be found under "Extracurriculars." Of course you will want to follow the "Student Homepages" link to find out what they have come up with.

Archbishop Chapelle High School, New Orleans
http://achs.chapelle.k12.la.us/

Probably the most cleverly designed homepage I've seen! It is in the form of a notebook in which you flip the pages. This makes the tour easy, and there are pictures also!

Archdiocese of New Orleans InfoPage Menu
http://www.catholic.org/neworleans/menu.html

You can find links to more schools here: Archbishop Rummel High School, Archbishop Blenk High School, Our Lady of Lourdes School, and Our Lady of Prompt Succor School. In New Orleans is a shrine of Our Lady of Prompt Succor (*succor* means help) that has been there for many years.

Brother Martin High School, New Orleans
http://www.gnofn.org/~brmartin

This school is run by the Brothers of the Sacred Heart, whom you can find out more about here. You can listen to the school's "fight song" and follow links for research by subject.

Notre Dame Seminary, New Orleans
http://www.catholic.org/neworleans/ndmay1.html

This link will take you to the Archdiocesan page. Select "Enter" and then "Seminaries" off the table of contents to finally find the seminary. You can flip through the seminary newsletter (which includes some pictures) page by page.

St. Rita Catholic School, Alexandria
http://www.timetrend.com/~strita

You may want to see the Catholic links here. The patroness of this school was left a widow after being married 18 years. She then joined an Augustinian convent. She is specially honored in Spain. She is called the "Saint of the Impossible" due to the wonderful favors obtained through her intercession.

Maryland

Georgetown Prep, North Bethesda
http://leonardo.gprep.pvt.k12.md.us

Make sure you select "The Campus" from the main menu. You will find an overhead view of the campus. By clicking on objects in this view, you can take a virtual tour of the campus. Try it!

St. John the Evangelist, Clinton
http://www.nmaa.org/stjohns

The school is run by the Servants of the Immaculate Heart of Mary. You can learn more about them here. This is a page well worth visiting, with histories of the school, church, and town, as well as pictures and other information. They have a good set of links, both on making homepages and for school-related things. There is advice written for kids about what to do and not to do on the Internet. If you are having trouble getting around on their homepage, follow the "Roadmap" they provide.

St. Louis School, Clarksville
http://www.stlouis.baltimore.md.us/school/

You'll want to read their issues of "Super Scribbles." Find out about how St. Louis School got wired! See a list of all the Catholic schools in the archdiocese of Baltimore (sorry, no links, just addresses). And if you haven't seen it already, you will want to follow the link to St. Louis Parish.

Massachusetts

*Bishop Stang High School, North Dartmouth
http://www.ultranet.com/~bshs/index.htm

This one is not far from the ocean.

Savio Preparatory High School, East Boston
http://www.tiac.net/users/savio

You will want to see "Savio's Hotlist" of useful links arranged by subject. And the curious will want to read their newspaper. Another link will tell you everything you ever wanted to know about Boston!

Michigan

St. Helen Catholic Elementary School, Saginaw
http://www.cris.com/~kruska/edu/school2.html

Although I wouldn't call it a virtual tour of the school, it is the next best thing. You can enter each room of the school, meet the teacher, and learn what he or she has to say. I like the door images too.

St. Hugo School, Bloomfield Hills
http://www.sthugo.k12.mi.us

It's always a good idea to see the students' homepages. One student has had only 14 visitors. Let's surprise him by swamping his homepage! Oh, by the way, if you check out "Candid Photo," you will see some students truly surprised to have their photo taken.

Minnesota

Saint John's Preparatory School, Collegeville
http://www.csbsju.edu/sjprep/

Alright! Another photo tour. Here you can take a tour of the campus and see scenes from the daily life at the school, which is run by the Benedictines of St. John's Abbey. You can learn more about them here also. For the curious, you can read the school's publications called *Prep Talk* and *Parent Talk*.

Missouri

The Network of Sacred Heart Schools, St. Louis
http://www.sofie.org/network/

An interesting and useful place to see. Visit the "Sofie Forum." It's a place where students, faculty, staff, and alumni can converse. Join an ongoing discussion, or begin a new one on a topic you propose. "Show" is the Network of Sacred Heart School's first online gallery. It provides a place where their students as well as new and established artists can share their work, not only with the Sacred Heart Network but also the worldwide Internet community. There are more forums here where you can both learn and share with others many subjects related to schools. You can read their *Network News* publication or download it.

Nebraska

Creighton Prep Homepage, Omaha
http://dante.creighton.edu/

This school is a private Jesuit college prep school for young men founded in 1878. If you click on the arrow for their "Mission and History," you can find links for Omaha and Jesuit information. This page uses frames, and its table of contents is found in the left frame. See the students homepage creations by clicking on "Students" under "People." You will find some photos under both "Athletics" and "Clubs & Activities."

Marian Catholic, Omaha
http://marian.creighton.edu/binfo.html

If you want to see a photo of a bunch of happy students, go here.

*Mary Our Queen, Omaha
http://www.top.net/psmutny

This is certainly a beautiful title to have for a school. The Fifth Glorious Mystery of the Rosary commemorates Mary being crowned as Queen in Heaven. There is even a feast called the Queenship of Mary celebrated on August 22.

Mount Michael Benedictine High School, Elkhorn
http://mountmike.creighton.edu/

Here you will want to look under the "Mount Michael Homepage" for a tour of the campus. Although you won't find a virtual tour, there are some pictures. You can enter each classroom and find many links to the subject taught there. "The Abbey" will give you Benedictine information.

*Skutt Catholic High School, Omaha
http://esu3.esu3.k12.ne.us/districts/skutt/home.html

I wonder what the history behind the name of this school is?

New Hampshire

Bishop Guertin High School, Danville
http://www.tiac.net/users/bg1/

Under "What is Bishop Guertin High School?" you will find "The Facilities" where you can see photos of the place with commentaries. Student pages are always worth seeing. Jessica Allan tells us on her page, "I do absolutely nothing interesting with my life, and I had to write a Web page to tell you this . . . If you want to talk to me, my e-mail address is at the bottom of this page. If you're looking for a date, forget it." Now isn't that great stuff?

St. Patrick School, Jaffrey
http://das.wang.com/users/ksquires/stpats

A straightforward page that's simple to follow. You can see pictures of various people of the school and follow regional and educational links.

New Jersey

Bishop Eustace Preparatory School, Pennsauken
FrDonioCC@aol.com

Address any e-mail you send here to the attention of Father Frank Donio, SAC.

Don Bosco Technical High School, Paterson
dbtpatnj@aol.com

Don Bosco was a great Italian priest who founded the Salesian Order to help poor boys in need.

Our Lady of the Assumption School, Bayonne
sysop@bayonne.net

Now here is a question for you. What is the difference between the Assumption of Mary and the Ascension of Jesus—that is, what's the difference between assumption and ascension?

New York

Holy Cross High School, Queens
http://www.panix.com/~hchs

A school operated by the Brothers of the Holy Cross, about whom you can find out more here. Also, you will find links to their other schools. Read the school's *Discovery* magazine, which I think is well laid out. You can also read some students' letters and essays on their homepage.

Iona Preparatory, New Rochelle
http://www.ionaprep.pvt.k12.ny.us

Look under "Programs & Activities" and "Extracurricular Activities" to see the photos from two plays put on by the "Prep Players." Also, you may want to read *NewsWire,* a collection of up-to-date news articles concerning the Iona Prep community.

St. Gregory the Great School, Williamsville
http://www.pce.net/users/stgregs

I like homepages that tell me what to do! This one told me to visit the library media center, art room, and students, which I did. There I met people from the library, admired the students' artwork in the art room, and saw what the students have created for homepages. Oh yes, under the latter, you will find the first ever Duffy the Dog homepage. A real dog! You can even e-mail him!

Ohio

Padua High School, Cleveland
http://members.aol.com/PaduaHs/index.html

To see a photo of the school, select "Padua Franciscan High School" on the opening page. You can find out "Who are the Franciscans?" or explore the "Area Profile" of Cleveland.

St. Francis de Sales High School, Toledo
http://dewey.sfs.utoledo.edu

There are Oblates of St. Francis de Sales on the teaching staff. You can learn more about them here. Under "Athletics" you can see pictures of the swimming and water polo teams in action. Under "Campus," select "Music: Marching, Concert, and Pep Bands; Chorus" to see pictures of the band and hear the school's song. Of course, there is a lot more here.

*Saint Ignatius High School
http://www.en.com/users/sihs/

St. Pius X School, Reynoldsburg
http://www.cd.pvt.k12.oh.us/schools/px/index.html

After looking at homepages all day, I had worked up an appetite so I looked at the "Lunch Menus" on this page. How about a virtual meal? Not quite as good as the real one. By the way, here you will find page links for the Web organized according to subject.

*Trinity High School, Garfield Heights
http://www.blarg.net/~trinity/thshome.htm

I think this is a great name for a Catholic high school. The Holy Trinity—Father, Son and Holy Spirit, one God—is a mystery that we cannot fully grasp this side of Heaven. Since God is infinite and we are finite, there is a good chance we will not be able to fully grasp this one in the next life either!

Oklahoma

*Christ the King, Oklahoma City
http://www.telepath.com/ckschool

Christ the King is the feast the Church celebrates at the end of the Liturgical Year. Jesus wants to be King of all hearts. He is the King of Love!

Oregon

St. Mary's School, Medford
http://www.stmarys.medford.or.us/

Under "Activities" and "The Arts," the theater page has plans for a picture gallery! If you're looking for a book on the Internet, you just have to see under "Clubs" the *Literary Magazine* where you can not only search for books but see many links with commentary of other places to find them. For those who like Latin, there is "The National Junior Classical League," an organization linking students of Latin across the country. Finally, you will want to see the sixth grade homepage, as well as individual students' homepages.

Pennsylvania

*Archbishop Ryan High School, Philadelphia
http://www.homepagecreations.com/ryan/index.html

There are a number of Catholic schools named after Bishops or Archbishops.

Cathedral School
http://www.enter.net/~cathedral

This is an elementary school serving the families of the Cathedral Church of St. Catherine of Siena, Allentown, and the Church of St. Joseph the Worker, Orefield. With over 18,000 visitors to this page, either a lot of alumni have computers or it's a good page! You will want to visit the "Saints Calendar" where you can listen to beautiful music while seeing and reading about the saints.

Drexel Hill School of the Holy Child, Drexel Hill
http://www.forum.swarthmore.edu/~joanna

Named for the Drexel family of Blessed Katharine Drexel.

*St. Lucy Day School for Children with Visual Impairments, Upper Darby
http://www.homepagecreations.com/stlucy/index.html

This patron saint was a virgin and martyr. She was chosen for this school because St. Lucy (d. 304) is popularly invoked for diseases of the eye.

*St. Luke's, Stroudsburg
http://catholic-church.com

Did you know that St. Luke the Evangelist is the patron saint of physicians and surgeons, and also of artists?

St. Martin of Tours, Philadelphia
http://www.voicenet.com/~gootba/stmart.htm

This page is under construction. It will be maintained by the sixth grade. The fourth-century patron saint of this school is the father of monasticism in France. He was also the first holy man who was not martyred to be publicly venerated, after he died, as a saint.

St. William's School, Philadelphia
http://www.voicenet.com/~gootba/stwill.htm

John O'Brien, a sixth grader at St. Williams School, seems to have designed this page. He can teach you about homepages. He has some links of interest and "Other Cool Sites" here.

Rhode Island

LaSalle Academy, Providence
http://www.loa.com/lasalle

Named after St. John Baptist de La Salle, the founder of the Christian Brothers. I like the motto below the sketch of the school here, "Live Jesus in our hearts—forever." Now there is a good pointer here for homepage designers—they give you a choice for viewing their homepage: with frames and 256 colors or just the simple site. Some people who have older computers or use browsers such as Mosaic and Lynx need the simple version of your homepage.

After you decide which way you want to view the page, you will find an interesting set of links on their table of contents. Of course, you will want to look at the "Student Pages." But there are also links to other Catholic schools as well as public/private ones in Rhode Island. There are tips on creating homepages and a "Software Closet" that attempts to identify good shareware (usually inexpensive) and freeware programs available to users of the Internet.

Father John V. Doyle School
frdoyle@ids.net

You can only e-mail this school. They should contact the aforementioned school to get a page on the Internet.

South Carolina

Summerville Catholic School
gnosotti@awod.com

This is another one of those e-mail only places. But that won't stop you from getting to know them.

Tennessee

Diocese of Nashville High School
http://www.serve.com/DIOCNASH/rtestsch.htm

On this page you will not only find a link to a high school but to several parochial schools in and outside of Nashville. Then there is also a link to the Dominican Campus and "Saint Bernard Non-graded School." If you want to find out more about these places, click on the square button next to them. I am almost sure you will want to see the high-school page. To start you off on this one, I recommend you choose "Anatomy and Physiology Class Project" and then "Pictures of Our School."

Father Ryan High School, Nashville
http://www.serve.com/nashfrhs

A colorful site indeed! Under "Father Ryan Soccer Web Site" and "Boys' Soccer" you can find a picture gallery. Select "More About the School" and "General Information" to get a virtual tour of the campus.

Texas

Bishop Thomas K. Gorman Middle School and High School, Tyler
http://www.gower.net/btkg

Here you will want to see "Pictures from Around Bishop Gorman." You're also going to want to see "Faculty and Student Resources on the Internet."

Saint Agnes Academy, Houston
http://www.st-agnes.org

With almost 20,000 visitors, you just have to believe there is something worth seeing here! Certainly the link to "Web Tutorials" would be popular. Perhaps I discovered why this is a popular page. Under "Study Hall" you can hear the S.A.T. exam FAQs and test-taking tips on Audionet. Besides this, they have a link to an extensive page on the S.A.T. exam along with other helpful information. Educators will want to see their "School Programs." They have a memory program (I should study this one—if I can remember to check it out later!), a speed-reading program, links to college and educational-related sites, and a FAQ section. Shortly they will be putting up A.C.T. exam preparation helps. Good thing I'm done with all that!

Virginia

All Saints School, Manassas
http://www.rc.net:80/arlington/all_saints/school/index.htm

You'll find some interesting tidbits under "Lunch." The main menu (no pun intended) makes it easy to tour this page. You can see some samples of student work from each of the grades. Also, you'll want to follow the link to the church.

Good Shepherd Catholic Church, Mt. Vernon
http://www.mnsinc.com/gscc/yacht.html

Here you will find "Y.A.C.H.T.," that is, Young Adult Catholics Hanging Together. You will want to see their group photos. The club is comprised of post-high school singles, couples, and young families from the Good Shepherd Parish community. Their mission is to provide spiritual and social fellowship to young adults, to encourage individual and group participation in standing committees and programs at the Parish and within the broader community, and to foster new relationships with other young adult organizations throughout the Arlington Diocese. Perhaps you can build a Y.A.C.H.T. in your parish!

Holy Trinity Parish School, Norfolk
http://www.infi.net/~gewkab/hts.html

Here you can view a picture of the school in JPG or GIF format. You can follow the link to Holy Trinity parish. If you go down the main page a little ways, you can click on "Visit Our Classes" to do exactly that. Finally, "Father Lou's Books" may be a link for the curious to explore.

Paul VI High School
http://www.ee.cua.edu/~paulvi/index.html

The school is run by the Oblates of St. Francis de Sales whom you can find more information about here. You will want to see the images of Paul VI High School and can also find out about the city of Fairfax and the surrounding area.

Washington

St. Philomena, Des Moines
http://www.halcyon.com/dale/Dales.html

Another page with a lot of visitors, almost 10,000. You will be entertained by music while you look around the main page. It is straightforward, making it easy to explore. Meet and see the whole staff. Check out the student homepages, too. Teachers, will want to view their teacher resources on the Web. The "Kids Page" offers links highly recommended to parents for their children. You are going to want to look at the "Art Page" and see works by students. There's a science and tall tales connection here as well.

*St. Luke School, Des Moines
http://www.cyberspace.com/stluke/

What animal is used to represent this Evangelist?

Visitation Catholic Schoo
visitatn@bess.net

Named after Our Lady's visit to her cousin Elizabeth. There is a feast commemorating this event in the Church calendar on May 31.

*Wisconsin: Divine Savior Holy Angels High School, Milwaukee
http://www.execpc.com/~msloan

Now this school didn't want to mess around. They didn't just take Our Lord for their patron under the title of Divine Savior but added the Holy Angels on top of that!

For updates or suggestions regarding this page, or if your school was previously but is no longer listed and you wish to see it reposted, e-mail the following:

Marty
mkirwan@capaccess.org

OTHER REFERENCES FROM THE INDEX

http://www.catholic-church.org/index.htm

The Catholic Internet Directory by Tim DeRyan
http://www.catholic-church.org/cid/

You can see my comments on this one in Chapter 6.

St. Luke's Church Virtual Tour
http://www.microserve.net/~fabian/

You will definitely enjoy seeing this one put together by Scott Fabian. See the inside and outside of this beautiful church, including its stained glass window and statues. Those who have parish homepages may want to include something like this on their page.

Southern California Catholic Singles Calendar
http://www.catholic-church.org/young_adult/

Find out what's happening with singles in southern California.

Holy Name Parish
http://www.catholic-church.org/holyname/

A very well-laid-out page with tons of information about parish life and ministries connected to it—pictures and music besides!

*St. Mel's Parish
http://www.catholic-church.org/stmel/

Who was St. Mel (d.c. 488)? He was the bishop of Ardagh. Mel is actually short for Melchus. He labored with St. Patrick in Ireland.

*Family of the America's Nature's Method Homepage
http://www.upbeat.com/family/

Even if you have difficulty getting to this homepage, there is plenty of information on the Internet on this subject.

The U.S. Pro-Life Directory
http://www.catholic-church.com/media/prolife1.html

Everyone you want to know from A to Z concerning the pro-life issue with contact information. The table of contents arranges the groups according to what services they provide regarding this issue. Clicking on them will jump you down the list to that section on the page. At the bottom of the page, you will find "Part 2" so you won't think that's the entire list. You might also want to follow the "Speak Out" link at the bottom of this page.

*A Catholic's Internet Book Review
http://www.catholic-church.com/books

If you like book reviews, this is the place for you. You can review their reviews!

12

RCNet

http://www.rc.net

What is RCNet? Founded in the spring of 1995, RCNet's mission is to provide Catholic dioceses, parishes, schools, and institutions an opportunity to have a homepage on the Internet. RCNet provides this service free of charge to qualified Catholic entities. RCNet also provides free filtered access (they screen out any junk) to the Internet for Catholic priests, parishes, and schools where practical (currently, this applies to Washtenaw and Western Wayne Counties in Southeast Michigan). RCNet does not create homepage files; they simply host the files once your parish or school has created them.

The Webmaster of this page tells us that RCNet is not trying to become the site with the most Catholic content on the Internet. Instead, his hope is that Catholics representing the thousands of dioceses, parishes, schools, and organizations in the world will take advantage of RCNet's offer to build a Catholic community, of sorts, across the Internet. If you would like more information on establishing a homepage for your Catholic organization, use their automated e-mail responder at homepage@rc.net or send them a more personal note at info@rc.net.

RCNet is a family run organization with an all-volunteer staff, namely Peter Wagner and his family. They are not an official arm of the Catholic Church but are at the service of the Church and enjoy very good relationships with the local priests, parishes, and their home diocese of Lansing, Michigan. Funding for RCNet comes

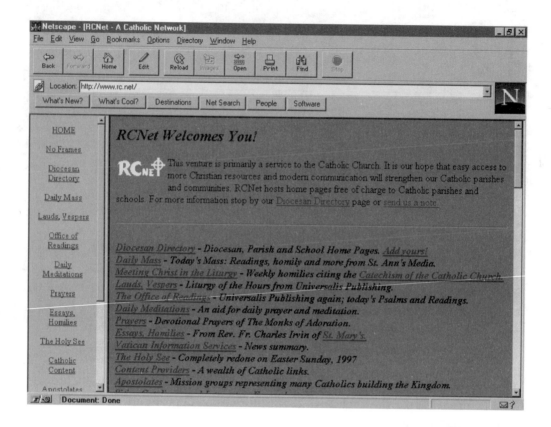

from the many parishioners in the area who subscribe to RCNet's Internet access services. They are grateful to these parishioners for their support, which has already enabled hundreds of Catholic parishes and dioceses from around the world to have free homepages.

They offer dial-up access to this network. RCNet will help to get you up and going by providing Windows software that you can use for e-mail, World Wide Web browsing, file transfer, newsgroups, and other "traditional" Internet applications. Membership in RCNet makes most sense for those able to reach the 332, 455, or 572 exchanges in the 313 area code with a local telephone call (essentially all of Washtenaw County and Western Wayne County).

RCNet will also host your diocesan or parish homepage free of charge as a service to the Church. They host our community's homepage. I started out by e-mailing it to Peter. But now I use FTP to put it up on their Internet site directly. Their physical mailing address is: RCNet, 3202 Hillside Drive, Ypsilanti, MI 48197-3732. Their phone number is: 313-572-0640. So if you don't have a homepage on the Internet, what are you waiting for? They're easy to create, and if you e-mail it to them, they'll get it up on the Internet right away.

If you check with the members of your parish or group you'll probably find somebody who can put a page together. There are also free software packages and utilities to help you out in Chapter 3. Once you have created the page(s), just attach the file(s) to an e-mail message (they use Eudora, a free package from Qualcomm) and send it to RCNet (see addresses below).

Qualcomm
http://www.qualcomm.com/

RCNet
webmaster@rc.net

Now with all that said, why did I choose this directory? Is it because they are located in Michigan, the state in which I grew up? Is it because they host our home-page? Those may be pretty good reasons for me, but perhaps not for you. Like Ecclesia, RCNet is actually an Internet service provider, which means their own computer is directly hooked up to the Internet so they don't have to go through someone else. And this computer is on all the time so people can access what's on it from the Internet. I am impressed that someone is using his technological talents for the Church. Peter set this up to enable others in his area to get on the Internet. Now that's a nice guy, don't you think?

Peter does have some directories on his homepage, probably the most impressive of which is the Diocesan Directory. This is not just a directory of diocesan home-pages, but uses the diocese as a method of sorting homepages. So under a particular diocesan name, you may find the diocesan homepage, schools, parishes, retreat centers, and so on. That was probably the most important reason I chose RCNet, though Peter has other good links off his main page, too.

You will notice on the opening page that Peter uses two frames, the left one as the table of contents. One nice feature here (I would hope others take the hint!) is that Peter gives you a "No Frames" option. Besides this, if you put your cursor on the line dividing the frames, you can drag the line either left or right. This enables you to resize either frame window.

As I've done with other Internet directories, I give detailed listings of only a chosen few from the index. You will find all the categories listed in the left frame window along with a short commentary in the right frame window on the Internet.

Any topics from his index that I do not address in detail appear under "Other References from the Index."

DIOCESAN DIRECTORY

http://www.rc.net/dioceses.html

Here are links to archdioceses and dioceses in North America and around the world. Not all have an Internet presence yet, but the numbers are growing. As I explained previously, you will find more than just diocesan homepages when you click on a diocese. You may wonder, aren't all these other things on the diocesan homepage anyway? They may not be. It would be a good idea for a diocesan homepage to include links to the homepages of all the institutions within it, but not all do this.

Now, if you aren't skipping sections of this book, you should have seen by now directories listing diocesan, parish, and school homepages. Many of the ones listed in Peter's directory can be found with my comments in other sections of this book. Here I make some comments and describe what you will find when you click on a particular diocese name. The number and type of links under each diocesan name varies, and listings will most likely grow, so be sure to check under the particular diocese in which you are interested.

Now when you go to this page on the Internet, you will find an alphabetical listing of United States dioceses and archdioceses by state. Because not all dioceses in Peter's listing have links under them, he has put a "+" next to the names of those that have content. If you click on one that does not have a plus sign, you will be taken to a page without any links on it. Because they have no content, I do not list the dioceses without a plus sign.

Since sites are arranged alphabetically by state, Peter has placed the letters of the alphabet at the top of this page so you can click on a letter and jump down to the states under it. Also, at the end of the dioceses listed under each letter of the alphabet, you will see the word "Top." If you click on this, you will return to the top of the page.

As I've said many times, directories are never static. Peter has added after the United States listings an index of countries. Click on any of these to find whatever Church links he has found for that country. As this has recently been added, you won't find the country listing following. But you can certainly explore on your own!

Canada

All Dioceses
http://www.rc.net/canada/index.html

If you want to know anything about the Church in Canada, this should be your first stop.

The Byzantine Catholic Church in America
http://www.epix.net/~byzantin/byzan.html

Interested in the Byzantine Catholic Church?

*A Directory of Personnel: Diocesan Personnel
http://pwa.acusd.edu/~rpgordon/pages/yellowpages.html

Obviously, this one helps those in Canada keep in touch.

United States

Note: (A) means "Archdiocese" following.

Alabama—Mobile (A)
http://www.rc.net/mobile

Here you can find links to about 21 parishes, one shrine, and the archdiocese itself. On the archdiocese page, among other things you can find out about their history and Bishops and get in touch with priests there. The Mobile diocese was founded on May 15, 1829, and became an archdiocese in 1980.

Alabama—Birmingham
http://www.rc.net/birmingham

You will find three parishes listed here. This diocese wasn't founded until 1969.

California—Los Angeles (A)
http://www.rc.net/losangeles

Links here to two parishes, a school, and an abbey. The archdiocese link will take you to the Department of Communications, Office of Vocations, Office of Justice and Peace, and Religious Education Congress. This was made a diocese in 1840 and became an archdiocese in 1936.

California—San Francisco (A)
http://www.rc.net/sanfrancisco

Here you will find Catholic charities, a parish, and an Alumni Club. This one was established in 1853. Its patrons are St. Francis of Assisi and also St. Patrick.

California—Oakland
http://www.rc.net/oakland

Links to two parishes and one Newman Hall. This diocese was established in 1962.

California—Orange
http://www.rc.net/orange

See five parishes and a high school. Established in 1976, this diocese chose Our Lady of Guadalupe for its patroness.

California—San Bernardino
http://www.rc.net/sanbernardino

A couple of parishes found here. The diocese was founded in 1978. Can you guess what saint this one is named after? It's St. Bernardine (d. 1444).

California—San Diego
http://www.rc.net/sandiego

Links to the Cursillo movement and to the same movement for Filipinos. Also, a pointer here takes you to the Tridentine Latin Mass Congregation sanctioned by the Bishop that provides the Tridentine Latin Mass for the faithful of the diocese. See their page for more information about this Mass. The diocese was established in 1936.

California—Santa Rosa
http://www.rc.net/santarosa

A parish and school link here. Established in 1962.

Connecticut—Hartford (A)
http://www.rc.net/hartford

There are three parishes listed here. Don't think there is a St. Hartford, because there isn't. This one is named after a city. It was established in 1843 and became an archdiocese in 1953.

Connecticut—Bridgeport
http://www.rc.net/bridgeport

One school to explore. This diocese was founded in 1953.

District of Columbia—Washington (A)
http://www.rc.net/washington

Links to five parishes and a high school. The archdiocese was established in 1939.

Florida—Miami (A)
http://www.rc.net/miami

The archdiocese homepage is available here in English or Spanish. As you can imagine, there is a lot of information. Founded in 1958, it was made an archdiocese 10 years later.

Florida—Pensacola-Tallahassee
http://www.rc.net/pensacola

One parish listed and the diocesan homepage. So many dioceses were recently founded, including this one in 1975.

Florida—St. Augustine
http://www.rc.net/staugustine

The diocesan page can be found here. Besides the usual information, you can look at "Religious Images." In 1870 this one became a diocese.

Georgia—Atlanta (A)
http://www.rc.net/atlanta

The Catholic Center at George Tech and the page of the archdiocese is here. Of particular interest on the latter page is the archdiocese's "Eucharistic Renewal" plans. I wonder why I found that interesting? Atlanta was established in 1956 and became an archdiocese six years later. For patrons, it has the Immaculate Heart of Mary and Pope St. Pius X.

Georgia—Savannah
http://www.rc.net/savannah

Here at the diocesan homepage you can find out about Supreme Court Justice Clarence Thomas' visit to the Catholic Pastoral Center. This diocese, established in 1850, has chosen Our Lady of Perpetual Help and St. John the Baptist for its patroness and patron. It has also been consecrated to the Sacred Heart of Jesus and the Immaculate Heart of Mary.

Idaho—Boise
http://www.rc.net/boise

Find out about the "Monastery of St. Gertrude" and visit a parish here. This one was erected as a diocese by Pope Leo XIII in 1893.

Illinois—Chicago (A)
http://www.rc.net/chicago

Here you will find links to three parishes, the "Calvert House" at the University of Chicago, and the Archdiocesan page—with the usual tons of stuff on it. Also, an interesting link is the "Newview regional ministry for those in their 20s or 30s." I can still join this one, but better do it soon! This archdiocese goes back to 1880.

Illinois—Joliet
http://www.rc.net/joliet

Eight parishes, two schools, and the diocesan page can be found here. This one took for its patron St. Francis Xavier when it was established in 1948.

Illinois—Peoria
http://www.rc.net/peoria

One parish listed along with the diocesan page here. This one goes back to 1877.

Indiana—Evansville
http://www.rc.net/evansville

A lone parish can be found here. In 1944 Pope Pius XII established this one.

Kentucky—Louisville (A)
http://www.rc.net/louisville

Links to a parish and the archdiocesan page. This one moved around. In 1808 it was established in Bardstown and then moved to Louisville in 1841. It became an archdiocese in 1937.

Louisiana—Alexandria
http://www.rc.net/alexandria

A couple of parishes here to look at. In 1853 this one also was established in another town and then moved to Alexandria in 1910.

Maryland—Baltimore (A)
http://www.realinfo.com/pope/

On the archdiocesan page you will want to look under "Related Links" to find "People in the Church," people who made a difference. This one goes back a ways, having been established in 1789 and made an archdiocese in 1808. Because this is such a historically important place for the establishment of the Church in this country, its archbishop takes precedence over all the other archbishops in the United States.

Massachusetts—Boston (A)
http://www.rc.net/boston

Seven parishes, a school, and the archdiocesan page are here. On the latter page, get the answer to the hot question of our times: "How can a marriage be declared null?" Boston was erected in 1808 and raised to an archdiocese in 1875.

Michigan—Detroit (A)
http://www.rc.net/detroit

Five parishes can be found here. I just happened to come across the Divine Child page's description of their stained glass windows with pictures that you may want to see. Established in 1833, Detroit became an archdiocese in 1937.

Michigan—Grand Rapids
http://www.rc.net/grandrapids

A couple of parish links here. This one was established back in 1882.

Michigan—Kalamazoo
http://www.rc.net/kalamazoo

St. Thomas More Student's Parish has a link. This one only became a diocese in 1971.

Michigan—Lansing
http://www.rc.net/lansing

See 12 parishes and a couple student centers. This one came into existence in 1937.

Minnesota—St. Paul Minneapolis (A)
http://www.rc.net/stpaul

At this archdiocesan page, you can learn some "Did You Know?" trivia about Catholics and find out about movies on the "Movie Review Line." Established in 1850, this one became an archdiocese in 1888.

Mississippi—Biloxi
http://www.rc.net/biloxi

Consists of three parishes and the diocesan page. It was established in 1977 and its Bishop took "Unity of God's People" for his motto.

Missouri—St. Louis (A)
http://www.rc.net/stlouis

Links to four parishes. This one has a few patrons in St. Louis of France (d. 1270), St. Vincent de Paul, and the recently canonized St. Phillipine Duchesne. It was founded in 1826 and became an archdiocese in 1847.

New Hampshire—Manchester
http://www.rc.net/manchester

A parish and the diocesan page are here. On the latter you might want to see "The Bookstore at Ste. Marie" if you are looking for religious books or gifts. Established in 1884, the present Bishop has taken "To Love and Serve" for his motto. I couldn't think of a better one.

New Jersey—Newark (A)
http://www.rc.net/newark

Links to a parish, a school, and the diocese. I have stopped at the airport in Newark more than once. Anyway, this one was erected in 1853 and raised to an archdiocese in 1937. The present archbishop has chosen "Come Lord Jesus" for his motto.

New Jersey—Paterson
http://www.rc.net/paterson

A couple of parishes and St. Mary's Abbey can be found here. This one was established in 1937. The present Bishop has chosen the Greek word "Maranatha," meaning "Come Lord," for his motto.

New Mexico—Santa Fe (A)
http://www.rc.net/santafe

A lonely parish is listed here—they must be taking a long siesta in Santa Fe. Established in 1850 and raised to an archdiocese in 1875, Santa Fe has been consecrated to the Immaculate Heart of Mary. Its patron is St. Francis of Assisi.

New Mexico—Las Cruces
http://www.cibola.net/alc

A page of facts about the diocese is here. Established in 1982. This city is named "The Crosses" in Spanish meaning the three crosses on Calvary.

New York—New York (A)
http://www.rc.net/newyork

Another lonely parish listed. This one was made a diocese in 1808 and an arch-diocese in 1850. The present archbishop has this for his motto: "There can be no love without justice."

North Carolina—Charlotte
http://www.rc.net/charlotte

A link to a parish and Mecklenburg area Catholic schools. This diocese was begun in 1972.

North Carolina—Raleigh
http://www.rc.net/raleigh

The diocesan page with an audio message from the Bishop, slide show, and photos of a Chrism Mass. Pope Pius XI (d. 1939) made this a diocese in 1924. The Bishop has chosen "To serve not to be served" as his motto.

North Dakota—Fargo
http://www.rc.net/fargo

One parish listed here. Formerly Jamestown, the diocese of Fargo began in 1897. The Bishop has taken "Lord teach us" as his motto.

Ohio—Cincinnati (A)
http://www.rc.net/cincinnati

Three parishes, the Catholic Kiosk page, and the archdiocese are here. On the latter, you can hear an audio of a monthly prayer and much more. This diocese was founded in 1821 and made an archdiocese in 1850. "Goodness, truth and justice" is the Bishop's motto.

Ohio—Columbus
http://www.rc.net/columbus

A link to the diocesan department of education here. This diocese was founded in 1868.

Ohio—Steubenville

http://www.rc.net/steubenville

Consists of the Franciscan University and a parish link. The diocese of Steubenville was begun in 1944. The Bishop's motto tells us that our strength comes from our Faith.

Oklahoma—Tulsa

http://www.rc.net/tulsa

Links to the cathedral and diocesan page. Some interesting things on the latter: "Articles on the Catholic Faith," "Explanation of Catholic Terms," and "Ask a Priest." This diocese was founded 1973, and the Bishop's motto is "You alone are holy."

Oregon—Portland (A)

http://www.rc.net/portland

A link to Our Lady of the Mountain parish that sounds like a great place to actually visit. The page will give you their history with six photos. Portland became an archdiocese in 1846. The Bishop's motto is "Brothers in Unity."

Pennsylvania—Philadelphia (A)

http://www.rc.net/philadelphia

Three parishes, a history of the archdiocese page, and the archdiocese itself. On the last one you can listen to some entertaining music while browsing the page. The patroness and patrons of the diocese are Our Lady under the title of her Immaculate Conception and Saints Peter and Paul. This archdiocese has been consecrated to the Sacred Heart of Jesus and the Immaculate Heart of Mary. Philadelphia was made a diocese in 1808 and an archdiocese in 1875.

Pennsylvania—Altoona-Johnstown

http://www.rc.net/altoona

Get connected to the Penn State Catholic Community here. This one was made a diocese in 1901 and the Bishop's saying is "Household of God."

Pennsylvania—Pittsburgh
http://www.rc.net/pittsburgh

Consists of two parishes and the diocesan page. The Bishop's motto is "Thy kingdom come." This one was made a diocese in 1843.

Pennsylvania—Scranton
http://www.rc.net/scranton

Two parishes and a school listed here. Scranton was made a diocese in 1868. The Bishop's motto is "Faith, hope, and charity."

South Carolina—Charleston
http://www.rc.net/charleston

You will find three parishes, a school, and the diocese listed. On the latter you can read their Catholic newspaper online. This diocese was founded in 1820.

Tennessee—Memphis
http://www.rc.net/memphis

Links to a parish and high school can be found. The Bishop's motto is "The Lord is my light." This one was made a diocese in 1971.

Texas—San Antonio (A)
http://www.rc.net/sanantonio

Three parishes can be found, one of which is Our Lady of The Atonement, a Roman Catholic parish that has permission for worship in what is called the Anglican Use. San Antonio was made a diocese 1874 and an archdiocese in 1926.

Texas—Galveston-Houston
http://www.rc.net/galveston

Another parish with Anglican use is found here. The Bishop's motto is "Thy kingdom come." In 1847 this one was made a diocese.

Texas—San Angelo
http://www.rc.net/sanangelo

The diocesan page found here has a lot of local information, including their newspaper that you might want to browse through. This Bishop's motto in Latin is similar to St. Louis Marie de Montfort's popular saying, "To Jesus through Mary." San Angelo was established as a diocese in 1961.

Virginia—Arlington
http://www.rc.net/arlington

Another diocesan page where you can find much information and read the newspaper. The Bishop's motto is "Be rooted in Him." Arlington was established as a diocese in 1974.

Virginia—Richmond
http://www.rc.net/richmond

Two parishes, a Newman community, and the diocese are located here. "To unite all in Christ" is the Bishop's motto. This one was made a diocese in 1820.

Washington—Spokane
http://www.rc.net/spokane

Another lonely parish on the Web here. This diocese was consecrated to the Immaculate Heart of Mary in 1948. Spokane was made a diocese in 1913.

Wisconsin—La Crosse
http://www.rc.net/lacrosse

Four parishes, a Newman community, and the diocese are here. This diocese was begun in 1868.

National Council of Catholic Bishops
http://www.nccbuscc.org

Look here for weekly updates of what's going on in the Catholic world, both locally and globally. I added this one; you won't find it on Peter's listing on the Internet.

CONTENT PROVIDERS

http://www.rc.net/home.html

I have shortened this list, as some items on Peter's Internet list have appeared more than once earlier in this book.

Catholic Christian Outreach
http://www.sasknet.com/~cco/

This is a wonderful student movement that challenges members to live in the fullness of their Catholic faith with a strong emphasis on becoming leaders in the renewal of the world.

Catholic World Wide Web Directory
http://www.catholic.org/colweb/links.html

Catholic Online's links to Catholic sites on the Internet. There are enough links here to keep you surfing the Net for awhile.

Envoy Magazine
http://www.envoymagazine.com/envoy

Catholic apologetics and evangelization magazine. This homepage catches your eye. You can select the magazine itself, other apologetic articles, or links to Catholic apostolates. They use frames so you will find the table of contents in the left-hand window.

Other Documents of the Catholic Church
http://www.rc.net/resource.html

Another link to links of Catholic resources. You can find links to the Bible, the early Fathers of the Church, and Church documents. There are also links to classic Christian books and more.

Spirituality for Today
http://www.spirituality.org/

A spiritually enriching homepage. You will find a link to their different monthly issues, following which is a short summary of what you will find in the issue.

 APOSTOLATES

http://www.rc.net/org/

The term *Apostolate* is derived from the word apostle, and not by an accident of language. Those in apostolates are in their own way like the apostles who tried to bring Christ to people through teaching, praying, and works of charity.

 Catholic Vision/Catholic Home Schooling Resources
http://pages.prodigy.com/web-source/home.htm

The Reyburns know about homeschooling—they have been doing it for 12 years with their own children. The Catholic Vision is a Catholic bookstore and study center. See their recommended books, tapes, magazines, games, and movies at the bookstore. At the study center you can see their monthly newsletter, read informative youth articles, ask a theologian, and more. Find coloring pictures and games for the whole family on their "Activities" page or meet pen pals and even see a picture of the whole family.

 The Divine Mercy Region, SFO
http://www.rc.net/org/dmercy

This one is put up by the Secular Franciscan Order located in lower Michigan and Toledo, Ohio. You can look at their newsletter and search for any SFO's closest to you.

 EWTN Global Catholic Network
http://www.ewtn.com/

I'm sure you know what this is! If you don't, I know you skipped to the end of the book!

 Focolare
http://www.rc.net/focolare

Far better known in Europe than in the United States. Be sure to see this homepage. Besides information about the Focolare themselves, you might want to read *The Word of Life*, their monthly publication.

*The Fraternity of Mary
http://pwa.acusd.edu/~rpgordon/fratmary.html

This sounds like a great group.

John Paul II Bible School
http://www.rc.net/org/jpiibs

In Alberta, Canada, some people, along with their Bishop, founded a residential Catholic Bible school. Each September students arrive for a nine-month interactive program in Scripture study, community life, and growth in the life of prayer. At the end you receive a diploma in Sacred Studies. You can read stories about how others came there, read their mission and vision, and find out details such as how much the program costs and how to apply.

Knights of Columbus Richard Council 788
http://members.aol.com/richard788

Besides finding out about this local council, you can find links to information about the Knights in general, other councils, the National Center for Missing and Exploited Children, their newsletter, and more.

Maranatha Renewal Center, Ontario, Canada
http://www.rc.net/maranatha

A charismatic center.

The Monks of Adoration
http://www.rc.net/org/monks

I can't help but recommend this one! I was happy to put together this homepage. You won't find frills here but, I believe, will find good Catholic information. I will put a form on this homepage so you can comment on it and submit your homepage address.

The Paulist Fathers Catholic Information Site
http://www.rc.net/org/paulist

Their mission is to reach out to those who are not Christian, to build new relationships with other committed Christians and their churches, and to minister to marginal Catholics or Catholics separated from the Church. You can find out more about the Paulist Fathers here, read their newsletter, and follow some Catholic links.

Queen's Chinese Catholic Community, Kingston, Ontario
http://www.ams.queensu.ca/qccc

See what the Chinese Catholics are doing in Canada. In case you missed my earlier discussion about this homepage, there are some interesting things you can do here, including taking a Bible quiz! Their table of contents goes across the top of the page, but you won't want to miss what's written on their blackboard farther down on the screen. This is what you might call a seamless frame page. There are two frames here but the dividing line between them is hidden.

Washtenaw Covenant Community, Ann Arbor, Michigan
http://www.rc.net/wcc

An international ecumenical community of communities dedicated to proclaiming the Good News of Jesus Christ and to raising a new generation for mission in the next millennium. They respect religious differences among members and acknowledge that there are serious disagreements among the churches. Nonetheless, they believe that much is shared among Christians. This was the same belief of Pope John XXIII, who opened the Second Vatican Council. See photos of community life in action, "Words of Life" (a Christian resource of art, literature, scripture, and teaching), and more.

World Wide Marriage Encounter, Region 6
http://www.rc.net/org/me6

Here you will find couples who believe very strongly in marriage—not just as an institution but as a way of life. This is the Midwest region of Marriage Encounter. You will find a map of the United States with points of contact for this movement, links to other Marriage Encounter resources, and downloadable artwork.

The Xaverian Mission
http://www.rc.net/org/xaverian

They take their name and inspiration from the patron of the missions, St. Francis Xavier. The Xaverians live in small communities spread throughout Africa, the

Americas, Asia, and Europe—sharing their Faith and witnessing to God's love as they do their part in continuing the mission of Jesus in the world. My policeman friend, Mike Farrell, put this page together. If I don't recommend it, I might get arrested!

And from Outside North America . . .

Fides et scientia (National University of Singapore Catholic Students' Society)
http://www.veritas.org.sg/~nuscss

Faith and science.

The Pontifical Filipino College, Rome
http://www.rc.net/rome/collegio_filippino

(In English, Tagalog, German, Spanish, French, or Italian) Here you can do research (libraries, academic journals, and dissertation abstracts), copy books or documents, visit the Philippines, and get some information on news, travel, and leisure.

Retrouvaille . . . A Lifeline for Married Couples
http://yarra.vicnet.net.au/~retro/welcome.htm

This is a helpful ministry that I have commented on before. If you don't want to go back and look at the comment, visit the page instead!

SEARCH ENGINES

http://www.rc.net/search.html

Peter Wagner has provided links to some popular search engines so that people visiting can find what they are looking for if they don't find it on his site. If you click on his links to the various search engines, you will be taken directly to them. He has an alternative, also. You can type in the subject you are looking for in one of the blank boxes he has provided then click on the name of the search engine next to that box. This will submit your subject to that search engine and return to you a page that lists Internet information about that subject. You can learn a lot more about this by going to "Searching the Net" found in Chapter 14.

Search.com

http://www.search.com

A bunch of useful search engines! I have used this one often because of this.

 Yahoo!

http://www.yahoo.com

The most popular engine! Imagine this one was started by some university students.

 Excite!

http://www.excite.com

Claims to be "100% smarter than Yahoo!" Now that's exciting!

 Webcrawler

http://www.webcrawler.com

Lightning-fast search engine.

 Altavista

http://altavista.digital.com

This used to be the largest. Like in everything else, somebody is always competing to one-up you.

 Hotbot

http://www.hotbot.com

This engine claims to be the largest!

OTHER REFERENCES FROM THE INDEX

http://www.rc.net

Today's Mass
http://www.christusrex.org/www1/mcitl/

Readings, homily, and more from St. Ann's Media. You know, we don't often think about the fact that St. Ann is Jesus' grandmother.

Meeting Christ in the Liturgy
http://www.christusrex.org/www1/mcitl/

These are weekly homilies citing the Catechism (see site following).

Catechism of the Catholic Church
http://www.christusrex.org/www1/CDHN/ccc.html

I think it's an excellent idea to use the Catechism in homilies. People need to know their Faith, especially these days.

Matins
http://www.universalis.com/cgi-bin/display/-600/USA/Matins.html

Vespers
http://www.universalis.com/cgi-bin/display/-600/USA/Vespers.html

Liturgy of the Hours from Universalis Publishing.

The Office of Readings
http://www.universalis.com/cgi-bin/display/-600/USA/Readings.html

Universalis Publishing again; the current day's Psalms and readings. There are two readings: one taken from Sacred Scripture and the other one from writings of the saints or Church documents.

Daily Meditations
http://www.rc.net/wcc/readings/index.htm

An aid for daily prayer and meditation.

Essays, Homilies
http://www.rc.net/lansing/st_fran/fr_charlie.html

From Rev. Fr. Charles Irvin of St. Francis of Assisi
http://www.rc.net/lansing/st_fran/

Priests go to such time and effort preparing their homilies. They can reach more people by putting them on the Internet.

The Holy See
http://www.vatican.va

Soon to be the biggest content provider of them all. Many times in common language usage we say "The Vatican" instead of Holy See. Strictly speaking, the Vatican refers to the country. The Holy See refers to the Pope and the congregations that help him govern the Church.

About RCNet
http://www.rc.net/about.html

You shouldn't need to look at this one as I have told you just about everything you need to know about them. Of course, Peter may have added a few things since I looked at this page.

13

Catholic and Christian
Resources on the Internet

http://user.bnoc.net/merlin/catholic

Danny Greene has put together this directory of Catholic links, set up to be an Internet directory. Danny had the bad luck of being the last directory listing in my book. I say bad luck because I had to omit sites he listed that were repeated elsewhere in the book. Given the fact that I already listed so many Catholic sites, his odds of repeating one were very high. I tell you this so you understand that his directory has many more listings than appear is this section.

When you go to this directory on the Internet, you will find it straightforward. The table of contents is listed along the left-hand side of the page; in the middle are comments. The diocese and student organization links have been so extensively covered earlier in this book that they are not detailed here, but you will find the links to them in "Other References from the Index." I have not included "General Christian Sites" from his table of contents because this book is concerned with Catholic sites.

Danny has a good system of updating his links. He puts the new ones on the top of the list. Want a site added to this listing or inform Danny of a link that doesn't work? E-mail Danny Greene at merlin@washington.xtn.net.

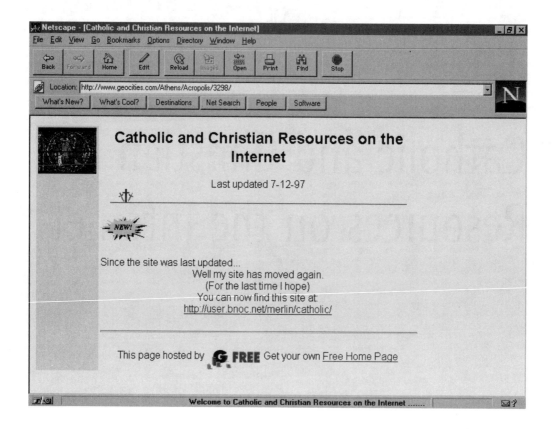

INFO GENERAL CATHOLIC SITES

http://user.bnoc.net/merlin/catholic/gener.htm

 Nazareth Resource Library
http://www.io-online.com/james/

If you like libraries, be sure to not miss this one. The opening page says, "I would like information about . . ." and then lists topics along the left-hand side with links to more information about them on the right. If you don't like this format, you will find the table of contents for this site across the top and bottom of this page. There is all kinds of information about the Church here. It also covers other groups and individuals. Finally, it has links to other Catholic sites.

PARISH AND CHURCH SITES

http://user.bnoc.net/merlin/catholic/church.htm

Now every parish I know has a church or place of worship attached to it. But the reverse does not hold true. You can have churches that are not parishes, for example, churches that are shrines.

St. John the Baptist Parish
http://www.SJBNewburgh.Org/

The feast of St. John the Baptist is June 24. This homepage has a nice sketch of the church on it. As you scroll down on this page you will see links organized in a table with topic headings like "What's Happening at St. John Parish." Here you may want to see the jumping letters on the "Fortress of Fun" page—this was the first time I had seen this special effect. You will most likely want to see the pictorial view of the parish events and perhaps send them a prayer request. There is more here, but I will let you explore it yourself.

St. Andrew's Parish
http://www.hooked.net/users/amdg85/st_andrw.html

Hear pleasant organ music as you explore their homepage. You can see pictures of the staff, read their bulletin and reflection of the Sunday Gospel, hear a good selection of English and Tagalog songs while reading the lyrics, submit a prayer request, follow a good selection of Catholic links, and laugh at their jokes and stories.

Holy Family Catholic Church
http://catholic-church.org/holyfamily/

As you know by now, I like photos. Here you can see a picture of the church and altar area. Also, there is a link to the Diocese of Nashville and the city of Brentwood. I thought I would check out the city and was greeted with a flashing "Need A Job?" Perhaps I should apply.

CATHOLIC SCHOOLS, COLLEGES, AND UNIVERSITIES

http://user.bnoc.net/merlin/catholic/coll.htm

As you know, I have already listed large directories for Catholic schools at all levels on the Internet, but perhaps I missed a few. So I'm giving you Danny's smaller list just in case.

Schools

The Soden Memorial Council for International Education at St. Joseph International School, Yokohama
http://www.dnai.com/~ainai/SJIS/SaveSJIS.html

This homepage is really a plea for you to help keep this school open. They seem to have forestalled the board of directors from closing it for a while anyway. They are working hard to make the school a success. You can read about what they are doing here.

St. Joseph International School Volunteer Organization
mendosan@erols.com

Related to the school above. A volunteer organization of active alumni committed to global "bridge building" through international Catholic education was formed for program development, recruitment, and fund-raising. It is based in Seattle, and Reston, Virginia.

St. Joseph International School of Yokohama, Japan, has been educating students in the Marianist tradition since 1901. They welcome inquiries from students from across Japan and around the world. You can e-mail them at the following address:

Father James Mueller, SM, Principal
sjislib@gol.com

Colleges and Universities

*Loyola University of New Orleans
http://www.review.com/college/index_survey_js.html

You know when you see "Loyola" in any title that Jesuits are somehow involved. This is because their founder was St. Ignatius of Loyola.

*Jesuit Universities
http://www.gonzaga.edu/AJCU/AJCUSchools.html

Of course, Jesuits run these universities! It came to my mind that perhaps people did not always have last names. Many saints were later given last names that represented where they were from—like Ignatius, who was from the town of Loyola, Spain, became "of Loyola." Does anybody know Mother Teresa of Calcutta's last name?

Dominican College of San Rafael
http://www.dominican.edu/

Run by the Dominican Sisters. You will want to see the little photos that go along with the table of contents. If you like pictures, you can almost bet there will be some on any school page under "Athletics." It looks like they are still working on this page, as some listings in the table of contents don't have links yet. But there is certainly enough to look at now.

CATHOLIC ORDERS, CENTERS, AND COMMUNITIES

http://user.bnoc.net/merlin/catholic/cocac.htm

Sometimes a smaller list is better, as a big list can be overwhelming to some people. There is a new technique that I have seen on the Internet of chaining homepages together to form a circle. So when you go to, say, one parish, you would find a link to the next parish and so forth. This is an interesting idea and can give you the sense of touring around a certain place.

The Benedictine Sister's Midwestern Region
http://www.benedictine.edu/mount.html

Here you can find some interesting links to spiritual leaders, the feminine perspective, the Benedictine world, Benedictine monasteries and abbeys for men and women and more.

Order of Saint Benedict Index
http://bingen.cs.csbsju.edu/~osb/index.html

Want to look something up about the Benedictines? You can find everything you want here. I like the clip-art picture of St. Benedict. You are greeted at the top of the page by a quote from the Rule of St. Benedict for his monks: "Let them prefer nothing whatever to Christ." Don't you think that is a good rule for everybody?

Sisters of the Blessed Sacrament
http://www.libertynet.org/~sbs/

The special concern of these sisters is for the poor and oppressed, to whom they reach out among the Native American, African American, and Haitian peoples. Blessed Katharine Drexel, who was from Philadelphia, founded this community. Find out more about her, learn a prayer to her, and read about her shrine. (I have visited it.) Educators can learn about "Workshop Way," an elementary school teaching method.

Legion of Mary
http://transporter.com/lom/

Truly a wonderful ministry mentioned before in this book. The spiritual life has been looked upon as a battle so many times that you will see names like "legion" or "soldiers" that appear to have come from the army.

Apologetics

http://user.bnoc.net/merlin/catholic/apol.htm

As you know, I am all for apologetics. When one has lived in areas where there are few Catholics, as I have, one can't help but be drawn into debates with other denominations who are trying to refute your beliefs. Unfortunately, for those who don't know their Catholic Faith well, the misguided arguments against the Church seem to have some plausibility. That's why we need to learn how to defend ourselves and the Church from these errors. On these pages, you will learn how to do this.

Catholic Evidence Guild in the Diocese of Lansing, Michigan
http://www.itd.umich.edu/~ximenez/ceg/index.html

Their aim is to help people learn more about the Catholic Church and get answers to their questions about the Church and her teachings.

 Catholic Answers
http://www.catholic.com/cgi-shl/index.pl

Get your questions answered here. Of course, you can't take all the mystery out of what we believe because then there would be no reason for Faith. But we can support *why* we believe what we do, even if we cannot grasp fully the mystery of, for instance, the Three Persons in One God.

CATHOLIC MEDIA SITES

http://user.bnoc.net/merlin/catholic/media.htm

The media basically runs our modern world. We probably get most of our information from TV and newspapers and now we can get a lot of it from the Internet. There has never been an age where people have so much information at their fingertips. But with such a glut of information, we have to be selective and not waste our time reading useless stuff. Rather we should use the advantages of technology to feed our soul with good spiritual information.

 *Good Earth Ministry Support
http://www.roysphones.com/homegems.htm

This one reminds me of *The Good Earth,* Pearl Buck's novel. Now it is true that some people have gone overboard about the earth, almost to the point of worshipping it. But the idea of caring for the earth that God has created originates with the Book of Genesis, in which God commands us to take care of it.

 *Catholic Engaged Encounter
http://www.roysphones.com/homeee.htm

Retreats for those engaged to be married. This is such a good idea that I would want every engaged couple to get involved in this before getting married. Marriage is a sacrament and a lifetime commitment. As with any vocation, marriage requires that we seriously reflect on the obligations we are taking upon ourselves. Sometimes this involves help from others.

CATHOLIC DOCTRINE, HISTORY, AND BIBLE RESOURCES

http://user.bnoc.net/merlin/catholic/bible.htm

Although the Internet provides so many useful Catholic sources, it sure is easier to learn all this in a school. Perhaps people with expertise in different fields of theology will give lectures or classes on the Internet. I know this is being done on a smaller scale on certain Catholic forums or chat areas offered through the big Internet access providers like CompuServe or America Online. Anyway, you can certainly find people to answer your questions if you find something difficult to understand.

 ## Catechism of the Catholic Church
http://www.christusrex.org/www1/CDHN/ccc.html

This site, representing a great source for the learning of the Faith, put a lot of information in its pages. Included here are references from many Church documents, saints, and so forth that obviously could not be quoted in their entirety. You can always use the Catechism as a jumping-off point to other sources on a particular topic of interest.

 ## Catholic Doctrinal Concordance
http://www2.best.com/~ipage/concorda.htm

This collection of basic Catholic doctrines (and where to find the Biblical support for them) is arranged by topic. You may want to print this one out so you are prepared for the many times Catholics are asked, "Where is that in the Bible?" Sometimes I would like to respond, "Where did we get the Bible?" or "How do you know it is the Word of God?" The answer to both comes from the Church. The Church existed before any of the New Testament was written. The Church decided which books and letters were inspired by the Holy Spirit, which of them would be included in the Bible. The Bible came out of this Tradition and in it we read that it is not the final word on everything (Cf. Jn. 21, 25).

 ## The Catholic Encyclopedia
http://www.csn.net/advent/cathen/cathen.htm

This one obviously includes a lot. I sure hope they were able to scan this in, as it would have taken a long time to type it all!

World Wide Study Bible
http://ccel.wheaton.edu/wwsb/

Here you will find the Old and New Testament books and Apocrypha (that the Church considers canonical and refers to as Deuterocanonical).

OTHER REFERENCES FROM THE INDEX

http://user.bnoc.net/merlin/catholic/

Diocese Sites
http://user.bnoc.net/merlin/catholic/dioc.htm

Just because this one has been covered before doesn't mean that you can't explore his listing here. He has a fair number of links in the United States and some in Canada, the United Kingdom, and other countries abroad.

Newman Centers and Catholic Student Organizations
http://user.bnoc.net/merlin/catholic/newman.htm

This page really can't beat the one found at Cal Tech that lists so many student organizations. The page's layout is similar with a listing by regions in the United States then by country.

14

Looking for Information on the Internet in General

I have already covered hundreds of places to look for Catholic information. If you have come this far in the book and haven't found what you were looking for, what do you do? Perhaps you are looking for a particular person, place, newspaper, magazine, or mailing list not mentioned in this book, or are curious to see if a particular topic is on the Internet. I hope this section can help you find it. I must admit I have not spent much time searching for items on the Internet, but I do know a few search engines that can direct me to what I am looking for. For example, at http://www.search.com, I found a meta-searcher, which passes the information you are searching for to multiple search engines. If you don't know what search engines are, read the section on them following. I typed in the phrase "search engine information" at search.com and found myself with links to various pages that had something to say about search engines. One in particular was helpful—a homepage at a Moscow State University. You really can travel around the world on the Internet! Here, I found a research study comparing different search engines and their ability to find scientific information. That was not very useful to me as I was *not* trying to build a spacecraft in order to become the first monk on the moon! But the homepage did contain useful links to other homepages that discussed how to find what one is looking for on the Internet.

A particularly helpful homepage called, appropriately enough, "The Search Page" was put together by J. Marcus Ziegler. It is an excellent directory or hotlist for people who want to search the Internet and World Wide Web (WWW) for something but don't know where to start. He wrote this page because he was interested in learning a bit about HTML. Since he had plenty of search information on hand for his own use, he decided to create "The Search Page." You can find it at http://www. accesscom.com/~ziegler/search.html. Much of the information following comes from Mr. Ziegler's wonderful homepage.

SEARCHING FOR INFORMATION

Have you ever wanted to know what happened on a particular day in history? Perhaps the day you were born? Well, somebody thought you just might want to ask such a question. The following sites are for general information. You might never need them, but who knows? You might want to invent your own trivial pursuit board game.

Anyday in History
http://www.scopesys.com/anyday/

Search by month and day to see lists of what happened on that day. Can be an interesting way to find events in Church history.

Consumer World
http://www.consumerworld.org/

Fifteen hundred consumer resources on the Internet. Are you looking for people selling religious goods? You might be able to track them down here.

FAQ Finder
http://ps.superb.net/FAQ/

Contains links to 1,800 lists of frequently asked questions in 28 categories. Have a question about something? Look here for the answer.

Links Dictionary/Encyclopedia
http://www.linksdic.com/

Thousands of links listed alphabetically by subject. Want to find more about something in particular? Look here for the information.

SEARCHING FOR INTERNET HELP

Although I have already mentioned some places to look for Internet help, here are more places to get some help on the Internet, the World Wide Web, or on Netiquette (that is, etiquette for the Internet).

15-Minute Series
http://rs.internic.net/nic-support/15min/

Forty-one slide presentations of Internet training materials.

Beginners Central
http://www.digital-cafe.com/~webmaster/begin00.html

Tells you how and where to find information.

Internet Books
http://www.northcoast.com/savetz/booklist/

Contains 560 book bibliographies about the Internet.

Internet Exploring
http://www.screen.com/understand/exploring.html

Subject indexes and search tools, links to resources on Netiquette.

Net Lingo
http://www.netlingo.com/

Internet lingo dictionary of acronyms and terms.

NetLinks
http://www.netlinks.net/

A lot of information for beginners.

Roadmap96
http://ua1vm.ua.edu/~crispen/roadmap.html

Free Internet training workshop for beginners.

SEARCHING FOR INTERNET DIGESTS

Digests include daily or weekly information about the latest things on the Internet and World Wide Web. If you like keeping on top of things, you will want to look at these places.

InfoSeek WebTimes
http://www.infoseek.com/webtimes

Daily guide to what's developing in the Internet world.

InterNIC News
http://rs.internic.net/nic-support/nicnews/

Monthly newsletter by experts on the Internet.

Net Happenings
http://www.gi.net/NET/

Daily report of what's new on the Internet and World Wide Web.

The Scout Report
http://rs.internic.net/scout/report/

Weekly pick of new Internet resources.

SEARCHING FOR INTERNET MAILING LISTS

I have already mentioned some places to look for mailing lists and newsgroups. Here are a few more places to find what you are looking for.

E-Mail Resources
http://www.ronin.com/pa-software/email.html

Contains links to e-mail–related resources and discussion groups.

Forum One
http://www.ForumOne.com/

Searches 41,000 online discussion forums.

Liszt

http://www.liszt.com/

Sixty-six thousand listserv, listproc, and majordomo lists from 2,200 sites.

Liszt of Newsgroups

http://www.liszt.com/cgi-bin/news.cgi

Fifteen thousand two hundred sixty-four Usenet newsgroups.

Reference.Com

http://www.reference.com/

Search Usenet, newsgroup, and mailing list directories.

SEARCHING FOR INTERNET SERVICE PROVIDERS

Find a local Internet Service Provider (ISP), or what I have often referred to as an Internet access provider. Living in a monastery in the middle of nowhere, I was calling long-distance to get Internet access (only a few surrounding towns were on the local exchange). Not exactly an ideal situation! Fortunately, I learned that Prodigy had an Internet access site in one of these towns. I then discovered that with Windows 95 I could go to "My Computer," then "Dial-up Networking" and connect to the Prodigy Internet access site. Once connected to the Internet, I could use either of the browsers Internet Explorer or Netscape Navigator to "surf the Net."

Even more amazing, I could access CompuServe from this local connection. (I had been dialing their Boston phone number before, which was a toll call!) First, connect with "Dial-Up" and then run the CompuServe program as you normally would. America Online will allow you to do this also. Click the "Setup" button on the "Welcome" screen. In the dialog box, enter TCP/IP then pick the highest possible modem speed. Click "Save." Just repeat the same steps as above with CompuServe and you're in. So for those living in the woods, even you can get Internet access! Here's where to look to find the Internet Service Provider nearest to your home.

Boardwatch Map

http://www.boardwatch.com/isp/usisp.htm

Displays 1,500 providers on a map of the United States.

The Directory
http://www.thedirectory.org/

Sixty-four hundred listings of providers and 47,000 listings of BBSs in 100 countries.

The List
http://thelist.iworld.com/

Forty-four hundred providers organized by different search criteria, such as area code and country.

Meta-List
http://www.herbison.com/herbison/iap_meta_list.html

A list of lists for providers. Also has some pointers on what to look for in a good provider.

SEARCHING FOR BROWSERS AND HTML

Get some help with browsers. Since computer programs no longer come with manuals, few of us know what we are doing with them. Of course, one can always read the "Help" files (but who would want to waste time doing that?) Why not learn from others who have been playing around with them for awhile and have learned the tricks of the trade?

Of course, just when you think you know your program, something new will be added that will throw you back into an ignorant state. As things change on the Internet, your browser may need to be updated—so you can see the latest fancy special effects, for example. You may need to add some "plug-ins," that is, programs that add features to your existing browser. As the old saying goes, "Where there is a need, someone will try to fill it." So some people find out what a browser can't do and write "helper applications" to fill that need.

Need help with HTML? For those who want to get into serious homepage design, why not look to people who have been working at it for awhile?

Browser Central
http://www.cnet.com/Content/Browser/

Info on browsers, plug-ins, helper applications, and reviews of new releases.

HTML Guide
http://www.sun.com/styleguide/

Tells you how to make better Web pages. This was put together by a group of homepage designers at Sun Corporation.

Web Development Resources
http://www.eborcom.com/webmaker/

Everything you wanted to know about HTML.

SEARCHING FOR JAVA AND VRML

This has to do with homepages and deals with making them a little more fun visually. If you play around with these now, or want to learn more about them, here is where to look.

Gamelan
http://www.gamelan.com/

An official directory for Java. Has lots of applets and links.

JavaSoft
http://java.sun.com/

Contains tutorials, FAQs, links, software, and Java information from Sun Corporation.

QuickTime VR
http://qtvr.quicktime.apple.com/

QuickTime VR news, links, files, tools, and authoring primer.

VRML Library
http://cedar.cic.net/~rtilmann/mm/vrml.htm

VRML browsers, editors, authoring tools, tutorials, and links.

VRML Review
http://www.imaginative.com/VResources/vrml

Tutorials, links, news, and reviews of VRML tools.

SEARCHING FOR PEOPLE

If you're looking for somebody on the Internet, you might first try the ordinary telephone book. It's easier to just ask the person for their e-mail address. But if you are really determined to find somebody on the Internet, there are certain places you can look to track a person down.

Finding Addresses FAQ
http://www.qucis.queensu.ca/FAQs/email/finding.html

You might find it helpful to read this before you search the following sites.

InfoSpace AccuMail
http://www.accumail.com/

Offers business, fax, personal homepage, and toll-free directories.

International Telephone Directories
http://www.infobel.be/infobel/infobelworld.html

Directories from 56 countries.

Netscape People
http://home.netscape.com/home/internet-white-pages.html

Links to 15 places to find e-mail addresses. Has good descriptions.

RTFM Usenet Addresses
http://usenet-addresses.mit.edu/

List of four million e-mail addresses at MIT from Usenet news.

Ultimate White Pages
http://www.theultimates.com/white/

Do regular or reverse searching or get a map of an address.

WorldPages
http://www.worldpages.com/

Find people, business, government, URLs, and e-mails all in one place.

SEARCHING FOR BUSINESSES

Perhaps you will never need to look up a business on the Internet, but you never know. So here are some places to look for them.

AT&T Toll Free
http://www.tollfree.att.net:80/

Search toll free numbers (1-800 and 1-888) by name or criteria.

Company Locator
http://www.netpart.com/company/search.html

Search for a company's Web or FTP site—even works with partial names.

MapQuest
http://www.mapquest.com/

Interactive atlas can display international locations on six continents.

Telephone Directories
http://www.contractjobs.com/tel/

Telephone, fax, and business directories from 60 countries.

Ultimate Yellow Pages
http://www.theultimates.com/yellow/

Fast access to nine different yellow pages.

World Yellow Pages
http://www.worldyellowpages.com/

Sixty-five countries in Asia, Africa, Europe, Middle East, and United States.

SEARCHING FOR GOVERNMENT INFORMATION

Politics is certainly not a field with which I am familiar. But I do know that governments at times implement policies that go against Church teachings. As Catholics, we need to let them know when they have overstepped the authority given them. Most people are familiar with the constant battle being fought over abortion. To aid us in helping our governments "see the light," there are places we can look to find information about the government and how to reach key government people.

GovBot
http://www.business.gov/Search_Online.html

Search 106,000 Web pages from government sites across the United States.

Government Resources
http://www.lib.umich.edu/libhome/Documents.center/govweb.html

Comprehensive state, federal, and international links.

MEL Government Resources
http://mel.lib.mi.us/government/GOV-index.html

Government, politics, and law (including international).

Pathway Services
http://www.access.gpo.gov/su_docs/aces/aces760.html

Connects to many sources of government information from one site.

U.S. Government E-mail
http://www.peaceday.org/govt_em.htm

The President, Vice-President, Senate, and House members.

SEARCHING FOR SOFTWARE

Although your hard drive is probably filling up fast, there is always another software program out there that you just have to have. On the Internet you will find many software programs, some of which are free. Shareware includes software programs that usually are offered on a trial basis. Eventually, you are expected to send in whatever fee they expect for the program.

Download
http://www.download.com/

Lots of software for the Mac and IBM.

File Mine
http://www.filemine.com/

Freeware and shareware meta-site that contains a searchable interface.

Filez
http://www.filez.com/

Search 5,000 servers and 75 million files for Mac, OS/2, or Windows.

Info-Mac
http://www.pht.com/info-mac/

The largest collection of software for the Macintosh on the Internet.

Pass the Shareware
http://www.passtheshareware.com/

Links to DOS, Mac, OS/2, Unix, Win3/95/NT sites, and beginners' help.

Software Directory Directory
http://boole.stanford.edu/nerdsheaven.html

Shareware, freeware, public domain, and high tech.

SEARCHING FOR NEWS

It seems many people want to know the latest in news. On the Internet you can get news to your heart's content, most of it current. Nobody likes old news! It's good to keep informed, but do we really have to know what's going on in every corner of the world? I thought only God needed to know that!

Media
http://www.sn.no/~thorie/media.html

Worldwide news links, including newspapers, periodicals, and more.

New Century Network
http://www.newcentury.net/

Providing content from 225 daily United States newspapers.

News Central
http://www.everest.simplenet.com/newscentral/

Links to more than 2,700 newspapers.

News Links
http://pppp.net/links/news/

5,300 links to newspapers around the world.

Worldwide Newspapers
http://www.voyager.co.nz/~vag118/news2.html

Comprehensive list of newspapers worldwide.

SEARCHING FOR MAGAZINES

Now if you have time after reading all that news, you might want to look at the Internet magazines. Of course, you may want to know whether your favorite magazine is on it so you won't have to subscribe to it by mail anymore.

E-mail Zines
http://propagandist.com/tkemzl/index.html

Links to 190 e-mail zines, newsletters, mailing lists, and journals.

E-zines
http://www.meer.net/~johnl/e-zine-list/

Links to 1,625 E-zines, organized in 40 categories, and updated monthly.

Monster Magazine
http://www.enews.com/monster/

Two-thousand links dedicated to print and electronic magazines.

Top 100
http://www.netvalley.com/netvalley/top100mag.html

Links to the top 100 computer magazines.

SEARCH ENGINES

Now we have arrived at the famous search engines. A search engine allows you to enter what you want to search for on the Internet. Of course, being somewhat limited, a single search engine will have its own database of information that it has compiled. Since you will be turning to these often, I thought a little more detail would be helpful. The following search engines should find 99 percent of what you are looking for.

Alta Vista
http://www.altavista.digital.com/

Thirty million Web pages and 3 million articles from Usenet news. It tells you how many matches it found for each word you specified. This can be helpful because a particular word may have so many matches that it is useless for the search. Alta Vista lists the results of the search. For each match it gives you a link with title and URL, the first few dozen words of the page's text, a file size, and the date on which Alta Vista inserted the entry into its database. The matches are ranked with the best matches appearing first. Alta Vista normally searches only the World Wide Web, but you can search Usenet newsgroups as well.

Now there are tricks to searching. You will soon find out that the more specific you can be in your search, the better. If I just search for the word "Catholic," I might find 200,000 matches. It could take me a few years to look through them. So it is better to limit the search. You can use the basic Boolean operators "and," "or," and "not" in your search. For example, I can search by entering the following: Catholic AND Augustine AND Hippo NOT Canterbury. This would find homepages with all the words Catholic, Augustine, and Hippo but not with the word Canterbury. This would help to screen out homepages that mention St. Augustine of Canterbury. When searching for a phrase, you should put the words in quotes. This tells this search engine to look for a phrase. Therefore the words in quotes must appear directly adjacent to each other in the homepage. So, for example, I can enter: "The Monks of Adoration." I would receive homepages only with these four words next to each other.

There are other tricks for searching with multiple words. You can type the word you're searching for prefaced with "+" to denote that this word must be present in the homepage. If you use "-" before a word, you filter out any results that include this word. So, for example, I could enter: Friars+Franciscans-Capuchins. Although Capuchins are Francisans, I would not receive homepages with them mentioned; I would only receive homepages that mentioned Friars along with the word Franciscan.

You can also limit searches by capitalizing words to force case-sensitive searches. Alta Vista lets you do even more. You can use additional terms to limit your searches to titles, URLs, links within a document, and so forth. Alta Vista also offers an advanced search form, which requires the Boolean operators mentioned previously. It allows you to limit your search by date and lets you specify criteria to use when ranking the results. (For example, you could specify a query requesting matches for the following: Jack AND Jill AND "ran up the hill" between the dates 1/1/96 and 12/31/96.)

Lycos
http://www.lycos.com/

This is an easy-to-use, powerful tool for locating information on the Web. It returns results ranked in order of relevance (which ranges from a low of 0.0 to a high of 1.0). It also indicates how many terms in your search expression were actually matched. This information can be helpful because, by default, Lycos searches for occurrences of any of the words you use, not all of them. You can change this by instructing Lycos to search for each word "and" the others instead of each word "or" the others. You can also set a limit for the minimum number of words that must be matched (this can range from two to seven). This will narrow down the search by making Lycos perform multiple-word searches or telling it to search for terms that could have multiple spellings.

Unless you change its settings, Lycos provides a linkable title, an outline, an abstract, and a URL for every page that it returns. You can tell it instead to show summary results, which include just the linkable title and Lycos's rating. Or you can get further information in a detailed results report that supplies you with the number of links a page has to other pages, as well as the words matched on the page. You probably won't need more information than that.

HotBot
http://www.hotbot.com/

Fifty million Web pages, as well as Usenet news and mailing lists.

*Infoseek Guide
http://guide.infoseek.com/

This guide lets you search the Web, Usenet (including FAQs), and Infoseek's reviewed pages. You can also search within a certain topics database while specifying which topic you want to search. This has the advantage of searching a smaller database that will lead to faster results.

Inktomi
http://inktomi.cs.berkeley.edu/

If you like easy searches, then this is the search engine to use. It returns fairly accurate results for the World Wide Web. The downside of its simplicity is the loss of ability to configure your searches as you can with Alta Vista. Further, it provides very limited information about results.

Infoseek Ultra
http://ultra.infoseek.com/

Index to 50 million Web pages, a real-time index of the Internet. If you can't find what you're seeking in this many homepages, I don't know what to tell you.

Excite
http://www.excite.com/

This search engine lets you search the World Wide Web, Usenet, Usenet classifieds, and Excite's own database of Web site reviews. Although you will probably find the information you want here, it doesn't offer the sophisticated searches Alta Vista does. Excite is set to look at homepages on the Web by concept. This contrasts to the traditional method of searching by key words. You can tell it to search this way also. Keyword searches return only those documents that include all or some of your search words. Concept searches, on the other hand, also give you homepages that don't include your search words but do include information about the words.

MetaCrawler
http://metacrawler.cs.washington.edu:8080/index.html

This search tool packs a lot of power. It can take your search words and at the same time feed them to sites, including Lycos, Infoseek Guide, and Inktomi mentioned previously. Once these sites have returned information, MetaCrawler then collates the results and eliminates all redundant URLs. That is a great feature. It even eliminates invalid URLs so you can avoid dead-ends from outdated links that you usually encounter on other search engines.

MetaCrawler searches can be configured. You can use either "+" or "-" before a word to limit the search. Here you use parentheses around a group of words to indicate that they are to be treated as a phrase. You can specify multiple phrases in your search terms. Other features offered include the ability to specify the time you're willing to wait for results (from 1 to 10 minutes), and the ability to restrict the search to particular domains or geographical areas.

EZ-Find
http://www.theriver.com/TheRiver/Explore/ezfind.html

Do your searches leave you up a creek without a paddle or even a canoe? You might want to turn to "The River" at EZ-Find. Finding what you want here is easy, at least the name says it's easy. Here you can submit several queries to a variety of search engines in rapid succession. EZ-Find processes these queries sequentially rather than simultaneously. This meta-searcher provides highly configurable search capabilities that span 11 different search engines. This is probably a good place to start your searches.

Yahoo
http://www.yahoo.com

Certainly a well-advertised search engine. They even publish their own magazine. This is, probably, the first search engine I learned of. It is easy to use and is a good search tool if you have a general idea what you're looking for. However, you may find yourself sorting through the results. It has information listed by category such as business, sports, and so forth. If you are searching for highly specific information, this probably isn't the tool to use. It doesn't rank the results. This means that you may have to wade through dozens of URLs that may or may not contain the detailed information you're looking for.

Yahoo Search
http://search.main.yahoo.com/

The new search engine for this famous all-around index.

LISTS OF SEARCH ENGINES

You can't find it? You'll have to try other search engines. The following sites list lots of search engines and meta-searchers.

a2z Search Engines
http://a2z.lycos.com/Internet/Indices,_Directories_and_How-To_Guides/
General_Indices_and_Search_Engines/

From Lycos, links to 240 search engines; includes great descriptions.

Asianet
http://www.asianet.net/search.html

Graphical interface to 40 search engines plus links to 100 more.

Beaucoup
http://www.beaucoup.com/engines.html

List of more than 500 search engines, organized into categories.

Best Search Engine
http://www.nueva.pvt.k12.ca.us/~debbie/library/research/research.html

List of search engines tied to specific strengths.

eDirectory
http://www.edirectory.com/

Search engines from around the world, listed by country.

Eureka!
http://www.best.com/~mentorms/eureka.htm

Contains 45 popular search engines, a great starting point.

Searches
http://members.tripod.com/~mike122/searches.html

Listing of United States and International search engines and directories.

WebScout
http://www.webcom.com/webscout/

Lists 100 specialized search engines; also offers 22 specific newsletters.

HOT LISTS

Now what is a hot list? A hot list is somebody's idea of what is interesting out there on the World Wide Web. The links are usually listed with no description. Hopefully, you can get your Catholic homepage listed on one of these hot lists.

Dan the Man
http://www.dantheman.com/

Beginner information, Web surfing aids, Web programming, people, and games.

Gary Shuster
http://www.datadepot.com/~shusterg/hotlist.htm

Search engines, entertainment, Internet tools, legal, and magazines.

Hot Internet Sites
http://web.idirect.com/~klg/index6aa.html

Sixteen thousand links to entertainment, shareware, and software.

Hot Sheet
http://www.tstimpreso.com/hotsheet/

Easy access to the best of the Web; organized collection of 300 sites.

The Info Service
http://info-s.com/

Thirteen thousand eight hundred links for 230 subjects, averaging 200 new links every week.

Reviews of Search Engines

There are people out there who test search engines and write reviews about them. These reviews will help you decide which search engine is best for what you are looking for.

clnet Reviews
http://www.cnet.com/Content/Reviews/Compare/Search/

Review of 19 various search engines.

Eureka!
http://www.best.com/~mentorms/eureka.htm

Lists 45 search engines and gives a description/review of each one.

Guide Reviews
http://www.iguide.com/insites/16/6/10/index.htm

Reviews of 26 search engines.

Internet Searching
http://www.netskills.ac.uk/resources/searching/

Describes the types of searches you can perform on the Web.

Search Description from Macworld's Charles Seiter
http://www.macworld.com/pages/december.96/Column.2893.html

Better, faster Web searching.

Search Reviews
http://www.dis.strath.ac.uk/business/search.html

Links to 15 different reviews of search engines.

Web Search Tools
http://www.hamline.edu/library/links/comparisons.html

Links about understanding and comparing Web search tools.

OTHER SEARCH PAGES

Besides search engines, there are search pages. These sites provide links to many different types of information. Just as you can feel overwhelmed by the amount of information on the Internet, so you can feel the same way about finding it. Hopefully, the following pages will make it a little easier.

Absolute Resource
http://www2.southwind.net/~miked/resource.html

Business, education, e-mail, general, Internet, magazines, multiple search, engine lists, software, specialized, text, white pages, and yellow pages.

All-in-One Search Page
http://www.albany.net/allinone/

This page provides access to a variety of search tools, as the name claims. You can't submit queries to multiple engines simultaneously, though. With the great number of search tools on this page, you will more than likely be pointed in the right direction to find what you are seeking. Unfortunately, this page is not well organized. This may mean you'll spend longer than necessary getting where you want to go.

Ampersand
http://www.10mb.com/sanx/amp/

Lists computer, entertainment, political, reference, and search sites.

Best Search Engines
http://www.wp.com/resch/search.htm

Sixty-two engines for the Web, newsgroups, mailing lists, people, and organizations.

Big Search
http://www.wp.com/resch/search.htm

Major search engines, world news, weather, financial information, and more.

Find-It
http://www.cam.org/~psarena/find-it.html

Don't you love these creative names? You can "find it" here. This homepage offers a search that combines Find-It's preferred tools. Here's what it uses. For the World Wide Web, your Keyword goes to "Lycos." If you are searching for a World Wide Web Phrase, it is sent to "Open Text." Queries for a World Wide Web Directory go to "Yahoo." Searches for software are sent to "Shareware.com," Usenet Newsgroups to "Déjà News," and people searches to "Internet Address Finder."

Internet Finder
http://www.lsu.edu/guests/poli/public_html/search.html

Find information, facts, stock quotes, books and articles, lyrics, universities, people, software, distances, lawyers, words and phrases, birthdays, businesses, street maps, weather, sunrise/sunset, ZIP codes, collections of search engines, Usenet, and e-mail lists.

Internet Search
http://www.islandnet.com/~pjhughes/search.htm

Large list of search engines, Web search, special search tools, search pages, and indices (no descriptions).

Internet Search
http://w4.lns.cornell.edu/~seb/search.html

Engines, people, databases, libraries, books, magazines, and news.

Internet Searching
http://www.mnsfld.edu/depts/lib/search.html

Great descriptions; has search engines, news, discussion groups, addresses, software, and jobs.

Internic Tools
http://www.internic.net/tools/

Lists of all sorts of Internet search engines.

Researcher's Toolkit
http://www.geocities.com/WallStreet/6100/

InfoAlert newsletter list of online research sites.

Search Services
http://www.simmons.edu/~schwartz/mysearch.html

Links to search service collections, meta-search services, simple search services, and information about all sorts of search services. Excellent annotations/descriptions of the links.

W3 Jumpstation
http://www.ultranet.com/~misfit1/jump.htm

A very comprehensive directory/browser homepage.

Windweaver
http://www.windweaver.com/

Search tools, reviews, links, and even a course about searching.

Wired Source
http://www.wiredsource.com/

Annotated links to search and index, news, Net issues, business, government, education, and the arts.

Yanoff's Internet Services List
http://www.spectracom.com/islist/

Lists 100 different topics, each with a few links.

EPILOGUE ▼▼▼

As I wind down this book, for some reason Star Trek and Captain James T. Kirk, sitting on the bridge, recording his captain's log come to my mind. This has been a long journey through Catholic cyberspace. I hope and pray that this book will be of service to Catholics around the world.

One result I would like to see emerge from this book would be a convention where all of us who provide Catholic services, homepages, and software can meet and discuss how to cooperate in our efforts. Further, this convention should be open to the public so that they too can learn about Catholics on the Internet and what's available to them.

Nobody could possibly speak more powerfully about the relationship between computers and the Church than Pope John Paul II. So I end this book with his statement issued in connection with World Communications Day—May 27, 1989.

The Church Must Learn to Cope with the Computer Culture

by Pope John Paul II

In one of her Eucharistic Prayers, the Church addresses God in these words: "You formed man in your own likeness and set him over all creatures."[1]

For man and woman thus created and commissioned by God, the ordinary working day has great and wonderful significance. People's ideas, activities and undertakings—however commonplace they may be—are used by the Creator

[1] Eucharistic Prayer IV

to renew the world, to lead it to salvation, to make it a more perfect instrument of divine glory.

Almost 25 years ago, the fathers of the Second Vatican Council, reflecting on the Church in the modern world, declared that men and women, serving their families and the community in their ordinary occupations, were entitled to look upon their work as "a prolongation of the work of the Creator . . . and as their personal contribution to the fulfillment in history of the divine plan."[2]

As the council fathers looked to the future and tried to discern the context in which the Church would be called upon to carry out her mission, they could clearly see that the progress of technology was already "transforming the face of the earth" and even reaching out to conquer space.[3]

They recognized that developments in communications technology, in particular, were likely to set off chain reactions with unforeseen consequences.

Far from suggesting that the Church should stand aloof or try to isolate herself from the mainstream of these events, the council fathers saw the Church as being in the very midst of human progress, sharing the experiences of the rest of humanity, seeking to understand them and to interpret them in the light of faith. It was for God's faithful people to make creative use of the new discoveries and technologies for the benefit of humanity and the fulfillment of God's plan for the world.

This recognition of rapid change and this openness to new developments have proved timely in the years that followed, for the pace of changes and development has continued to accelerate.

Today, for example, one no longer thinks or speaks of social communications as mere instruments or technologies. Rather they are now seen as part of a still-unfolding culture whose full implications are as yet imperfectly understood and whose potentialities remain for the moment only partially exploited.

Here we find the basis for our reflections on this 24th World Communications Day. With each day that passes, the vision of earlier years becomes ever more a reality. It was a vision which foresaw the possibility of real dialogue between widely separated peoples, of a worldwide sharing of ideas and aspirations, of

[2] "Gaudium et Spes," 34
[3] cf. "Gaudium et Spes," 5

growth in mutual knowledge and understanding, of a strengthening of brotherhood across many hitherto insurmountable barriers.[4]

With the advent of computer telecommunications and what are known as computer participation systems, the Church is offered further means for fulfilling her mission. Methods of facilitating communication and dialogue among her own members can strengthen the bonds of unity between them. Immediate access to information makes it possible for her to deepen her dialogue with the contemporary world.

In the new "computer culture" the Church can more readily inform the world of her beliefs and explain the reasons for her stance on any given issue or event.

She can hear more clearly the voice of public opinion and enter into continuous discussion with the world around her, thus involving herself more immediately in the common search for solutions to humanity's many pressing problems.[5]

It is clear that the Church must also avail herself of the new resources provided by human exploration in computer and satellite technology for her ever-pressing task of evangelization. Her most vital and urgent message has to do with knowledge of Christ and the way of salvation that He offers. This is something she must put before the people of every age, inviting them to embrace the Gospel out of love, ever mindful that "truth cannot impose itself except by virtue of its own truth, which wins over the mind with both gentleness and power."[6]

As the wisdom and insights of past years teach us: "God has spoken to humanity according to the culture proper to each age. Similarly the Church, which in the course of time has existed in varying circumstances, has used the resources of different cultures in her preaching to spread and explain the message of Christ."[7]

"The first proclamation, catechesis or the further deepening of faith cannot do without the (means of social communication) . . . the Church would feel guilty before the Lord if she did not use these powerful means that human skill is daily rendering

[4] cf. "Communio et Progressio," 181, 182
[5] cf. "Communio et Progressio," 114 ff.
[6] "Dignitatis Humanae," 1
[7] "Gaudium et Spes," 58

more perfect. It is through them that she proclaims 'from the housetops' the message of which she is the depository."[8]

Surely we must be grateful for the new technology which enables us to store information in vast man-made artificial memories, thus providing wide and instant access to the knowledge which is our human heritage, to the Church's teaching and tradition, the words of Sacred Scripture, the counsels of the great masters of spirituality, the history and traditions of the local churches, of religious orders and lay institutes, and to the ideas and experiences of initiators and innovators whose insights bear constant witness to the faithful presence in our midst of a loving Father who brings out of His treasure new things and old.[9]

Young people especially are rapidly adapting to the computer culture and its "language." This is surely a cause for satisfaction. Let us "trust the young."[10] They have had the advantage of growing up with the new developments, and it will be their duty to employ these new instruments for a wider and more intense dialogue among all the diverse races and classes who share this "shrinking globe."

It falls to them to search out ways in which the new systems of data conservation and exchange can be used to assist in promoting greater universal justice, greater respect for human rights, a healthy development for all individuals and peoples, and the freedoms essential for a fully human life.

Whether we are young or old, let us rise to the challenge of new discoveries and technologies by bringing to them a moral vision rooted in our religious faith, in our respect for the human person, and our commitment to transform the world in accordance with God's plan.

On this World Communications Day, let us pray for wisdom in using the potential of the "computer age" to serve man's human and transcendent calling, and thus give glory to the Father from whom all good things come.

John Paul II
Vatican City

[8] "Evangelii Nuntiandi," 45
[9] Cf.Mt 13, 52.
[10] "Communio et Progressio," 70

Why Saint Albert the Great?

Why did I dedicate this book to St. Albert the Great? Primarily because he is the patron Saint of scientists. He was so interested in all knowledge that I believe if he were alive today he'd be online.

Who Was He?

Who was he? I did not know the answer to that question until recently. I went to a Catholic grade school named after him, yet nobody ever told me about him. Usually he is remembered as the teacher of St. Thomas Aquinas, who wrote the famous *Summa Theologica*. Because of the fame of his student, St. Albert probably lost some of the credit he deserved for himself.

The Early Years

Albert the Great was born in 1206 at his family's castle in Lauingen, a small village on the Danube in the province of Swabia in southern Germany. He was the son of a wealthy nobleman, the Count of Bollstadt. From his youth, Albert had an inquisitive mind. Early on he displayed a keen interest in the beauty and order of nature. His youthful wandering through the forest and along the river in the area of his birth undoubtedly contributed to his later achievements in botany and natural science.

Albert attended the University of Padua, the greatest center for scientific learning at the time. Here the Dominican Blessed Jordan of Saxony, who was looking for young scholars for the new Dominican community, recruited him for the Order. Blessed Jordan, the Father General, was the immediate successor of St. Dominic, the founder of the Order. Albert joined the Dominicans at age 16. After completing his studies, he taught theology at Hildsheim, Freiburg, Ratisborn, Strasburg, and Cologne.

Synthesis of All Knowledge

In 1245 Albert was sent to Paris where he obtained a doctor's degree. It was at this time that he began the tremendous task of gathering together the whole of human knowledge that embraced all branches of natural science, logic, rhetoric, mathematics, ethics, economics, politics, and metaphysics. He would labor at this work for the next 20 years.

St. Albert regarded himself as a disciple of the Greek philosophers Aristotle and Plato. He said that one could not make progress in philosophy without knowledge of these thinkers. St. Albert's study and use of Aristotle's philosophy influenced St. Thomas, who used it as the philosophical basis of his theology.

The Scientist

Albert's scientific works fill 40 volumes. For him, natural science was not just limited to collecting facts. He considered this just the beginning of the investigation. According to Albert, collecting facts had to be followed by relating all the facts to each other. The correlation of these facts lead to the proposal of several probable causes. These causes were tested by experiment. From here a single conclusion was drawn and said to be the true cause. St. Albert, by reasoning this way, increased and improved the scientific knowledge of medieval man by introducing a systematic method entailing inductive (from particular to general) and deductive (from general to particular) reasoning.

Albert had a great interest in nature. His greatest success was in the areas of botany and zoology. He was an enthusiastic supporter of observation and experimentation. His recognition of the importance of facts pioneered the way for the scientific revolution that would emerge in the seventeenth century.

"The Great"

His contemporaries called St. Albert "the Great" and this title referred to the scope and depth of his learning. As a great scientist, he stands beside Friar Roger Bacon, the Franciscan, who referred to some of Albert's works as "original sources." Albert was, in his own lifetime, and for several centuries after, the authority on geography, physics, mineralogy, astronomy, biology, and chemistry. He even traced the chief mountain ranges of Europe and explained how climate was influenced by latitude. Amazingly, St. Albert gave a superb description of the earth, which he was able to demonstrate as spherical. Ulrich Engelbert, a contemporary of Albert, called him "the wonder and the miracle of his age."

In theology, St. Albert the Great is known for his great devotion to, and writings about, the Blessed Sacrament. Not only a great scientist and scholar, Albert was a holy man.

In 1248 Albert set up a house of studies for the Dominicans in Cologne. In 1254 he was made the provincial superior.

Bishop Albert

In 1256 St. Albert, along with his famous student St. Thomas Aquinas and the great Franciscan theologian St. Bonaventure, defended, in Rome, the right of the mendicant Orders to beg for financial support from the faithful. While there, he was the personal theologian of Pope Alexander IV. As a result of his brilliant defense of the mendicant Orders, the Pope consecrated him a bishop and appointed him to the archdiocese of Ratisbon.

The Final Years

In 1262, after Albert had settled the most urgent problems within his archdiocese, he resigned from it and returned to teaching. He was asked by Pope Gregory X to attend the Council of Lyon in 1274 and took an active part in the deliberations there.

He outlived his famous student, St. Thomas Aquinas, by several years and defended his former student's writings when they were challenged.

After 1278 he suffered a lapse of memory and his strong mind gradually became clouded. On November 15, 1280, at the age of 73, he died among his religious brothers in Cologne. He was beatified in 1622. In 1931, he was declared a Saint, a Doctor of the Church, and given the title "Universal Doctor" by Pope Pius XI. He is called, in Latin, *Albertus Magnus,* and his feast day is November 15.

GLOSSARY

Here are definitions of terms that you may come across either on Internet access providers or on the Internet. Listed first are files extensions, abbreviations appearing at the end of filenames that identify the file type. Next are terms you may encounter while using the Internet. Even if you don't come across them, you can impress your family and friends with your knowledge of computer trivia.

FILE EXTENSIONS

.ARC files   Files compressed using the program ARC.

.ARJ files   Files compressed using the ARC compression.

.ART files   Graphic files that are compressed using the Johnson-Grace compression scheme.

.AU files   Audio files used on UNIX workstations.

.AVI files   Windows-based audio and video files.

.BAT files   Batch files, or scripts run in DOS that are designed to automate tasks.

.BMP files   A Windows bit map, a type of graphics file used by Windows for backgrounds.

.COM files   Small programs for DOS. Used in the same way as .EXE files.

.CPT files   Macintosh files that have been compressed using the Compact Pro compression format.

.DLL files   Dynamic Link Library. Files that give functionality to other programs. Usually need to be installed into the WINDOWS/SYSTEM directory.

.DOC files   Document. The default file extension for Microsoft Word. Most files with this extension will be Microsoft Word files.

.DOT files   Document Template. Files that are templates for Microsoft Word.

.EPS files   Encapsulated Postscript File. These are vector graphics, a format used in most drawing programs.

.EXE files   Executable files, or applications. Most programs end with this extension.

.GIF files   Graphics Interchange Format. A type of graphic image very common on online services and the Internet.

.HQX files   Macintosh files that have been converted from ASCII to binary (or vice versa) with the BinHex encoding process.

.HTM files   Extension given to Web page files saved to your hard drive or floppy disk.

.INI files   Initialization file. Used by programs to set parameters and preferences.

.JPEG files   Joint Photographers Experts Group. A graphics format designed to take up as little space as possible while retaining as much quality as possible.

.ME files   A commonly used extension in DOS programs that tells you to do something like READ.ME.

.MID files

Musical Instrument Digital Interface. These files are songs for most sound cards and MIDI equipment.

.MOD files   Music Modules. Music files that include the instruments as well as the score, and play through a sound card, not MIDI.

.MOV   An Apple Quicktime movie file.

.MPEG files   Motion Pictures Expert Group. A format for the digitization and compression of video images.

.PCX files   Older graphics files, commonly used for clip art.

.S3M files   Music files similar to MOD files except they support up to 16 tracks.

.SCR files   Windows Screen Saver files.

.SEA files   Self-Extracting Archive. Macintosh files that automatically decompress when double-clicked.

.SIT files   Stuffit files. Macintosh compressed files.

.SND files   Sound. Macintosh System sounds.

.SYS files   System file. Drivers used by DOS and Windows.

.TIF files   Tagged Image File Format. Bit-mapped graphic images.

.TTF files   True Type Font. Scaleable fonts commonly used in Windows.

.TXT files   Text files. Usually just plain text.

.UUE   An UUencoded file. A method of converting binary files to text for transfer across the Internet.

.WAV files   Wave files. Windows sound files.

.WKS (WK1, WK3) files   Worksheet files. Lotus 1-2-3 spreadsheet files.

.WP files   WordPerfect file.

.XLS files   Excel spreadsheet file.

.ZIP files   PKware zip archive. The most common format for compressed files.

COMMON INTERNET TERMS

account   Like your credit card account, Internet access providers use accounts to keep track of who is doing what on their system. When you sign up with a provider, you will be given an account name. Of course, the provider will also use this account to bill you for the service.

access number   The phone number that your modem calls to connect to an Internet service provider.

address   Code used to identify Internet locations of people so you can send them e-mail. It normally looks like username@hostname. Username would be your username, login name, or account number. Hostname is the Internet's name for the computer or Internet provider you use.

address book A feature that holds frequently used Internet addresses and is particularly helpful when sending mail to several people at once.

alt A type of newsgroup that discusses alternative-type topics. They are not official newsgroups.

America Online (AOL) The number one public Internet access provider that offers its own subnetwork of utilities, libraries, chat areas, and other services.

anonymous FTP Using the FTP program to log on to another computer to copy files even though you don't have an account with that computer. Usually what you can do on that computer will be restricted.

applet A small program that performs a simple task.

Archie A system that helps you find files that are located anywhere on the Internet. After you find the file, you can use FTP to access it.

ARPANET The predecessor to the Internet funded by the United States Department of Defense.

ASCII America Standard Code for Information Interchange. The most common code for text on computers. In common usage, ASCII means a text file that doesn't include any formatting.

automatic mailing list A mailing list that is maintained by a computer program. The most common programs are LISTSERV and Majordomo.

bandwidth The amount of data that can travel through a channel in a given period of time. Measured in cycles per second (hertz) or in bits per second (bps).

baud A variable unit of data transmission speed (such as one bit per second).

BBS Bulletin Board System. An information service you connect to directly with your modem.

BCC (Blind Carbon Copy) Used in e-mail to send a copy of a message to one or more people without the other recipients knowing about it.

beta A pre-release version of software, distributed to a select group of users for testing purposes.

binary file A file containing data or program instructions in a computer-readable format.

bit   The smallest unit of measure for computer data.

BPS   Bits Per Second. A measurement of the speed that data is transmitted and received by a modem. The larger the number, the faster the data is sent and received.

browser   An application used to view information on the Internet.

byte   A series of bits of a particular length. Computer storage is usually measured in bytes.

cache   A storage area for frequently accessed information on your computer. Retrieval of the information is faster from the cache than the originating source.

CD-ROM   Compact Disk-Read Only Memory. A storage medium popular in modern computers. One CD-ROM can hold 600MB of data.

chat room   An access-provider area in which you can chat with other members in real-time.

cookie   A file on your computer that records information, such as where you have been on the World Wide Web.

com   When this appears as the last part of an address (for example AOL.com), it means that the host computer is run by a company.

CompuServe Information Service (CIS)   The second largest Internet access provider, with its own subnetwork containing libraries, forums, chat areas, and so forth.

CPU   Central Processing Unit. The main "brain" of the computer, where information is processed and calculations are done.

cut and paste   A method of copying data from one window to another.

cyberspace   Cyberspace refers to the 'place' you go when you use your computer and modem to communicate with others.

DARPA   Defense Advanced Research Projects Agency. Organization that provided the funding for the original precursor to the Internet.

DHCP   Dynamic Host Configuration Protocol. A network configuration that allows maintenance to be performed from a central site rather than by end users.

digest   A compilation of mailing list messages into a single file.

directory   An index of the files on a disk. A directory can contain individual files as well as other directories.

domain name   Official name identifying the site of a specific computer connected to the Internet.

DNS (Domain Name Service)   A behind-the-scenes Internet service that translates Internet domain names (such as business.com) to their corresponding IP addresses (such as 125.100.6.123), and vice versa.

DOS   Disk Operating System. One of the operating systems found on computers that takes care of the computer's basic tasks.

downloading   Transferring files from a host computer to your personal computer.

drop down box   A window that appears when you click on a menu item; offers additional menu choices.

dynamic rerouting   A method of addressing information on the Internet so that if one route is blocked or broken, the information can take an alternative route.

e-mail   Electronic mail. Messages, usually text, that are sent from one person to another through the computer.

error-correcting   A modem protocol that will check data to make sure that data being sent are the same as data being received.

FAQ   Frequently Asked Questions. Often included on Internet sites to explain what is to be found in the area and how to use its features.

FAX modem   Modems that allow you to receive or send scanned documents over phone lines (faxes) as well as communicate with other computers.

file   A collection of data stored on a disk with a unique filename.

firewall   Allows only certain messages in and out of a system attached to the Internet.

forum leader   An access provider's representative responsible for the content and management of an online area.

freeware   A file made available to the public free of charge from the author.

FTP   File Transfer Protocol. A method of transferring files from the Internet.

gateway   A link from one computer system to a different computer system.

gopher   Internet databases that can be accessed by the WWW as well as other gopher clients.

GPF   General Protection Fault. An error that occurs when a program or driver tries to access memory addresses outside the range that Windows has assigned to it.

hacker   Originally used to describe a computer enthusiast. Now becoming synonymous with 'cracker,' a term used to describe people who break into secured computer systems.

hardware   The physical computer itself with all its components.

hard disk drive   The main storage device located inside most computers.

homepage   The index or table of contents of a collection of Web sites and pages particular to one person or business.

HTML   Hyper-Text Markup Language. The scripting language of the World Wide Web.

HTTP   Hyper-Text Transfer Protocol. The format of the World Wide Web.

Hyperlink   A colored section of text that, when clicked, will take you to another area of a Web Page.

Internet Domain Name   The unique name that identifies an Internet entity. For example, compuserve.com is the Internet domain name for CompuServe.

Internet Explorer   A popular computer program from Microsoft used to explore the Internet.

Intranet   A computer network used within one company or organization.

IP   Internet Protocol. A scheme that enables information to be routed from one network to another.

IRC   Internet Relay Chat. A tool that allows you to chat with others on the Internet by typing messages to them.

ISDN   Integrated Services Digital Network. A fast method of transferring data.

ISP   Internet Service Provider. An organization that provides access to the Internet via dial-up telephone lines.

Java   An object-oriented programming language.

keyword   Words identifying topics or other important information that are used in Internet searches. Also the fastest way to get from one area of AOL to another.

line noise   Noise on a phone line that can interfere with modem communications.

LISTSERV   An automatic Internet mailing-list manager.

lurker   One who sits in a chat room but does not participate.

mailbomb   Sending a large amount of e-mail to a mailbox with the intent of harassing a person. Never do it!

mailer-daemon   An automated program that returns to the sender Internet mail that is undeliverable for one reason or another.

Majordomo   Like LISTSERV, it is an automatic mailing list program.

megabyte (MB)   A measurement of storage capacity equal to approximately 1 million bytes (1,048,576 bytes). A typical floppy disk holds about 1.44MB of data; a typical CD-ROM holds over 600MB of data. A 1MB file takes about 10 minutes to download at 28,800bps.

message boards   A feature some access providers offer that allows members to post public messages for other members to read and respond to.

MIME   Multipurpose Internet Mail Extensions. A method of encoding a file for delivery over the Internet.

modem   Modulator-Demodulator. A device that converts a digital computer signal to analog, then sends it across the phone line.

modem profile   The settings your modem uses to communicate with an access provider.

modem string   The actual commands that configure your modem to communicate with other computers.

Netscape   The most popular WWW browser.

network   A set of computers linked to one another for data sharing. Also used to refer to the link itself.

newsgroups   Internet message boards. Also known as Usenet.

no carrier   Indicates no signal (carrier) between your modem and the computer modem you are connected to. A 'dropped carrier' or 'lost carrier' message simply means that the modem signal was interrupted for some reason.

node   A collection of modems that provide local access to a system. When you dial a local access number, you are dialing into a node that connects you to an access provider. Also refers to a single computer on the Internet.

operating system   The basic software on your computer that enables you to perform basic tasks such as copying files.

page   A document or piece of information available on the World Wide Web. Each page can contain text, graphics, sound, or video.

Parental control   Parental control allows a parent to restrict a child's access to certain areas of an access provider and the Internet.

phish   An attempt to illegally obtain someone's password by false representation.

pixel   A pixel is the smallest unit of space on a computer screen, represented by each little dot. Resolution is a measure of how many pixels you can fit on your screen.

plug-in   Software programs that extend the usability of a program.

posting   An article in a newsgroup.

PPP   Point-to-Point Protocol. One of two standard methods of connecting to the Internet.

Prodigy   A popular Internet Access Provider with its own subnetwork for its members.

progressive rendering   A download method where the file begins to display itself before the download is completed.

protocol   A set of rules that governs how information is to be exchanged between computer systems. Also used in certain structured chat rooms to refer to the order in which people may speak.

punt   Another term for being disconnected during your online session.

Quicktime   Apple's video format. These .MOV files can be played on the Macintosh or Windows PC.

RAM   Random Access Memory. The computer's main memory where program data is stored for quick retrieval. RAM, often confused with hard drive space, is actually temporary storage. When the computer is turned off or restarted, anything in RAM is lost.

ROM   Read Only Memory. A section of memory that is permanent and will not be lost when the computer is turned off. The computer's start-up instructions are stored in ROM.

screen name   The name you use to represent yourself within an access service.

search engine   A database or index that you can query by entering keywords to help you find information on the World Wide Web.

serial line   A connection between two computers using the same protocol.

serial port   The outlet (port) on your computer into which you plug a serial line.

server   A computer or software package that provides a service to other computers on a network.

shareware   A try-before-you-buy program. If you decide to keep and use the program beyond the trial period (usually 10 to 30 days), you are requested to pay a fee to the author.

SLIP   Serial Line Internet Protocol. One of two standard methods of connecting to the Internet.

SMTP   Simple Mail Transfer Protocol. Method by which mail is delivered from one computer to another.

snert   A rude or malicious user who disrupts chat rooms or message boards. Don't do it!

software   A collection of files that allow a computer to perform a certain task or tasks.

spam   Unnecessary posting of messages or e-mail. Posting a message that says "Me too!" is an example of spam.

SSL   Secure Sockets Layer protocol. A standard for transmitting confidential data such as credit card numbers over the Internet.

Stuffit   A specific method of compressing files on the Macintosh platform. Files compressed in this manner will usually end with .SIT.

surfing   Exploring the World Wide Web. Also referred to as Surfing the Net.

SVGA   Super Video Graphics Array. These monitors can display a resolution up to 1,028x768 and up to 16.7 million colors.

sysop   System operator. The manager of a bulletin board service or forum.

TDD/TTY   Tone Dialing for the Deaf/Teletype. A method by which the hearing impaired can type messages over normal phone lines using special equipment.

thread   An article posted to a newsgroup or message board, along with all its follow-up articles.

UART   Universal Asynchronous Receiver/Transmitter. The chip that controls the data sent to and received from a serial port.

Unstuffing   The extraction of files compressed with Stuffit, primarily on the Macintosh. Most Stuffit files end in the .SIT command.

Unzipping   The extraction of files compressed with PKzip. Most Zip files end with .ZIP.

upload   To transfer a file from one computer to another via modem or other telecommunication method.

URL   Uniform Resource Locator. An HTTP address used by the World Wide Web to specify a certain site.

Usenet   A worldwide network of discussion groups on all topics, also called message boards or newsgroups.

VGA   Video Graphics Array. This monitor has a 480 × 640 display resolution and can display up to 256 colors simultaneously.

virus   A computer program written to secretly reproduce itself across many computer systems. Viruses can cause serious damage to files and computers.

WAIS   Wide Area Information Servers. A system that lets you search documents that contain the information you are looking for.

WebCrawler   A search service that helps you find personally relevant information on the World Wide Web. WebCrawler also contains reviews of sites and features.

Webmaster   The person in charge of a Web site.

World Wide Web (WWW)   A graphical method of exploring the Internet. A World Wide Web browser allows you to view, download, and execute files coded for the WWW.

Yahoo   A very popular World Wide Web search engine.

ZIP file   A file that has been created by using WinZip, PKzip, or a compatible program.

INDEX

▼▼▼

author's favorite homepages and directories,
continued
Catholic Online, 62–63
as access provider, 7–8
free homepage sites, 33
Christus Rex et Redemptor Mundi, 65–66
Eternal Word Television Network (EWTN),
10–11, 63–64
Franciscan Custody of the Holy Land, 72–73
Mary Page, 74–75
New Advent Catholic Website, 66
Office for Vocations, Archdiocese of Los
Angeles, 76
Real Presence of Christ in the Eucharist,
73–74
Saint's Lives, 72
Saint Patrick's Parish in Dublin, Ireland, 71–72
Ultimate Pro-Life Resource List, 70–71
University of St. Thomas—Archbishop Ireland
Memorial Library, 64
Vatican Homepage, 58–59

B

BBS (Bulletin Board System), 60
bookmarks, 89–90

C

Catechism of the Catholic Church. *See also various Internet directories*
Christus Rex et Redemptor Mundi site, 69
doctrine, 4, 28
obtaining electronic version, x–xi
**Catholic and Christian Resources on the
Internet,** 375–383
apologetics, 380–381
Catholic orders, centers, communities,
379–381
doctrine, history, and Bible resources,
382–383
general sites, 376

media sites, 381
miscellaneous, 383
parish and church sites, 377
schools, colleges, and universities, 378–379
Catholic Kiosk: From Cincinnati, 273–314
Bishops, 311–312
Cincinnati Web/Catholic Cincinnati, 275–278
Cincinnati Catholic organizations, 278
former Archbishops, 278
historical interest, 276
parishes, 276–277
schools and universities, 277–278
general resources, 279–297
art and architecture, 282–283
book and video distributors, 296–297
Divine Mercy Chaplet, 285–286
education, 287–288
Gregorian chant, 286
hierarchy and organization, 288
history and tradition, 279–281
Latin resources, 284
liturgy and liturgical year, 286–287
media resources, 292–296
organizations' resources, 290–292
prayers and missals, 283–284
pro-life and resources, 288–290
Rosary, 284–285
theology, 283
Way of the Cross, 286
What is Catholicism?, 281–282
miscellaneous, 313–314
Our Lady, 298–300
Pope John Paul II, 300–301
Religious, *The,* 306
saints, 306–311
by individual saint, 307–311
top ten recommended sites, 274–275
Vatican, 302–305
general Vatican information, 302
sources for Vatican documents, 303
Vatican news sources, 303
Vatican statements, 303–305

notification of new pages
- CATH-URL, 40
- Usenet, 42

publications to help create Web site, 39

retrieving a homepage, 36, 46–47
- memory limitations, 47

I

international users. *See also* translations
- Rankin (Bob) e-mail instructions, 45–46

Internet, 3–14. *See also* computers; e-mail; homepages; Internet access providers; Internet directories; mailing lists; news and broadcasting services; search engines; Web browsers
- Catholic Net Review (of sites), 75
- Catholic Resource Network, 63
- helper programs and plug-ins, 390
- help on the Internet, 387
- hot lists, 75, 402–403
- Internet digests, 388
- publications to help create Web site, 39
- reviews of sites, 75, 402–403
- screening with Surfwatch and Cyber Patrol, 4
- searching for general information, 386

Internet access providers, 5–14. *See also* Web browsers
- America Online (AOL), 5, 8–9
  - Catholic Community on America Online, 9–10, 84
  - creating a homepage with, 33
- Catholic Connect!, 11–13, 59–60
- Catholic Online Forum, 6–7
- CompuServe, vii–viii, 5, 6
  - Catholic Online, vii, 7–8, 62–63
  - creating a hompage with, 33
- Eternal Word Television Network (EWTN), 10–11, 63–64
- graphics, turning off, 8
- NETCOMplete Netscape (Netcom), 8

Peace Communication Network, 13–14
- Prodigy, 389
- searching for providers, 389–390
- WOW for inexperienced users, 7

Internet directories, 41–42, 77–87. *See also* author's favorite homepages and directories; homepages; mailing lists; search engines
- All in One Christian Index—Catholic Indices, 80–81
- Catholic Community on America Online, 84
- Catholic Connection, 40–41
- Catholic Goldmine, 81–83
- Catholic Internet Directory, 78–79
- Catholic Media Directory, 79–80
- Catholic Web Directory, 62
- DioceseNet, 83–84
- error messages, 86
- methods of organization and headings, 77–78
- navigating a directory, 85–86
- Official Catholic Directory, 78
- places to list your new homepage, 41–42, 62

Internet Service Providers (ISPs). See Internet access providers

J

Java, 391–392

M

Magisterium of the Roman Catholic Church, xi, 33

mailing lists, 15–30
- bulk mailing, 29
- CatholiCity lists, 27–28
- Catholic mailing lists (sites listed), 20–27
- Catholic Spirituality list, 19
- College Theology list, 20
- digest mode, 19
- getting off a list, 19
- lists of lists, 20
- "Listserv" in address, 19

mailing lists, *continued*

    Majordomo system, 20

    manual vs. automatic, 19

    monitoring, 20

    notification of new pages (CATH-URL), 40

    searching for mailing lists, 388–389

    starting your own mailing list, 28–29

malls, 42

Marian Library/Institute, University of Dayton, 74–75, 298

Mary Foundation, 33, 66

media. *See also* news and broadcasting services

    Catholic Media Directory, 79–80

modem. *See* computers

Monastery of Christ (Benedictine), 76

N

Netiquette, 387

news and broadcasting services, 9

    Catholic Media Directory, 79–80

    Catholic News Service (CNS), 9

    Catholic World News, 63, 75

    Electronic Newsstand, 43

    Eternal Word Television Network (EWTN), 10–11, 63–64

    magazine lists, 396–397

    National Catholic Reporter (NCR), 10

    newspaper lists, 396–397

    Vatican Information Service, 63

    WEWN short-wave station, 63

newsgroups. *See* mailing lists

nodes, 60

O

online services. *See* Internet access providers

Orthodox Church, 72

R

RCNet, 351–373

    apostolates, 367–370

    content providers, 366

    diocesan directory, 354–365

        Canada, 355

        National Council of Catholic Bishops, 365

        United States (listing by state), 355–365

    free homepage, viii–ix, 33

    international, 370

    miscellaneous, 371–373

    search engines, 370–371

S

search engines, 397. *See also* Internet directories; mailing lists; Web browsers

    address searches

        businesses, 393–394

        people, 392–393

        Whois and Netfind, 48

    limiting your search, 398–399

    list of search engines, 401–402

    on RCNet, 370–371

    programs

        Alta Vista, 397–398

        Excite, 400

        EZ-Find, 400

        HotBot, 399

        Infoseek Guide and Infoseek Ultra, 399

        Inktomi, 399

        Lycos, 47–48, 398–399

        MetaCrawler, 400

        WebCrawler, 48

        Yahoo, 41, 401

        Yahoo Search, 401

    meta-searcher, 385

    reviews of engines, 385, 403–404

    Search Page (hot list), 386

search pages, 404–407

WebCrawlers (obtaining list of), 42

Summa Theologica (Thomas Aquinas), 66

T

Telnet, 11

Totus Tuus (papal texts), 61

translations, 58

Our Father and bulletins, 65–66

U

URL (Uniform Resource Locator), 31, 85

V

Vatican. *See also various directories*

Annuario Pontificio (Vatican directory), 13

unofficial guide to website, 168

Vatican homepage, 58–59

Vatican Information Service, 63

Vatican (nonofficial), 238–239

viruses, 29–30

VRML, 391–392

W

Web browsers, 31–32. *See also* Internet access providers; search engines

DOSLynx, 49

graphics, turning off, 31–32

Microsoft Internet Explorer, 31–32, 85

bookmarks, 90

homepage creation, 36, 39

Minuet, 50

Mosaic, 50

Netscape Navigator, 31–32, 50, 85

bookmarks, 89

homepage creation, 36, 39

Net-Tamer, 49

searching for browsers, 390–391

streamlining the settings, 50–51

Web (World Wide Web/WWW). *See also* e-mail; homepages; Internet; Internet directories; search engines; Web browsers

WWW Frequently Asked Questions sites, 4, 386

ABOUT THE AUTHOR

Brother John Raymond studied electrical engineering and participated in the University of Michigan's co-op program working at the Environmental Research Institute of Michigan. There he assisted in the testing of a computer-generated simulation program of small aperture radar imaging. After switching his major to mathematics, he received his B.S. in mathematics and a high school teaching certificate from the University of Michigan. He taught high school mathematics and physics, tutored college students in math, and helped adults prepare for their high school equivalency diploma.

Brother John worked for the Educational Computer Corporation as a simulation analyst and computer programmer. He was instrumental in programming and designing simulators for an electrical power plant and various types of airplanes.

Brother John also has a M.A. in Theology from Holy Apostles Seminary and College in Cromwell, Connecticut. In addition, he has given talks at conferences, been a guest on several television programs, and writes a bi-weekly column on prayer for the *Catholic Twin Circle*. He enjoys weight lifting and running.

Brother John Raymond is the co-founder of The Monks of Adoration, whose vocation is to adore Jesus. It is a contemplative life of praise, worship, and intercessory prayer. He lives in Petersham, Massachusetts.